Learn Visual dBASE® Programming

A Hands-on Guide to Object-Oriented Database Programming

Martin L. Rinehart

Addison-Wesley Publishing Company
Reading, Massachusetts • Menlo Park, California • New York
Don Mills, Ontario • Wokingham, England • Amsterdam
Bonn • Sydney • Singapore • Tokyo • Madrid • San Juan
Paris • Seoul • Milan • Mexico City • Taipei

Many of the designations used by manufacturers and sellers to distinguish their products are claimed as trademarks. Where those designations appear in this book, and Addison-Wesley was aware of a trademark claim, the designations have been printed in initial capital letters or all capital letters.

The author and publisher have taken care in preparation of this book, but make no expressed or implied warranty of any kind and assume no responsibility for errors or omissions. No liability is assumed for incidental or consequential damages in connection with or arising out of the use of the information or programs contained herein.

Library of Congress Cataloging-in-Publication Data

Rinehart, Martin L.
   Learn Visual dBASE programming : a hands-on guide to object-oriented database programming / Martin L. Rinehart
   p. cm.
   Includes index.
   ISBN 0-201-60836-7
   1. Object-oriented databases. 2. Visual programming (Computer science) I. Title.
QA76.9.D3R546 1995   95-30401
005.75'65—dc20   CIP

Copyright ©1995 by Martin L. Rinehart

All rights reserved. No part of this publication may be reproduced, stored in a retrieval system, or transmitted, in any form or by any means, electronic, mechanical, photocopying, recording, or otherwise without the prior written permission of the publisher. Printed in the United States of America. Published simultaneously in Canada.

Sponsoring Editor: Keith Wollman
Project Manager: John Fuller
Production Coordinator: Ellen Savett
Cover design: Barbara T. Atkinson
Set in 11 point Times New Roman by Martin L. Rinehart

1 2 3 4 5 6 7 8 9 -MA- 9998979695
First printing, August 1995

Addison-Wesley books are available for bulk purchases by corporations, institutions, and other organizations. For more information please contact the Corporate, Government, and Special Sales Department at (800) 238-9682.

This book is dedicated to Virginia, the Grin and Virgrinegar.

Summary Table of Contents

1	Your First Windows Program	1
2	Back to Procedural	21
3	Easing Into Objects ---- Analysis	47
4	Easing Into Objects ---- Generation	67
5	We Get Set	109
6	Object-Oriented and Event-Driven	121
7	On to the Calendar	139
8	The Calendar Comes Alive	163
9	Finishing the Calendar	193
10	Beginning an Application	219
11	Building a Speed_bar Class	261
12	Polishing the Speed_bar	293
13	Building Tree Classes	309
14	Critical Path Charting	343

Contents

1 Your First Windows Program — 1
- Windows Programs Are Simple — 3
- Classes and Objects — 5
- Constructor Functions — 6
- Object Properties and Methods — 6
- Let's Write a Program — 7
- Your Tools — 8
  - The Editor — 9
  - The Compiler and Linker — 11
  - The Form Designer — 11
  - Crystal Reports — 12
  - Experts — 12
  - Other — 13
- You Use the Tools — 13
- Summary — 18

Back to Procedural — 21
- Numbered Listings — 22
  - In and Out — 23
  - Line Numbering — 30
  - User Interface — 33
  - LISTER for LISTER — 38
- Visual dBASE Scopes — 39
  - LOCAL Variables — 39
  - STATIC Variables — 43
  - Improving LISTER — 43
- Summary — 45

Learn Visual dBASE Programming

3 Easing Into Objects ---- Analysis   47

- Why Action Diagrams?   49
  - Keeping Your Code Sound   49
  - Scrambling Your Sound Code   50
  - Defining Action Diagramming   50
- Designing an Action Diagramming Utility   51
  - The Lexer   51
  - The Parser   52
  - The Stack Machinery   53
  - The Output Machinery   54
  - Design for Debugging   54
- Implementing the Lexer   54
  - The Test Loop   55
  - Using an Object Class Object   55
  - Adding Properties   57
  - Tokenizing   58
- Implementing the Parser   63
  - The Parser Output   64
  - Completing the Parser   65
- Summary   66

4 Easing Into Objects ---- Generation   67

- File Input in the Mainline   68
- The Stack Machinery   69
  - A Stack Class   70
  - Using the Stack Class   74
  - Adding the Other Tokens   78
- The Output Machinery   89
  - Simple Output   90
  - Building the Prefix   92
  - Testing and Fixing   96
  - Finishing DO CASE Blocks   100
- On Your Own   106
- Summary   106

Contents

5 We Get Set — 109
- Setup — 110
  - Windows — 110
  - DBASEWIN.INI — 111
  - The Navigator — 112
  - The SpeedBar — 113
  - The Command Window — 114
  - The Program Editor — 116
- Summary — 119

6 Object-Oriented and Event-Driven — 121
- Form Basics — 122
  - An Intelligent Windows Window — 123
  - Creating a New Class — 123
- Writing Event Handlers — 126
  - Responding to a Move Event — 126
  - Assigning Properties in the Event Handler — 126
  - Using STATIC Variables in the Event Handler — 128
- Using Named Subroutines — 130
  - Using Subroutine Reference Variables — 130
  - Codeblocks Add Another Subroutine Type — 132
- Attaching Another Object — 135
- Summary — 137

7 On to the Calendar — 139
- Creating a Calendar Class — 140
- Adding a Grid of Line Objects — 141
  - Drawing the Vertical Lines — 142
  - Drawing the Horizontal Lines — 144
- Letting the User Resize the Calendar — 146
- Labeling the Days of the Week — 148
- Adding Date Objects — 151
  - Adding Date Calculation Functions — 151
  - Calling with a Date Parameter — 153
  - Creating Day Objects — 153

Setting the Day Objects	154
Drawing the Day Objects	155
Improving Performance	156
The Whole Calendar Class	157
Summary	161

8 The Calendar Comes Alive — 163

Selecting Dates with the Mouse	164
Highlighting the Selected Day	164
Moving the Selected Day	165
Improving the Day Spacing	167
Adjusting the Month	169
Displaying the Month	169
Changing Months	173
Adjusting the Year	179
Adding Home and End Pushbuttons	179
The Full Listing	182
Summary	191

9 Finishing the Calendar — 193

Keystroke Events	194
How Not to Handle Keystrokes	194
How to Handle Keystrokes	197
Other Keys	199
Adjusting the Buttons	202
Moving the Existing Buttons	202
Adding the New Buttons	203
The Full Listing	207
Summary	218

10 Beginning an Application — 219

Creating a Scratch Form	220
Creating an Empty Form	221
Saving Your Form	225
The Output of the Form Designer	226

Contents

Creating a Menu System	231
Finding the Menu Designer	232
Using the Menu Designer	234
Help About Menu Objects	244
Creating Modal Windows	247
The Not_Yet Window	247
A Help/About Window	254
Tying It All Together	256
Summary	259

11 Building a Speed_bar Class — 261

The Speed_bar's Button Object	262
Bouncing Rectangles	263
Adding the Image	265
The Speed_bar	275
Designing the Speed_bar	275
Building the Visual Components	276
Bringing the Speed_bar to Life	285
The Full Listing	289
Summary	292

12 Polishing the Speed_bar — 293

The Speed_bar's Spacing	294
The Surround Width	294
Status Messages for Speed_bar Buttons	297
Setting the Status Message	298
Goof-Proofing the Speed_bar	300
Calling a Clean_up() Method	301
The Full Listing	304
Summary	308

13 Building Tree Classes — 309

Designing the Tree	310
Overall Object Design	310
Tree Detailed Design	310
Recursion	311

Programming the Tree Classes 314
Programming the Tree_display_form Class 322
    The Tree_display_form Constructor 323
    The Tree_display_form Display Methods 327
    The Tree_display_form Event Handlers 330
The Full Listing 334
Summary 342

14 Critical Path Charting   *343*

Designing the Class 344
    A Simple Data Structure 344
    A Simple Class 345
Drawing the Chart 345
    Building a Test Project 346
    Creating the Form 348
    Adding the Header Lines 349
    Adding the Component Names 353
    Plotting the Project Components 354
    Showing the Dependencies 357
Doing the Calculations 359
    Following Dependencies 359
    Finding the Critical Path 364
Closing the Form 366
The Full Listing 367
Summary 375

Index   *377*

Acknowledgments

The people at Addison-Wesley who worked with the author to bring you this book include Editor-in-Chief Keith Wollman, Acquisition Editor Julie Stillman, and Project Editors Eleanor McCarthy and John Fuller.

Of course, without Borland's Visual dBASE, we wouldn't have had a project. Going back to the original dBASE for Windows we're indebted to Michael Gardner, Randy Stolton and Lloyd Tabb, to name just three of many. And we'd be remiss not to mention Ray Love, too. Thanks to all.

No one works alone on a project like this. Without my family I couldn't have done it. And I'd also like to thank my friends, particularly the many eFriends on Borland's CompuServe forums who are about as helpful a bunch as you could ever expect to meet.

Chapter 1

Your First Windows Program

This book is about doing Visual dBASE programming. I assume that you know dBASE (or Clipper or Fox) basics and aren't in need of any instruction in the USE and SKIP commands. On the other hand, I assume that you're new to object-oriented programming and want to upgrade your skills out of the old procedural paradigm.

I also assume that you actually like programming and that you won't mind at all if we have some fun along the way. Each chapter will start with a quick look at where we're going.

Learn Visual dBASE Programming

For instance, in this chapter you will:

- Launch your first window
- Use the NEW operator
- Meet object constructor functions
- Use object.property syntax
- Program an event handler
- Meet the new scopes

Then we'll get to the meat of the chapter, which is actually doing the programming. At the end, I'll give you a quick summary of what we've done and what you've learned.

Are you ready to start programming Visual dBASE? Good! We'll get started in just a second. First, there are a couple of things you should know. The good news is that if you know any Xbase programming, you already know almost all the Visual dBASE language. Before we're five pages into this chapter, you'll have learned about 80% of the language that is new with object-oriented dBASE.

The other news is that this is *not* your father's dBASE. While the language stays the same, the programming paradigm is *completely* different. You are walking into a new world of objects and events, a new way of designing and programming, a new way of *thinking*. Before you've finished this chapter, you'll be profoundly worried that you simply don't understand how any of this works.

Fear not! In this book we'll build lots of Visual dBASE classes. I believe that you learn to program by programming, not by studying isolated examples of language syntax. We'll build lots of useful classes, beginning with a popup calendar class. As you build these classes you'll see how the new paradigm works. Before you're done, you'll be as comfortable building object-oriented, event-driven Windows programs as you are now building procedural programs.

Better yet, you'll see that object-oriented methods move you into a new level of productivity. In building classes, you'll get a start on creating your own library of reusable objects, a library that will carry forward into all your Visual dBASE work. Now let's find out just how easy this can be.

Chapter 1   *Your First WINDOWS Program*

Windows Programs Are Simple

OK, turn your computer on and launch Visual dBASE. If you haven't changed the original setup, you'll see the Navigator window over the Command window. If you've changed things, you may see one or neither. We want to get the Command window active.

    Minimize the Navigator, if it's on screen. If the Command window isn't visible, click on the Aladdin's lamp icon on the speedbar. (Get it? "Your wish is my Command.") The Command window is the Visual dBASE equivalent of the dot prompt that we knew since 1980 when dBASE II was launched. Let's try it out.

    Type "? 2+2" in the Command window. As you see in Figure 1-1, the answer, "4," shows in the results pane.

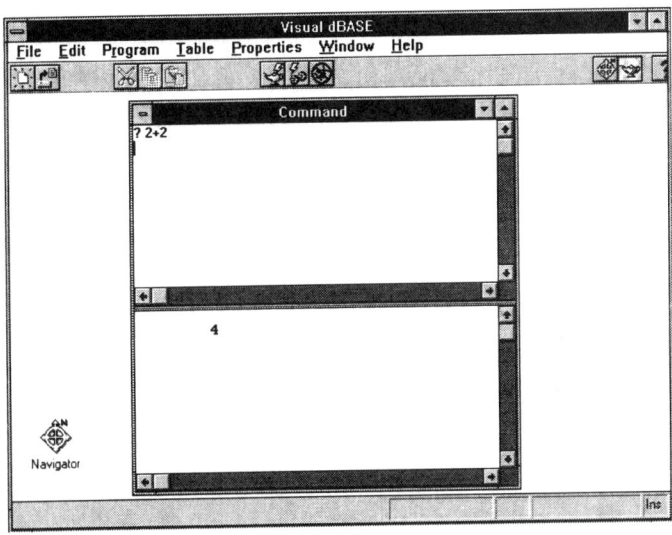

Figure 1-1: The Command Window is the new dot prompt.

If your Command window doesn't look like the one in Figure 1-1, position the top by dragging on the title bar. Then drag on the sides or corners to size it appropriately. Now drag the bar that separates the two panes to allocate the space between commands and results. To fine-tune things, choose Properties/Command window... from the menu and set up fonts to suit yourself.

3

Learn Visual dBASE Programming

Warning: There are lots of choices of fonts and font sizes, and most of them are substantially worse than the defaults!

The dot prompt was a marvelous place for programmers to work. You could test out just about anything before you placed your commands in a program file. The Command window continues that tradition. We'll use it to build our first window. You'll need exactly two commands to launch a window. One to create it, and another to open it. They are:

```
win = NEW form()
OPEN FORM win
```

As you see in Figure 1-2, that's all it takes to build a true Windows window and turn it over to the user. In this case, of course, you are the user.

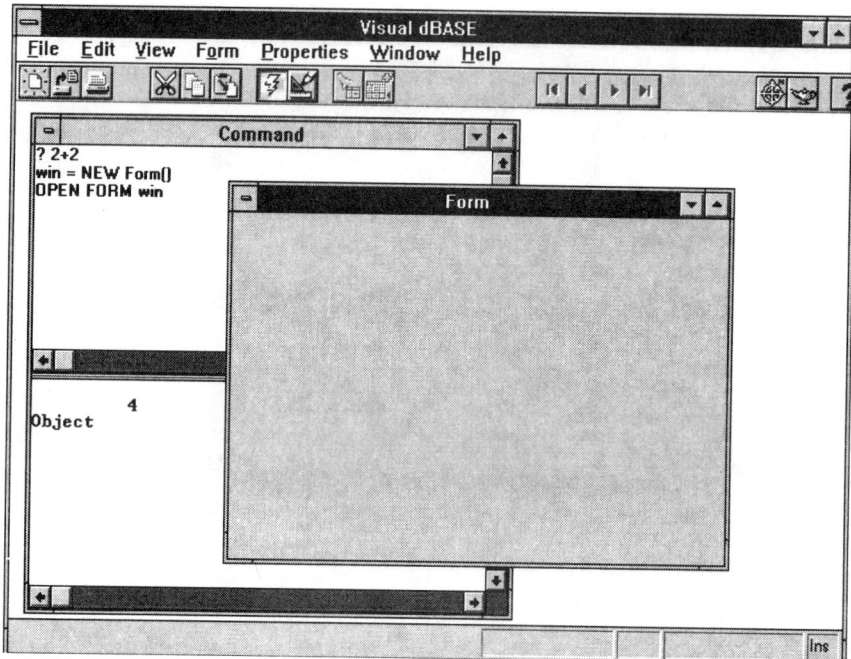

Figure 1-2: Window launched from Command window

Yes, your form is a true Windows window, and it already has all the basic capabilities you expect.

Try each of these:

- Drag the title bar to position the window
- Drag the corners and edges to resize the window
- Click the Maximize button to fill your screen
- Click the Resize button to return to normal
- Click the Minimize button to reduce it to an icon
- Double-click the icon to return to normal
- Minimize the form and single-click the icon to get the menu
- Choose Restore and return to normal
- Single-click the System button to get the system menu
- Choose Close

By the way, your friend with the C compiler and the original Windows Software Development Kit (SDK) got this far in about a month. Visual dBASE gets high marks for reducing the complexity. Now let's consider what we actually did.

Classes and Objects

I'm about to fire all the key object-oriented jargon at you. Read slowly, but don't waste your time taking notes. We'll be using all these terms and concepts continuously. They'll be second nature to you before you finish this book. Ready? Let's start.

A *class* describes how *objects* are built. The object is a single *instance* of the class. In Visual dBASE as in C++, the NEW operator creates a new object, or *member* of its class. We created win, a member of the Form class. (Actually, win is an *object reference* variable, but we'll get to that detail in due course. For now, consider it as the object.)

Visual dBASE provides 28 built-in classes, each with a vast store of knowledge. As you just saw, the Form class object knows how to behave like a Windows window. When you create a new object, the object *inherits* all the behaviors, or *methods* known to the class. Your form inherited the methods that let it respond apropriately to all the different clicks and drags that you expect from a Windows window.

Constructor Functions

Both the twenty-eight built-in classes and every class you'll program have constructor functions. The name of the constructor is the name of the class. You create a member object of a class with the NEW operator and a call to the function's constructor. These are some samples:

```
win = NEW Form()
rec = NEW Rectangle(win)
my_obj = NEW my_class()
```

As you can see, the parentheses enclose parameters. A Rectangle is an object that must be attached to a Form, so you need a Form as a parameter to the Rectangle constructor.

By the way, Visual dBASE is, as dBASE always has been, *not* case-sensitive. I capitalize NEW, since it's a dBASE keyword. I use lowercase for my own names. For Visual dBASE's built-in objects and their properties, I use mixed case. In the above examples, you see that Form and Rectangle are built-in classes, but my_class is not. This distinction gets more important when we use the built-in properties and methods.

Object Properties and Methods

Visual dBASE's objects have "properties." One of the properties of a Form object is called Text. A property, such as Text is referred to with dot operator syntax:

```
<object>.<property>
```

You can make assignments to properties. Let's try one. Figure 1-3 shows you assigning "Hello, world!" to a Form object's Text property.

Try this yourself. You see that the Text property for a Form sets the title in the title bar.

If you look closely, you see that I switched from OPEN FORM win to win.Open() — this shows that the Open behavior is a special type of object property, called a *method*. A method is something that the object knows how to do.

Chapter 1   Your First Windows Program

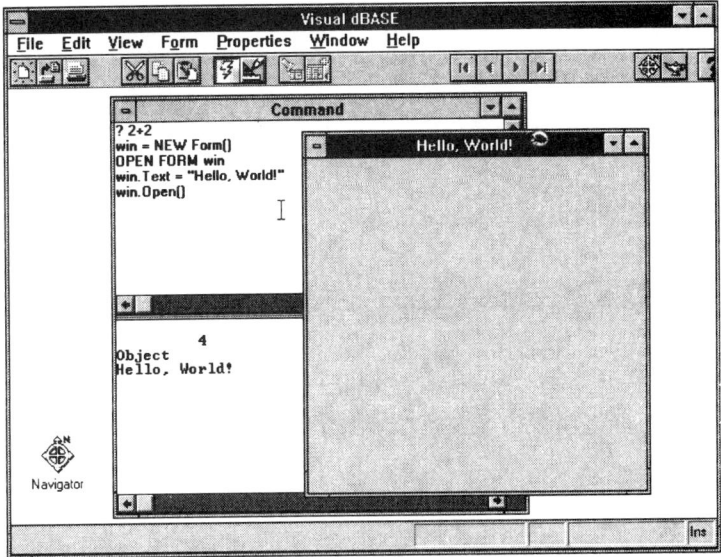

Figure 1-3: Win.Text = "Hello, World!"

Visual dBASE classes already have lots of useful methods, and we'll program lots more.

Like other properties, the dot operator lets you name the object to which the method applies. The parentheses distinguish a method property from a data property. And, as with other subroutine calls, you place any parameters inside the parentheses.

Well, there you have about 80% of the new language features of object-oriented dBASE. Don't worry, there won't be a quiz. This is the material that we'll be using constantly as we build our classes. It will be as much a part of your working vocabulary as @ SAY is today.

Let's Write a Program

We're ready to write our first Visual dBASE program. Before we do, though, let me mention that the Form class constructor takes the value of its Text property as an optional parameter. That means these two examples are equivalent.

7

```
w = NEW Form()
w.text = "Form Title"

* same as:

w = NEW Form("Form Title")
```

With that fact, let's write HELLO.PRG, a program that creates a Hello, World! window.

The listings are on the floppy disk in the back of the book. This one is L01-01.PRG. As you see in Listing 1-1, typing both lines is usually faster than copying in the listing.

Code Listing 1-1
```
win = NEW Form("Hello, World!")
win.open()
```

Of course, to enter, compile, link, and run a program, we'll need to know the tools that Visual dBASE provides. (Can't wait? Go ahead and try to enter and run that program before you read the next section.)

Your Tools

The first problem you face with any programming environment is mastering the tools. I don't think you'll find any programming system that makes this easier than Visual dBASE. Before you get started, create a \DBWORK directory where you can work. In Visual dBASE, use the Command window to enter this command:

```
md c:\dbwork
```

(Use your own disk drive letter.)

Then open the Navigator window. (If it's closed, click on the compass rose icon on the speedbar, or, from the keyboard, choose it from the Window menu.) Click the button to the right of the default directory, and use the dialog box to select \DBWORK as your default directory.

You want to access the pushbutton with the tool icon next to the default directory entryfield. The tool icon looks a little like a wrench.

Chapter 1   *Your First Windows Program*

From the keyboard, you can press Tab in the Navigator until the tool icon button has focus (watch closely, the added black around the button is subtle) and then press the spacebar. If you are a confirmed mousaholic, let me pass on a bit of advice. I've started to do more and more work from the keyboard, and find that it generally lets me work faster than I can with a mouse. I only go to the mouse for true graphic operations, such as using the Form Designer.

When you exit Visual dBASE, your default directory setting will be saved. You can find this setting in the text file \VISUALDB\BIN\DBASEWIN.INI. Visual dBASE lets you put a copy of DBASEWIN.INI in each directory where you'll be working, so you can have multiple defaults for different projects. It looks to \VISUALDB\BIN for this file if it doesn't exist in the current directory.

For starters, copy \VISUALDB\BIN\DBASEWIN.INI to \DBWORK\DBASEWIN.INI. You can use Windows File Manager or, in the Command window, type "modi file \visualdb\bin\dbasewin.ini" to read the file into the Text Editor. Then use File/Save As to save it into the \DBWORK directory. You could also use a COPY FILE command or think of some other alternatives. Visual dBASE, as any good event-driven, graphic-interface program, supplies lots of ways to get your job done.

Now we're ready to get to work.

The Editor

First, of course, you need a text editor to enter and edit programs. The included editor is a competent GUI programming editor. It includes syntax highlighting, clipboard access, and the other things you've come to expect in a modern editor.

You can get to the text editor in several ways. From the Command window, type "MODIFY COMMAND <name>[.ext]". The extension defaults to .PRG if you don't supply one. Of course, in reality you'll abbreviate and not waste time on capitals. You'll type "modi comm foo" to edit FOO.PRG. Being efficient, you'll set up a function key like this:

```
SET FUNCTION F2 TO "modi comm foo;"
```

With that done, you just press F2 and you're in the editor. (Without the semicolon (;) at the end of that command you'll have to press Enter after you press F2. You wouldn't want to waste two keystrokes when one will do, would you?)

9

Learn Visual dBASE Programming

You can also get to the editor from the File menu. This is a good choice if you need to wander around in a complex directory structure to locate a particular program. Select the Program file type in the Navigator, and then try File/Open. Note those two little radio buttons in the lower-right corner of the dialog box. The default says "Do" and the other says "Design Program."

By default, Visual dBASE runs executable files, which include, of course, .PRGs. The Design mode is available for tables, forms, reports and so on. For programs, Design mode means use the Program Editor. So be sure to click the Design Program button, before you click on OK. (From the keyboard type Alt+P, Enter.)

For those of you who, like me, think that your personal favorite editor is the only reasonable choice, Visual dBASE agrees with you. It makes it easy to use your own editor. You choose Properties/Desktop and then the Files tab to get to the right dialog box to pick another editor.

I use a DOS editor for my heavy editing, but I leave the default programming editor blank, so the built-in editor is chosen. Why? There are two key reasons. First, if your code has a syntax error, the compiler will happily return you to the exact line where it encounters the error and let you fix it. You correct the typo, press ^W, and you are right back in business. The same applies to runtime errors.

Second, the built-in editor is ideal for small test programs. (The Command window is great, but you can't build a loop without a program.) In the editor, ^D means Do — save, compile, and run. So you try something and then press ^D. Does it work? Exit from your window and you are right back in the editor. The turn-around time for the edit-compile-run-edit cycle is only a couple of seconds — several times faster than any C++ Windows environment.

The editor is documented in the on-line help. Click Help/Contents or press Shift+F1. The editor information is under Keyboard (although you'll have to wade through a lot of other information to find it). It's also covered in the *User's Guide*.

I recommend that you use the built-in editor for the work in this book. When you do get ready to do your own work, if you still want to use your editor for heavy editing (as I do), use the Command window to establish one or more function keys that invoke your editor with something like the following:

```
SET FUNCTION F10 TO "!my_editor \my\path\my_prg.PRG;"
```

Then you just press F10 (or whatever key you chose) and you are in business. Modi comm and the compiler/runtime system still can take advantage of the built-in editor, which you will become comfortable using.

I also launch a separate edit session from Windows, using my favorite text-mode editor. (I like text mode for working with text.) Pressing Alt+Tab lets me cycle between Visual dBASE and my editor.

The Compiler and Linker

One of the beauties of dBASE has always been that you could almost forget that the compiler existed. Borland's other language packages could learn a lot from dBASE in this regard. It's simplicity itself. From the Command window, you simply type "DO my_prog" and dBASE checks to see if the source .PRG is more recent than the compiled .PRO. If needed, it will recompile the .PRG.

If you want to compile without running (for a syntax check) you can give an explicit compile command in the Command window:

```
COMPILE my_prog
```

Linking is done with SET PROCEDURE and SET LIBRARY commands, as it has always been done. If you're a Clipper programmer who has never seen these, look them up in the *Language Reference*. You'll see that they are completely straightforward.

The Form Designer

The Form Designer will be one of your favorite tools. It's a totally visual tool: you click and click/drag things around, resize things and fuss with the fonts, see if it looks better if you align the text at right center and so on.

It's fun to use and completely visual. It's also a "Two-Way Tool": you run the Form Designer and it generates source code. You edit the source code and the Form Designer reads your edits and reflects them the next time you run the Form Designer.

Through the Form Designer you have access to lots of other tools. You'll see a tool bar that includes entry fields, combo boxes, editor controls and all the other gadgets that make up Windows dialog boxes. These are all available for dropping into your form where they are needed.

You'll launch the Menu Designer from inside the Form Designer. You'll find menu creation incredibly simple. That includes the main menu, pull-downs and nested menus, keystroke defaults and accelerator keys, and all the other features of Windows menus.

Most importantly, you'll find the object Inspectors. While Visual dBASE supports the dBASE IV language for backward compatibility, you'll see that a tremendous amount of the old language has been replaced by objects and their properties. The beauty of this is that you don't need to memorize the list of objects (which would be hard) and you don't need to memorize all their properties (which would be nearly impossible).

The tool bar shows you all the available objects. You pick one and the object Inspector shows you all its properties. This means that Visual dBASE is a much more capable system than dBASE IV, but it gets its capabilities through a smaller language!

That said, we're not going to start using the Form Designer right away. When I was learning Visual dBASE, I started with the Form Designer, instead of with .PRGs. That was a mistake. The Form Designer let me *not* know enough of the language so that I wasn't able to enter quick little test programs to see how things work. I would have mastered Visual dBASE a lot faster if I'd started with the language and then used the Form Designer, which is exactly what we'll do here.

Crystal Reports

Crystal Reports was a third-party report writer sold as an add-on for dBASE and other report writing. Borland liked the product so much it licensed it for use in Visual dBASE.

Crystal Reports is a first-class, Windows-capable report writer, fully able to handle graphical, multi-font reporting. While Visual dBASE has the tools so that you can program your own reports from scratch, I can't see any reason to do so.

Experts

Visual dBASE has Experts, menu and form-based intelligent dialogs, for forms, reports, tables and labels. You may be tempted to ignore them at first. That would be a mistake.

If you have a .DBF, you can employ the Form Expert to do your initial layout. There's nothing hard about using the Form Designer to place an Entryfield object on your form and establish a DataLink property that attaches it to your .DBF. But the Form Expert will do this for every field in your .DBF (or just the fields you specify) in a few seconds, so you can concentrate on the more creative work.

Other

There are lots more tools in Visual dBASE. You'll use the Query Tool to link multiple .DBFs, for instance. While the Expression Builder is not of much use to a programmer, your programs will be better if you remember that you can include it so that end users can build dBASE expressions (such as for searching their data). You can call the Expression Builder and know that it will return a syntactically correct dBASE expression that your code can then use.

But now, let's get back to programming.

You Use the Tools

Use the Program Editor to place these two lines in T.PRG in your \DBWORK directory:

```
win = NEW Form("Hello, World!")
win.open()
```

(From the Command window, type "modi comm t" to start the Program Editor on T.PRG in the current directory. From the Navigator, double-click Untitled after selecting the Program file type.)

When your two lines are ready, press ^D. That initiates this sequence:

- If changed since last save, save the source file.

- If changed since last compiled, recompile.

- Run the program.

You should now be looking at something like what you see in Figure 1-4.

This would be a good time to fiddle with that window without taking your hands off the keyboard. (You'll work faster if you know both mouse and keyboard alterna-

Learn Visual dBASE Programming

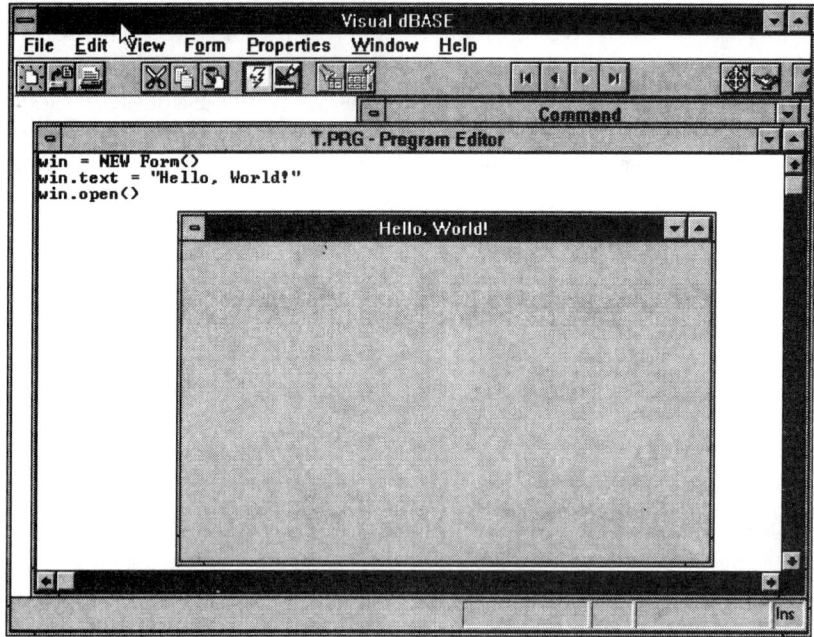

Figure 1-4: "Hello, World!" window launched

tives, and there are some things you can do from the keyboard that you just can't do at all with the mouse.)

First, open your window's system menu with Alt+hyphen — the hyphen looks a little like the bar in the system button. Use the indicated letter to move your window. Use the arrow keys to move your window around. Press Enter when you are done, or press Esc to have the window return to its original position.

Now let's go beyond what you can do with the mouse. Use Alt+hyphen again to get to the system menu and choose Size. The first arrow key will get you to an edge. Once you are on an edge, the appropriate pair of arrow keys lets you drag the edge.

Press the Down arrow to grab the bottom of your window. Now the Up and Down arrows move the bottom up and down. Press enough Down arrows to push your window right on down below the bottom of the screen. Press Enter and your window is now too big! There's no way to use the mouse to grab that bottom edge — the mouse literally can't touch it.

14

Let's retrieve that window edge. Press Alt+hyphen, Size. Now one Down arrow will grab the bottom edge, and then press Up arrow until you get that bottom edge back into the visible client area of Visual dBASE. Got it back? Good.

Finally, you can exit by pressing Ctrl+F4, the standard Windows keystroke to close a child window. Since this is dBASE, you can also exit by pressing Esc. I like the simplicity of Esc, but this is an option that you can turn off if it's not appropriate for your application.

Let's return to our program to make some changes in the properties of the window. The new and changed lines are shown in lighter shading in the printed listings, to make it easy for you to add them yourself.

First, let's add some color to our window. Listing 1-2 shows the addition of the ColorNormal property.

Code Listing 1-2

```
win = NEW Form("Hello, World!")
win.ColorNormal = '+W/B'
win.Open()
```

In the Visual dBASE text editor, add the new line and press ^D. You should now have a blue window. You can do lots more with colors in Visual dBASE than you could with dBASE IV, but one of the nice things about Visual dBASE is that you can still use the old, familiar 16-color specifications, like +W/B.

Listing 1-3 shows us positioning the window over to the right side of the screen.

Code Listing 1-3

```
win = NEW Form("Hello, World!")
win.ColorNormal = '+W/B'
win.Left = 35
win.Open()
```

In Visual dBASE, the coordinates are the old, familiar 25 rows and 80 columns. Or at least they seem to be, at first. As you'll see in due course, this is really a rather sophisticated scheme; it maps Windows proportional font capability to our old DOS coordinates.

Learn Visual dBASE Programming

One adjustment you'll have to make right away is to think about object's top, left, height and width (not top, left, bottom and right). Enter the changes shown in Listing 1-4 and you'll have a new, wide-body window.

Code Listing 1-4
```
win = NEW Form("Hello, World!")
win.ColorNormal = '+W/B'
win.Top = 5
win.Left = 5
win.Height = 10
win.Width = 90
win.Open()
```

Press ^D in the built-in editor and you should get the 747-version window. Let's move that over to the right a bit, so we can see our Command window. We'll want it for the next topic. Change the two lines highlighted in Listing 1-5.

Code Listing 1-5
```
win = NEW Form("Hello, World!")
win.ColorNormal = '+W/B'
win.Top = 5
win.Left = 25
win.Height = 10
win.Width = 50
win.Open()
```

This stuff is really pretty simple, isn't it? You create an object, then fiddle with its properties until it's just right. What's the big deal?

Well, fasten your seatbelt; put your seat and tray table in their full-upright, locked positions for this next one. Ready?

Add the line highlighted in Listing 1-6 and press ^D again. Be prepared for a shock.

Code Listing 1-6
```
win.Height = 10
win.Width = 50
win.Open()
```

Chapter 1   *Your First Windows Program*

```
? "T.PRG is done."
```

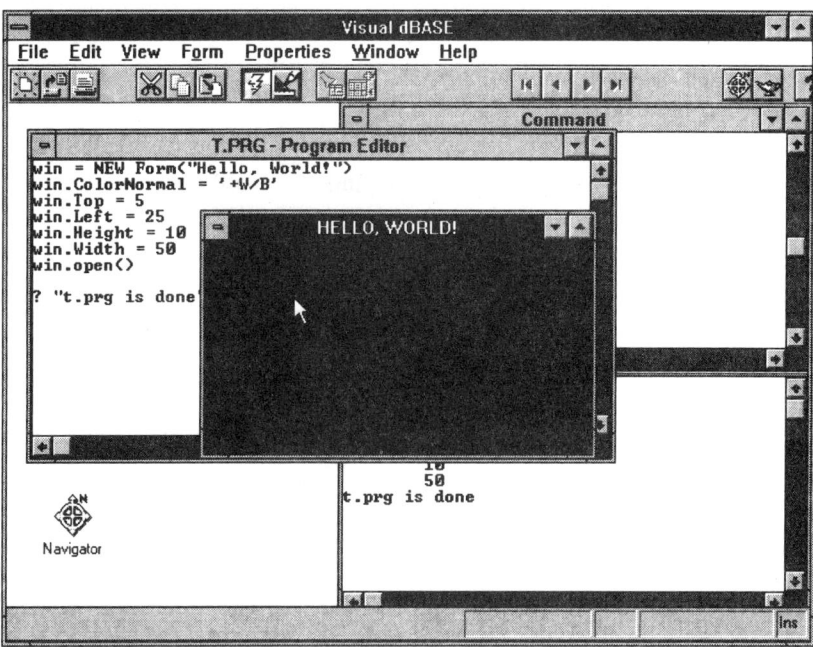

Figure 1-5: Window launched. Program halted.

As you see in your Command window's results pane, the message "T.PRG is done" appeared immediately after your window opened. It may have even gotten there first, depending on the exact state of Windows when Visual dBASE sent the messages that triggered painting your form and putting that text in the Command window. Figure 1-5 shows this result.

So your program has run to completion, but your window is very much alive and well. If you don't believe it yet, go ahead and put your window through its paces — move it, resize it, minimize it, restore it — while you stare at that message "T.PRG is done."

What's going on here? Your windows outlive the program that creates them? How do you know what's happening if you don't even have a running program?

17

No, this isn't a mistake. This is the *fundamental structure* of a Visual dBASE application. And it's why I've been using the word "launch" to describe what we do with a Window. Your code will launch windows, and then the windows are on their own.

I promise you, this will all work out in the end. I rather suspect you're a little bit (or maybe a lot!) nervous at this point. I know I was. If you've done this sort of thing in C++ or FoxPro 2.x, your program is alive and well and very definitely in charge. In Visual dBASE, your program launches the window and says goodbye.

But fear not! You'll learn how to design and build in this new paradigm, and you'll eventually wonder why we ever did it the old way. The C++ and other programmers with their complex event loops will be writing a whole lot of code that Visual dBASE pushes down underneath your level of concern.

As we go forward, you'll see that you can launch a window that is fully equipped without a program running underneath it. You'll see that you are giving the user control, but that you build the controls.

Summary

You've seen about 80% of the new language syntax and semantics that Visual dBASE uses. It's not really very much.

You've overcome hurdle number one in any programming environment — saying "Hello, World!". We didn't just say "Hello," we launched a fully-featured window — a very stylish "Hello, World!" indeed.

Along the way you've learned that objects are instances of a class. You used their data properties and their method properties.

You used the dot operator and saw that it can specify both data and method properties of individual objects. You saw that trailing parentheses distinguish method properties from data properties.

You used the built-in dBASE editor and compiler to create, run, and change programs. And you read about some of the other tools that we'll be meeting and using along the way.

All of this makes a very good start and would probably have you feeling a lot better if you hadn't just seen that the programming paradigm is not at all like the one you're used to for dBASE IV or other Xbase programs.

That makes a pretty accurate description of Visual dBASE. It's the same dBASE language, but it's in a brand new paradigm. Before we're done, you'll see that the old language and the new paradigm work together beautifully.

In the next chapter, we're going to do some old-fashioned procedural coding. We'll build a useful listing utility, and along the way, you'll get more comfortable with the Visual dBASE tools.

Of course, we'll sneak in a Windows dialog box so that you'll have a utility that looks and feels like a genuine Windows program.

Chapter 2

Back to Procedural

Before we get going into our brave new world of Windows programming, we're going to need some tools. In this chapter we'll build a program listing utility. In Chapters 3 and 4, we'll do a more ambitious program control flow utility.

These will be useful programs to put in your toolkit, and while you're building them you'll become much more comfortable with the built-in programming environment. We'll use procedural coding, so you won't have to worry about too many new things all at once.

Well, we'll sort of stick to the old-fashioned code. In this chapter we'll grab one of the pre-built dialog boxes, for the very good reason that a simple function call will replace several hundred lines of procedural code. Beginning in Chapter 3, we'll also sneak the occasional object into our procedural code. Basically, though, we'll be concentrating on building tools while you get the hang of the programming environment.

In this chapter you will:

- Build and use a program skeleton
- Use the low-level I/O routines
- Write a listing utility
- Add a first-class dialog box front end
- Meet and use the LOCAL and STATIC scopes

You dBASE and Fox programmers will find this code familiar, if you are used to using the low-level I/O routines. The Clipper programmers in the audience will be surprised at how easy this can be. (Clipper introduced the low-level I/O routines, but it never included an FGETS() and FPUTS() — which actually aren't that low-level.)

The listing utility we'll create in this chapter will be the first of a suite of programming tools that you can tune to your preferences. I like my own tools because they are minuscule, lightning fast, and do their job *exactly my way*. I've no doubt that the third-party add-on market will begin to supply tools like these, but they'll have to program in a huge supply of switches, toggles and options to make these things satisfy a reasonable number of programmers.

I'm going to satisfy an audience of one: me. I hope as we build these tools that you'll satisfy *you*, not me. Let's begin with our listing generator.

Numbered Listings

I like listings with line numbers so that I can refer to line numbers in text. This is obviously useful if you're writing a book, and it's also useful if you just want to write a little documentation, such as, "The loop on lines 35-47 does...."

But I'm opposed to line numbers on the left. In books, line width is a scarce resource. All the listings here are 60 characters wide, max. Your output device probably is more generous, but it's also probably finite.

Tip: Visual dBASE accepts program lines up to 4K characters long. At 15 characters per inch, that will run about 22 feet wide (7 meters). This wouldn't make a very convenient size for a book.

If you put the listing numbers on the right, you can number the majority of your lines, but skip the numbers if the lines take all the width you need.

The next listing's not on disk. It's a bit of code swiped from my typesetting software. This reads the text that I type in my favorite editor and emits properly tagged input for the desktop publishing program that actually prepares the masters for production. It shows how this right-number scheme can work.

```
CASE input_line = 'app'                                            1
   chapter_name = LTRIM(RTRIM( SUBSTR(input_line,5,3) ))
   chapter_number = IIF( LEN(chapter_name)=1, ;                    3
                         '0'+chapter_name, ;                       4
                         chapter_name )                            5
                                                                   6
   emit( 'Appendix ' + ;                                           7
       chapter_name + ;                                            8
       ': ' + ;                                                    9
       LTRIM(RIGHT( input_line, LEN(input_line)-7 )))
   emit()                                                         11
```

In and Out

I program in little pieces. If all problems were equally divisible, I'd always write exactly six lines at a time. I write debugging code into everything I do and never use the built-in Visual dBASE debugger. (dBASE programmers for whom I have great respect tell me that they use the debugger constantly and consider it indispensable. Don't ignore the debugger just because I do.)

Whether you add debugging code as you go or use the built-in debugger, plan your work in tiny increments. I'll guarantee that it will increase your output rate.

For example, a small listing utility will need to get the name of a source file, validate it, open and read the source, and open and write a listing file. Of course, there's also that part about adding the line numbers.

The basic idea is that you read one file and write another. This requires the low-level file I/O routines, which you may or may not already be using. Let's start with the lowest-level functionality.

Build a Test File

We're going to start by building a test file. Before we do, let's set a couple options. Choose Properties from the menu and choose Desktop from the pulldown. (Desktop is always there. The other choices, if any, are determined by the active window when you choose Properties.)

Click the Programming tab, or press the Tab key until you get to the tabs, and then use the left or right arrow keys to get to Programming. Set Decimals to 4. Set Space on, Talk off and Headings on. Set Coverage off and Ensure Compilation on. Set Design and Safety on. Press F1 for a complete explanation of any of these topics.

For starters, let's open an existing file, TESTIN.PRG and write it out a line at a time to a new output file, TESTOUT.TMP. As we go along, we'll treat short and long input lines differently, so let's set up an appropriate input file, as you see in Listing 2-1.

Code Listing 2-1

```
* TESTIN.PRG -- test file for lister

some short lines
with an

occasional looooooooooooooooooooooooooooooooooooooooooooong
line

* eof TESTIN.PRG
```

I pushed that long line out to my 60-character limit. Choose your limit (think about the font you'll use, the printer, page width and so on).

Building a Program Skeleton

Now that you've got a test file, let's try to read it. Start with a program skeleton, as you see in Listing 2-2.

Code Listing 2-2

```
* SKELETON.PRG --
* copyright 1995, Martin L. Rinehart

* end of SKELETON.PRG
```

Chapter 2 — Back to Procedural

To create this, type "modi comm skeleton" in the Command Window, or double-click the Untitled choice in Program files in the Navigator. Enter the text and press Ctrl+W to save. If you launched Untitled from the Navigator, you'll be prompted with the Save As dialog. Figure 2-1 shows how I save my skeleton program.

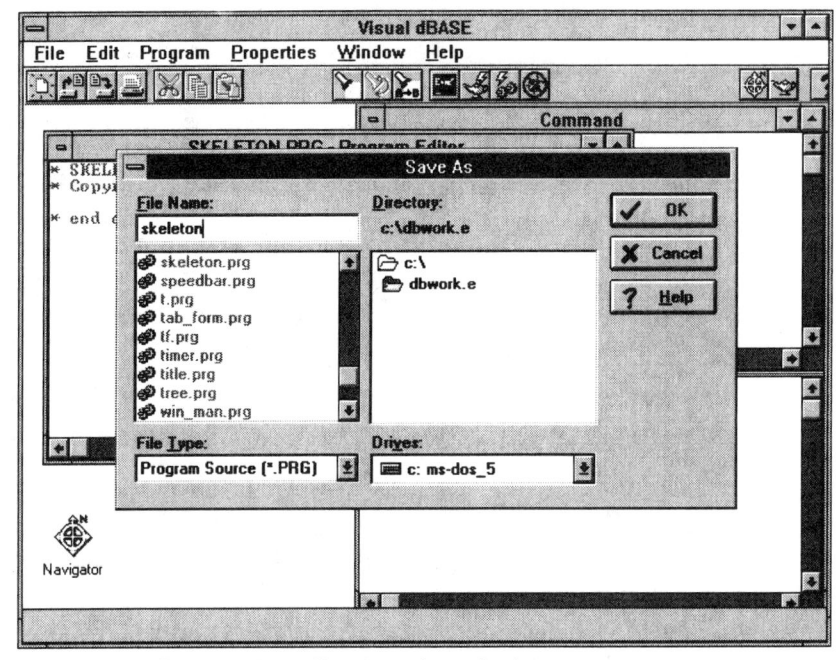

Figure 2-1: Saving the skeleton program

Some programming shops and some programmers use much more elaborate skeletons. They include what it is, who wrote it, the date it was written, a revision history and some documentation, among other items. Make your skeleton suit your own needs. At a minimum it should name the program and state its purpose.

Let's use the skeleton to create LISTER.PRG.

Creating LISTER.PRG

Launch the SKELETON.PRG in the Program Editor. Either type "modi comm skeleton" in the Command Window or double-click SKELETON.PRG in the Navigator's Program files.

Press Ctrl+R to launch the Replace Text dialog. Enter SKELETON in the Find entryfield, then press Tab to go to the Replace entryfield and enter LISTER. Click the Replace All choice and your job is done. Press Esc to exit from the Replace Text dialog. Figure 2-2 shows the Replace Text dialog being used this way.

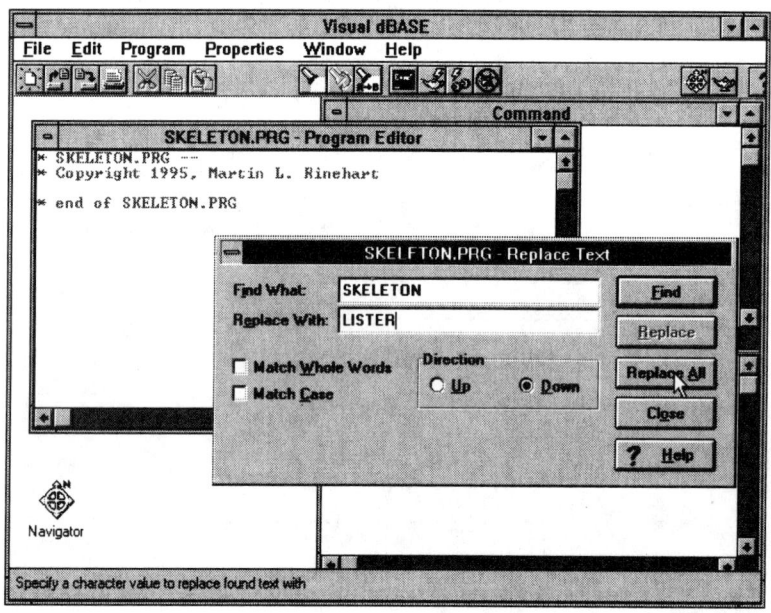

Figure 2-2: Changing SKELETON to LISTER

Now add a comment on the top line that explains the purpose of your program. To save, use Alt+F to get to the file menu, then press A to get to Save As. Type "lister" (.PRG is the default) and press Enter. You've now got a program that should look like the one in Listing 2-3.

Code Listing 2-3

```
* LISTER.PRG -- line numbered code listings
* copyright 1995, Martin L. Rinehart

* end of LISTER.PRG
```

Read the Input File

Now we're ready to open our test input file and read it with the low-level I/O routines. I think that calling these routines "low-level" was a major mistake. It's kept a lot of less intrepid programmers from using them. You can use these to create some mischief, but you have to work at it. If you've sense enough to not open for output critical files like DBASEWIN.EXE these are fine, simple routines for accessing, among other things, text files.

The FOPEN() function opens existing files and the FGETS() function gets a text string from an ASCII file. FOPEN() lets you supply an access parameter, but it defaults to read-only if you omit the parameter, which is a good way to open files you don't want to damage. It returns a handle identifying the file for future read (or other) operations.

The FGETS() function can also do complicated things, but will happily read one string at a time from a text file if you don't override its defaults.

Listing 2-4 is code that reads our test file and writes it into the Command Window's results pane.

Code Listing 2-4

```
* LISTER.PRG -- line numbered code listings
* copyright 1995, Martin L. Rinehart

in_handle = FOPEN('TESTIN.PRG')

DO WHILE .NOT. FEOF(in_handle)
   ? FGETS(in_handle)
ENDDO

* end of LISTER.PRG
```

Launch LISTER.PRG in the Program Editor if it is not already there. (If LISTER.PRG is already launched in the Program Editor, you can click on it, if it's visible, or try Alt+W to choose the Windows menu and then click on the appropriate window — it will be 3 or higher since 1 and 2 are always the Navigator and the Command Window, respectively.)

Add the four lines in the lighter shading in Listing 2-4 and press Ctrl+D. You'll probably want to adjust your Command Window to a larger size so you can see all of the input file. Figure 2-3 shows my run of this code.

Learn Visual dBASE Programming

```
in_handle = FOPEN('TESTIN.PRG')
DO WHILE .NOT. FEOF(in_handle)
    ? FGETS(in_handle)
ENDDO
```

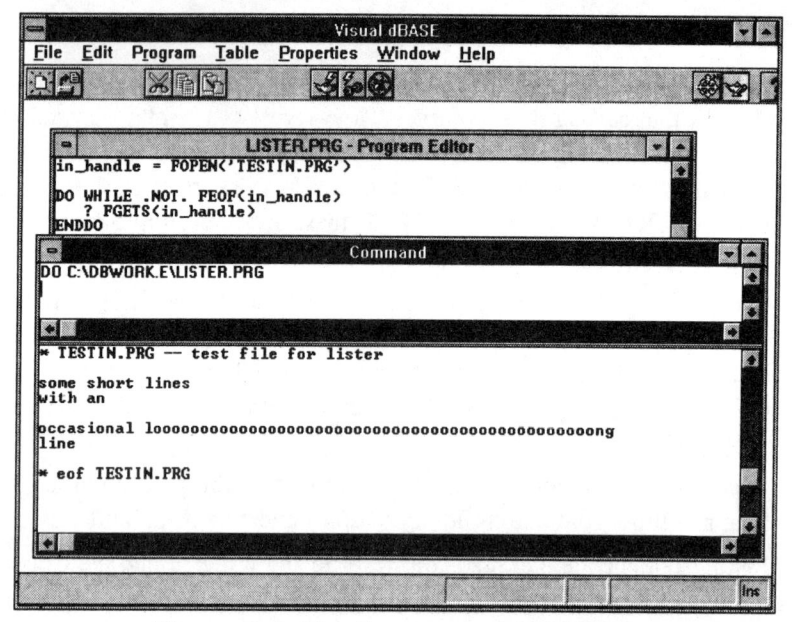

```
DO C:\DBWORK.E\LISTER.PRG
```

```
* TESTIN.PRG -- test file for lister
some short lines
with an
occasional looooooooooooooooooooooooooooooooooooooooong
line
* eof TESTIN.PRG
```

Figure 2-3: Testing an early LISTER

This reads the file. If you're not a complete beginner, you're probably thinking that a little error-handling code would be in order. What happens if the file doesn't exist?

This will work out, as you'll see, when we add the file opening dialog. For the moment, our test file does exist.

Writing the Output File

Now we need to write to the output file. For this we'll just create our test output file and write to it. If there was an existing file, we'll destroy it. This is another item that will work out before we're done.

The FCREATE() function creates a file. By the way, you can get the full details on this function by typing "help fcreate()" in the Command Window. Again, you can supply more parameters but the default case does exactly what we want.

The FPUTS() function is the appropriate opposite of FGETS(). Listing 2-5 shows the simple addition to write our output file.

28

Code Listing 2-5

```
* LISTER.PRG -- line numbered code listings
* copyright 1995, Martin L. Rinehart

in_handle = FOPEN('TESTIN.PRG')
out_handle = FCREATE('TESTOUT.TMP')

DO WHILE .NOT. FEOF(in_handle)
  s = FGETS(in_handle)
  FPUTS(out_handle, s)
ENDDO

* end of LISTER.PRG
```

This works, but it's got bugs. It will crash with an Already Open message when it tries to open TESTIN.PRG the second time. To get it to run, use the CLOSE ALL command in the Command Window. Here's the sequence:

- Ctrl+D from the Program Editor (crashes)
- Cancel the run
- Select the Command Window
- Type CLOSE ALL
- Select the Program Editor
- Ctrl+D again (runs)

From the Command Window, type "MODI FILE TESTOUT.TMP" and you can check the output file that you generated. Well, you could if you remembered to close it first. Again, back to the Command Window and CLOSE ALL, then MODI FILE TESTOUT.TMP.

After you look at TESTOUT.TMP, be sure you close it. Press Ctrl+F4, or double-click its system-menu button (upper-left corner) or open the system menu (single click, or press Alt+hyphen) and choose Close. In general, keep closing your windows behind you or your desktop will end up a hopeless mess.

You can repeat any command in the Command Window by clicking on it and pressing Enter. For keyboard-free operation, click the command you want and then right-click to get the SpeedMenu. Click on Execute Selection to run the command.

This is very useful in the, "Oh darn! I forgot to close the stupid file." type mistake we just saw.

Let's make our LISTER the sort of clever fellow that cleans up after himself. Listing 2-6 shows the two lines you need to add.

Code Listing 2-6

```
* LISTER.PRG -- line numbered code listings
* copyright 1995, Martin L. Rinehart
...

FCLOSE( in_handle )
FCLOSE( out_handle )

* end of LISTER.PRG
```

With that modification, you can run LISTER repeatedly and it won't fail. There's only one small item left.

Line Numbering

Now we're rolling. Line numbers were our original goal, so let's add them now. We'll add a counter to the mainline and then call a function to paste the line number onto the right side of the output line.

Let's start by just slapping the number on the right side of the line. That will get our framework right. Once that works we can worry about getting a neatly right justified number.

Structuring for Line Numbers

We're going to use the classic structure of procedural programs: a mainline and supporting subroutines. In this case we'll have a mainline and a function that adds line numbers on the right side of the line.

As I talk about routines, I'll try to be consistent in my terminology. If the routine is called by another, it's a subroutine. If a subroutine does not return a value, it's a procedure. A subroutine that returns a value is a function. As you'll see, there's not much distinction left in dBASE itself, but I use these terms and the corresponding keywords to keep my code clear.

Listing 2-7 shows LISTER with a line counter and a new function added.

Chapter 2 **Back to Procedural**

Code Listing 2-7

```
* LISTER.PRG -- line numbered code listings
* copyright 1995, Martin L. Rinehart

line_number = 0

in_handle = FOPEN('TESTIN.PRG')
out_handle = FCREATE('TESTOUT.TMP')

DO WHILE .NOT. FEOF(in_handle)
  s = FGETS(in_handle)

  line_number = line_number + 1
  FPUTS( out_handle, add_num(s,line_number) )

ENDDO

FCLOSE(in_handle)
FCLOSE(out_handle)

* end of mainline

FUNCTION add_num(line, number)

RETURN line + STR(number) && end of add_num

* end of LISTER.PRG
```

As you can see, I've added the parameters to the add_num function on the same line as the function statement, by enclosing them in parentheses. You can still use a PARAMETERS statement after the function statement, but for reasons I'll get to in this chapter, that's generally not the best way to go. For the moment, the syntax shown here is just a nicer looking way of naming the parameters that receive the values you're passing to the function with the call.

When you add these lines and press Ctrl+D, your output will look something like this:

```
* TESTIN.PRG -- test file for lister         1
     2
some short lines          3
with an          4
```

31

```
              5
occasional looooooooooooooooooooooooooooooong        6
line            8
            9
* eof TESTIN.PRG          9
```

(I chopped the long line to get this listing to fit in the book.)

Neat Numbers

This is quite ugly, but it shows that we're doing the right thing at the right time. Now let's make it look good.

To start, I'll add a variable, max_chars, to the mainline. In Visual dBASE you could make this a constant, which would be better unless you thought that you might want to change it from time to time. My magazine articles require formatting to different numbers of characters, so I need a variable. You decide for yourself.

With the length specified, I'm going to write the simplest number appender I can that will work. I'll use five digit numbers and simply not put them on if I don't have five characters free. Listing 2-08 shows the revisions.

Code Listing 2-8

```
* LISTER.PRG -- line numbered code listings
* copyright 1995, Martin L. Rinehart

line_number = 0
max_chars   = 60

in_handle = FOPEN('TESTIN.PRG')
out_handle = FCREATE('TESTOUT.TMP')

DO WHILE .NOT. FEOF(in_handle)
  s = FGETS(in_handle)

  line_number = line_number + 1
  FPUTS( out_handle, add_num(s,line_number) )

ENDDO

FCLOSE(in_handle)
FCLOSE(out_handle)
```

```
* end of mainline

FUNCTION add_num(line, number)

IF LEN(line) > max_chars - 5
  RETURN line
ELSE
  RETURN line + SPACE( max_chars-5-LEN(line) ) + ;
         STR(number, 5)
ENDIF   && end of add_num

* end of LISTER.PRG
```

Now when I run my listing utility, I get this result:

```
* TESTIN.PRG -- test file for lister                             1
                                                                 2
some short lines                                                 3
with an                                                          4
                                                                 5
occasional looooooooooooooooooooooooooooooooooooooong
line                                                             7
                                                                 8
* eof TESTIN.PRG                                                 9
```

This is exactly the result I want. (And it's about time, too. Once it works, I won't have to clutter up the book with full listings, which will obviously become a problem as our code goes to hundreds, then thousands of lines long. I'll just leave the numbers over there on the right. You'll know that they're not part of the code.)

User Interface

LISTER is doing a fine job, but it's not too bright. Suppose we didn't want to just process a routine called TESTIN.PRG? Now comes the hard part. If you've done any DOS programming you know that asking the user for a file name, checking for existence, handling different drives and directories — it all gets very complicated, very fast.

At least it does if you want to make your user's life easy.

At least it did, until dBASE 5.0.

Try this command at the dot prompt:

```
? getfile('*.prg')
```

When you do, you'll see that you have a sophisticated, Windows-style dialog box. It's the same one that Visual dBASE uses for all file selection. As you see, the *.prg specification provides the default extension. Figure 2-4 shows my getfile() from the Command Window.

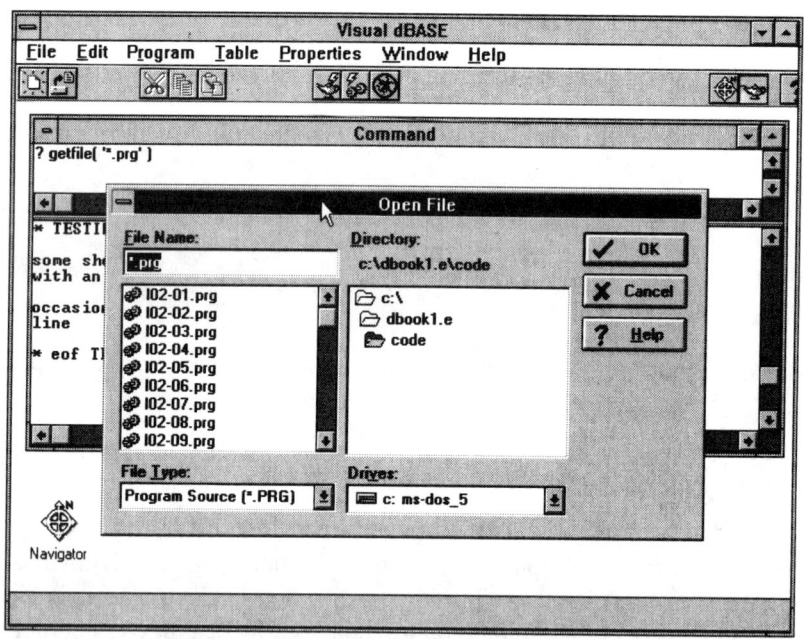

Figure 2-4: Simple command generating sophisticated dialog

Try this Command Window command and pick a file. Try again without picking a file. In the first case, it returns the file you chose, disk and directory included. In the second case, it returns a null string. Now we've got something to work with.

Testing the Names

Let's modify LISTER to call the GETFILE() dialog for an input file name. If the user cancels out of the dialog, we'll cancel out of the program. We know that this is

Chapter 2   **Back to Procedural**

the case if we don't get a name back. If we do get a name, we know it's an existing file, so we don't have to check.

We'll strip the extension and add .TMP to get an output file name. We won't worry about overwriting an older .TMP because we're in the business of creating a temporary file here.

I'm not using the .LST extension since that is used by other programs that expect a permanent list of files, such as PKZIP, MAKE files and linkers. The .TMP extension's history for temporary files goes back to the DEC operating systems that CP/M emulated before DOS emulated CP/M.

Listing 2-9 is my first cut at code that adds the GETFILE() capability. You'll see that I didn't try to run this code. I stopped it after building the output file name. When you run it, you'll see that was a smart decision.

Code Listing 2-9

```
* LISTER.PRG -- line numbered code listings
* copyright 1995, Martin L. Rinehart

line_number = 0
max_chars   = 60

fname = GETFILE('*.prg')

IF EMPTY(fname)
   RETURN
ENDIF

in_handle = FOPEN(fname)

oname = LEFT( fname, RAT('.',fname) ) + '.TMP'
? oname
RETURN

out_handle = FCREATE(oname)

DO WHILE .NOT. FEOF(in_handle)
```

When you run this improved edition, you get the GETFILE() dialog. If you cancel out of that dialog, your program terminates immediately. (If EMPTY() is new to you, it returns True for a string that is all blank or zero length.)

35

If you choose a file, you see the error in the name I've built. It doubles the period. It's simple enough to fix it so that I won't give you another listing. Just change the constant .TMP to TMP. Now when you run it you should get exactly what you wanted.

To get a fully operational program, delete these two lines:

```
? oname
RETURN
```

Title the Dialog

A couple more changes and we'll call LISTER a finished program. I'd like a sensible title on the dialog box. (As you see in Visual dBASE, the Open File dialog comes up under many names, appropriate to the type of file being opened.)

Luckily, that's just a parameter added to the GETFILE() call. The changed line is highlighted in Listing 2-10.

Code Listing 2-10

```
* LISTER.PRG -- line numbered code listings
* copyright 1995, Martin L. Rinehart

line_number = 0
max_chars   = 60

fname = GETFILE('*.prg', 'File for Listing')

IF EMPTY(fname)
```

Press Ctrl+D with that addition, and your Open File dialog should have a more descriptive title. Mine is shown in Figure 2-5.

Close with a Message

The last change I want is an indication that LISTER has actually done some work. Right now I'm not in doubt, but perhaps a month from now I could look at this and forget that I created a .TMP file and think that LISTER wasn't doing anything.

Let's have LISTER report that it has completed its job in the results pane of the Command Window. Listing 2-11 shows the line to add.

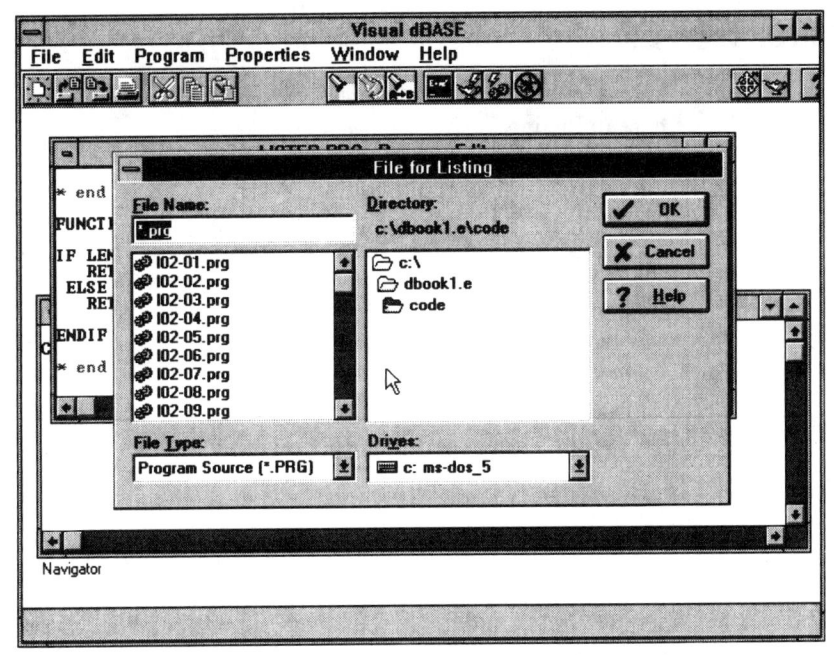

Figure 2-5: Properly titled open file dialog

Code Listing 2-11

```
FCLOSE(out_handle)

? oname + ' prepared.'

* end of mainline
```

With this line, the preparation of your listing file is announced on completion. That's all I care to do for now.

Someday down the road, when we get LISTER munching away at really big files, we might put some sort of message in the status bar showing how much work has been done as LISTER goes along. For small files, however, LISTER is virtually instantaneous. The Visual dBASE low-level I/O functions are very fast.

LISTER for LISTER

The first thing I've done with my finished LISTER is to build the full listing of itself. It's shown here in Listing 2-12.

Code Listing 2-12

```
* LISTER.PRG -- line numbered code listings           1
* copyright 1995, Martin L. Rinehart                   2
                                                       3
line_number = 0                                        4
max_chars   = 60                                       5
                                                       6
fname = GETFILE('*.prg', 'File for Listing')           7
                                                       8
IF EMPTY(fname)                                        9
  RETURN                                              10
ENDIF                                                 11
                                                      12
in_handle = FOPEN(fname)                              13
                                                      14
oname = LEFT( fname, RAT('.',fname) ) + 'TMP'         15
                                                      16
out_handle = FCREATE(oname)                           17
                                                      18
DO WHILE .NOT. FEOF(in_handle)                        19
   s = FGETS(in_handle)                               20
                                                      21
   line_number = line_number + 1                      22
   FPUTS( out_handle, add_num(s,line_number) )        23
                                                      24
ENDDO                                                 25
                                                      26
FCLOSE(in_handle)                                     27
FCLOSE(out_handle)                                    28
                                                      29
? oname + ' prepared.'                                30
                                                      31
* end of mainline                                     32
                                                      33
FUNCTION add_num(line, number)                        34
                                                      35
IF LEN(line) > max_chars - 5                          36
```

```
   RETURN line                                              37
ELSE                                                        38
   RETURN line + SPACE( max_chars-5-LEN(line) ) + ;         39
          STR(number, 5)                                    40
ENDIF && end of add_num                                     41
                                                            42
* end of LISTER.PRG                                         43
```

This listing is not on disk. The full program is in L02-11.PRG, which will write Listing 2-12 if run against itself.

Visual dBASE Scopes

In the bad old days (before Clipper 5) the only scopes we could use in Xbase were PUBLIC and the default PRIVATE. Either type of variable was fair game for any called routine to change. No one who worked very long with any Xbase dialect lacks for stories about how some perfectly well-behaved routine suddenly started crashing because some lower-level routine happened to use a variable of the same name as one in the calling hierarchy.

Clipper 5.0 introduced LOCAL and STATIC variables to Xbase, and dBASE has now adopted them.

LOCAL Variables

A LOCAL variable is *visible* only to the routine in which it is declared. Any other routine in your system (or every other routine, for that matter) can have a variable of the same name, but they will not be the same as the LOCAL variable.

Declaring LOCAL Variables

A LOCAL variable is created by the routine in which it is declared. It is discarded when its routine ends. No other routine can read or write it. In fact, no other routine is even aware that it exists (unless you use it as a subroutine argument). LOCALs should be used whenever they are appropriate.

Here's an example of bad code with PRIVATE variables:

```
i = 1
DO WHILE i < 5
```

```
    DO my_subr

    i = i + 1    && i = 4; it's an endless loop

ENDDO

PROC my_subr
i = 3           && this resets i, above!
RETURN
```

The calling routine looks like it will step i from 1 to 4 and then stop. But the called routine has a surprise in store. It never lets i get past 4 in the calling routine, so it will run until you reboot. Let's hope you didn't have too many files open.

Here's the same example, with a LOCAL i:

```
LOCAL i
i = 1

DO WHILE i < 5

  DO my_subr

  i = i + 1    && bulletproof!

ENDDO

PROC my_subr
i = 3           && this is another, separate variable
RETURN
```

Using LOCAL variables is a far better software engineering practice than using PRIVATEs. LOCALs are not subject to inadvertent damage by routines you can't see or by routines written by someone else for some other purpose.

Clipper is like C in insisting that LOCAL declarations come at the very top of the routine, before any executable lines. dBASE is like C++ in that it lets you declare your LOCALs just before you use them. This is a great convenience.

Another convenience is that you can use the semicolon to separate lines of code, as well as to continue lines.

Chapter 2 — Back to Procedural

Here's one example:

```
x = 1; y = 2
```

I'd very seldom want to write two different lines of code on a single line of file, but there are exceptions. Here's one:

```
LOCAL x; x = 1
```

With this combination, you think of a variable you need and on the spot declare it LOCAL and initialize it. I agree with those who say that this next one would be even better, but unfortunately you can't do it:

```
LOCAL x = 1 && Not allowed!
```

Declaring LOCAL Parameters

We now have two ways of declaring subroutine parameters:

```
PROCEDURE my_proc( param1, param2, ... )
```

&& or

```
PROCEDURE my_proc
PARAMETERS param1, param2, ...
```

Don't use the second way (the traditional way) except in very rare circumstances. If you put the parameters in parentheses on the same line as the PROCEDURE or FUNCTION statement, the parameters are local variables. In the older way, the parameters that follow the PARAMETERS statement are still PRIVATE variables.

If you use the parentheses method, any called routine that happens to use a variable of the same name as one of your parameters will not know that the parameter exists. It won't be able to inadvertently change it. In the older way, a called routine could destroy the value in a parameter, if it happened to use a variable with the same name.

Warning: Parameters are still a software engineering danger in dBASE, because variables are passed by reference.

Learn Visual dBASE Programming

Don't assume that because everything is LOCAL, it's all bullet-proof; it's not. Strings are passed by reference, which let's this example change June to Julie, even though everything is LOCAL:

```
LOCAL dt; dt = 'June'
pick_up_date(dt)

PROCEDURE pick_up_date(d)
IF mistakes = possible
  d = 'Julie'
ENDIF
...
```

In the calling routine, June was changed to Julie, even though you used a LOCAL variable for protection. In the called routine, your value was passed by reference, so d is a reference to the value in the calling routine. When you assign Julie to d, you assign Julie to dt in the calling routine.

You can avoid this source of error by passing by value. To pass by value, enclose the argument in parentheses:

```
LOCAL dt; dt = 'June'
pick_up_date( (dt) ) && passes value of dt
```

This makes it impossible for your called routine to change the value of your dt variable. Alternatively, make it a rule that your called routines will always copy their parameters:

```
LOCAL dt; dt = 'June'
pick_up_date(dt)

PROCEDURE pick_up_date(d)
LOCAL my_d; my_d = d
IF mistakes = possible
  my_d = 'Julie'
ENDIF
...
```

This will also ensure that the calling routine's values are not inadvertently changed.

STATIC Variables

Variables in dBASE can have dynamic or static temporal scopes. The *scope* of a variable is a range over which it exists. Visibility, such as PRIVATE or LOCAL, controls the grammatical units that can access the variable. Temporal scope controls the time(s) at which you can access the variable.

PUBLIC variables and STATIC variables are alive from the time they are declared to the time the application stops running. Their temporal scope is permanent. PRIVATE and LOCAL variables, on the other hand, are created when the routine that declares them starts running until the routine that declares them stops running.

You use STATIC variables when you don't want the variable's value to be lost at the completion of a routine:

```
PROCEDURE date_handler(params)

STATIC days_per_year = 365
...
RETURN
```

In this example, the variable days_per_year is set to 365. It is created and set the first time the date_handler() routine is called. (Presumably, someplace else you have logic that will change it back and forth between 365 and 366 when you encounter leap years.)

If you haven't counted, days_per_year is over the old limit of 10 (or 11) characters for a variable name. The name length limit is not documented in Visual dBASE. I started to experimentally find the limit, but I lost interest in my own experiment somewhere out at about 50 characters long. Make your names long enough to describe your values, but short enough to type.

Improving LISTER

With this knowledge, let's use a little bit of better software engineering, in an im - proved version of LISTER. It's shown in Listing 2-13.

Code Listing 2-13

```
* LISTER.PRG -- line numbered code listings          1
* copyright 1995, Martin L. Rinehart               2
                                                    3
```

```
LOCAL line_number; line_number = 0                          4
                                                            5
PRIVATE max_chars   && used in add_num()                    6
max_chars    = 60                                           7
                                                            8
LOCAL fname, oname                                          9
fname = GETFILE('*.prg', 'File for Listing')               10
                                                           11
IF EMPTY(fname)                                            12
  RETURN                                                   13
ENDIF                                                      14
                                                           15
LOCAL in_handle, out_handle                                16
                                                           17
in_handle = FOPEN(fname)                                   18
                                                           19
oname = LEFT( fname, AT('.',fname) ) + 'TMP'               20
                                                           21
out_handle = FCREATE(oname)                                22
                                                           23
LOCAL s                                                    24
                                                           25
DO WHILE .NOT. FEOF(in_handle)                             26
  s = FGETS(in_handle)                                     27
                                                           28
  line_number = line_number + 1                            29
  FPUTS( out_handle, add_num(s,line_number) )              30
                                                           31
ENDDO                                                      32
                                                           33
FCLOSE(in_handle)                                          34
FCLOSE(out_handle)                                         35
                                                           36
? oname + ' prepared.'                                     37
                                                           38
* end of mainline                                          39
                                                           40
                                                           41
FUNCTION add_num(line, number)                             42
                                                           43
* max_chars is declared in LISTER.PRG's mainline           44
                                                           45
```

```
IF LEN(line) > max_chars - 5                              46
   RETURN line                                            47
ELSE                                                      48
   RETURN line + SPACE( max_chars-5-LEN(line) ) + ;       49
       STR(number, 5)                                     50
ENDIF && end of add_num                                   51
                                                          52
* end of LISTER.PRG                                       53
```

At line 4, the line_number variable is declared local and initialized. Lines 6 and 7 declare max_chars PRIVATE and tell me where I've used it. Lines 9 and 16 declare more LOCALs in advance of their use.

At line 24, s is declared LOCAL. I use short names, like s, when a variable is declared, used and forgotten in a very short span of code.

Line 44 again documents the source of the max_chars variable. Purists will object, arguing that all variables should be passed as arguments to the called function. I'm not a purist. I object to cluttering up your subroutine calls with extraneous parameters, especially when they are truly global variables, such as the character limit for your output.

Summary

In this chapter, we've built a code listing utility. Along the way, you've become more familiar with the built-in editor and are getting used to writing, compiling, and running programs in Visual dBASE.

We started with a program skeleton that will serve as the starting point for all our programs. Then we moved on to our listing utility.

We built it using the so-called low-level routines, FOPEN(), FGETS(), FCREATE(), FPUTS(), and FCLOSE(). You saw that these are not very low-level, and that they make short work of handling text files.

When it came time to add a user-friendly (for programming utilities, the users are you and me) front-end routine, we used the new GETFILE() function. This launched a sophisticated, Windows-style file selection dialog that made our program look great with only a trivial effort on our part.

Finally, we took a close look at the new scopes, LOCAL and STATIC. You saw that LOCAL variables are generally the ones you want to use, replacing the older PRIVATE variables. The new parentheses syntax for subroutine parameters gives you another way of adding LOCAL variables, although it still leaves some work to us.

In the next chapter, we're going to do some more procedural coding, but we're going to use objects to help us with our work.

Chapter 3

Easing Into Objects — Analysis

Visual dBASE includes the CLASS/ENDCLASS control construct, which is key to Visual dBASE programming; it also means that your old diagramming utilities won't work. The DO/UNTIL loop also is new, but you could probably live without that one being correctly handled. You won't be able to live without CLASS/ENDCLASS.

In this chapter, we'll continue to do procedural programming, building the first half of an action diagrammer. We'll ease into objects, using them in their simplest form — as an immensely useful tool in procedural programming.

In this chapter you will:

- Find out why we use action diagrams
- Learn about the analysis and generation phases of code analyzers
- Learn about lexical analysis and parsing
- Write a lexical analysis routine
- Write a parser
- Use small objects as part of procedural systems

We're going to have some fun here. This is just a useful little utility, but we'll build it as if we were working on a real compiler. We'll structure it with a lexer (lexical analysis routine) and a parser (grammatical analysis routine) for a couple of reasons.

First, using official compiler terms like lexer and parser will make our software impressive to talk about, even though we'll keep it dead simple. (I'll define these terms when we get to them.)

Second, the structure will be there for you to improve over time. We'll code for IF statements where the word IF is the first two non-blank characters on a line. A general routine could handle what I consider truly bad code style:

```
x = 2; IF y = 3
x = 4; ENDIF
```

If you ever write like that, please don't tell me. I'll tell you what I think about it. It's dumb. On the other hand, if you need to generalize this utility to handle all valid input, you'd only need to fix up the lexer and it would handle that dumb code — the rest would work unchanged.

In this chapter, we'll build the lexer and parser: the analytical components. In Chapter 4 we'll get on to build the generation components. First, let's see where we're going.

| Chapter 3 | Easing Into Objects -- Analysis |

Why Action Diagrams?

When I first began writing dBASE (that was dBASE II, circa 1981) I found that it was too simple to misplace an ENDIF, or to cross an ENDDO and ENDIF. We all learned to take defensive action against these mistakes.

Keeping Your Code Sound

When I wrote the code I normally typed the commands in pairs, so there was no chance for confusion. Many editors will do this for you today. The idea is to start like this:

```
DO WHILE ??

   SKIP
ENDDO
```

With the loop shell in place, you move your cursor into the loop and start typing, as these comments point out:

```
DO WHILE ??

   * this is where you continue
   * your work, adding
   * lines as needed

   SKIP
ENDDO
```

When you enter an if, or any other nested structure, you repeat the process:

```
DO WHILE ??

   * this is where you continue
   * your work, adding
   * lines as needed

   IF ???

      ELSE
```

49

```
    ENDIF

    SKIP
ENDDO
```

    Again, either you or your editor completes the IF/ENDIF block before you get to entering the contents of the block. This process is almost foolproof.

Scrambling Your Sound Code

    Of course, "almost foolproof" in programming means it's a rich source of errors. The problem comes when someone looks at your running code, tells you how good it looks and then says, "Oh, yeah. There's this one thing I didn't mention....." and then goes on to tell you about the five conditions under which your program's existing logic does and doesn't apply.

    Then you go into your code and start marking and moving large blocks to accommodate the new logic. Before you know it, you've achieved spaghetti.

    At any rate, before I knew it, I'd achieved spaghetti. Meticulous indenting helps. Complex logic, where your indenting is deep, helps defeat the value of indenting. There's no way around the problem — you need to put your computer to work to help you out.

Defining Action Diagramming

    The simplest form of an action diagram is one that we've all used, even without having a nice name to put on it. You make a printout and then starting at the deepest level you can find, you draw a line from an IF to an ENDIF. You try to do all the deepest logic blocks first, connecting the start and end of each logical construct.

    After you've done all the innermost blocks, you back up a level and start connecting those that enclose just one level of other blocks. Then you go to the next level, and so on. When you are done, your logic is pretty clear (or you've found where an ENDCASE precedes a needed ENDIF, or whatever).

    More sophisticated action diagrams show what type of construct each logic block is, and add other information. For example, the True and False portions of an IF block can be separately labeled.

Designing an Action Diagramming Utility

We'll build this utility as if it were a compiler. This gives us a theoretically sound basis for making it more sophisticated over time. A compiler is generally built in two main parts:

- Analyzer (asks what the code means)
- Generator (implements the meaning)

The analyzer, or analysis phase, generally has two parts:

- Lexical analysis (tokenizes the code)
- Semantic analysis (parses the tokens)

The Lexer

Compiler writers call the lexical analysis machinery a lexer or tokenizer.

Tokenizing breaks the input stream into atomic chunks, such as numbers, keywords, variable names and string constants. You can think of this process as breaking the program statement (sentence) down into words. Here's a sample input line:

```
IF last_name="Smith"
```

Here are the tokens:

- IF (a keyword)
- last_name (a variable name)
- = (an operator)
- Smith (a string constant)

The job of the lexer is to pass the right tokens to the parser, no matter how screwball the input line. The lexer will pass the preceding four tokens for all these forms of the previous statement:

```
IF last_name="Smith"
IF last_name = "Smith"
   IF last_name='Smith' && indents and comments ignored
      IF LAST_NAME = "Smith"
IF last_name           =          "Smith"
```

The lexer also skips over blank lines, tosses comments, and does any other cleanup, all designed to make the parser's life easier

The Parser

The parser makes sense of the tokens. In the preceding example, it would decide that the = sign was a relational operator, not an assignment operator.

Our parser is going to have to worry about the keyword DO, for instance. Here are four possibilties for the token that follows DO:

- the keyword CASE

- the keyword WHILE

- a name

- the end of the statement

DO CASE is the start of a DO CASE switch. DO WHILE is the start of a loop. DO <name> is a subroutine call. DO all by itself is the start of a DO/UNTIL loop.

What? DO/UNTIL?

Have you seen the DO/UNTIL loop? It's a nice addition to the language, though nothing very radical. Here's how you write it:

```
DO
   * code to do
UNTIL <condition>
```

Chapter 3 Easing Into Objects -- Analysis

DO/UNTIL is first cousin to DO WHILE/ENDDO. As its appearance suggests, the logical test comes at the bottom. Here's a way to process all the records in a file:

```
DO

    * process records here

    SKIP

UNTIL EOF()
```

Beware! This loop may fail on an empty table, because the EOF() test isn't made until the first pass through the loop is complete. Use DO/UNTIL only if you always want at least one pass through your loop.

Don't decide that this restriction means you don't want to bother with DO/UNTIL. The very first loop we write for our lexer is a perfect use for DO/UNTIL.

Our parser will handle these DO problems, separating DO WHILE from DO/UNTIL and DO <name>.

The Stack Machinery

The lexer and parser will handle the analysis phase. Now let's consider the generation phase.

As we come to the start of a block statement, such as the IF in an IF/ELSE/ENDIF, we'll push it onto a stack. When we come to a mid-block modifier, such as the ELSE, we'll notify the top element of the stack. When we come to the end of a block, such as ENDIF, we'll pop the stack.

With a stack, we won't have to worry about the depth of nesting, unless, of course, our stack runs out of space. Since this is a small utility with trivial data requirements we should have a couple megabytes free for our stack, so I won't worry about it running out.

When we come to a mid-block modifier or an end of block statement, we'll also check for errors. ELSE had better not show up in a DO WHILE; LOOP had better not be in an IF. UNTIL is the only way to end a DO/UNTIL, and so on.

We'll use a Visual dBASE object to implement the stack. You'll see that this makes the code dead simple.

The Output Machinery

Output machinery, together with the stack machinery, are our utility's generator portion. I hope that one of you will be inspired to make a very nice, graphical output backend and post it in the DBASEWIN forum on CompuServe.

The one I'm going to show you here is an old-fashioned, character based output. It works and it meets my needs.

Design for Debugging

The most important part of my design work is figuring out how to code the system in my preferred six-line increments. As you saw in Chapter 2, I do just one little thing at a time.

In my younger days, I wrote large blocks of code and then debugged them. Now that I only do itsy little pieces, I average about twice as many lines of finished code per day as I used to, and I almost never find serious structural bugs late in the coding process.

Here's how I'm going to do this one. We'll build the lexer, and type input lines in the Command Window, looking at the lexer's results in the results pane of the Command Window. Then we can hook the parser onto the lexer to see that they both work.

After they both work, we can hook them up to real file input. With file input, we can add the stack machinery. We'll have to build a display that shows us the stack and a stepper that lets us work through one line at a time, watching the stack grow and shink.

Finally, with that running, we can build the output machinery. Are you ready to get started? Let's go.

Implementing the Lexer

First, load SKELETON into the Program Editor, change the SKELETONs to ACTION_Ds and File/Save As ACTION_D.PRG. Next, type this command in the Command Window:

```
SET FUNCTION F2 TO "modi comm action_d;"
```

That will let you press F2 to launch ACTION_D in the Program Editor. Test it, and you are ready for efficient work.

The Test Loop

Start by adding the lines shown in Listing 3-1.

Code Listing 3-1

```
* ACTION_D.PRG -- Action Diagrammer for dBWin Code
* copyright 1995, Martin L. Rinehart

x = ''
DO

   ACCEPT 'line: ' TO x

UNTIL x = 'quit'

* end of ACTION_D.PRG
```

Quite a coincidence, isn't it? Our very first loop is a new DO/UNTIL. It's just what we want — a loop that executes first and tests at the end.

When you press Ctrl+D for this program, it should sit in the Command Window's results pane and calmly prompt you for lines, until you enter quit.

With that running, it's time to add a lexer. I'll begin the lexer with a skeleton that will pretend to break the lines into tokens and then display the tokens. I'm going to use an object from the Object class as the vehicle for passing around our tokens.

Using an Object Class Object

The Object class is the base class for a plain object. This built-in class has no properties of its own. It does know how to create itself, and when you are done with it, how to release its memory. Along the way, you can attach properties to it. The Object class also has the intelligence to release the attached properties when you are done with the object.

Note here that I'm using the UpperLower capitalization to denote a Visual dBASE built-in class or property. For instance, objects are created from the Object class. All of this is more trouble to explain than to do. The code is in Listing 3-2.

Code Listing 3-2

```
* ACTION_D.PRG -- Action Diagrammer for dBWin Code
* copyright 1995, Martin L. Rinehart

x = ''
DO

   ACCEPT 'line: ' TO x
   y = tokenize(x)
   show_tokens(y)

UNTIL x = 'quit'

* end of action_d mainline


FUNCTION tokenize(input)
LOCAL toks ; toks = NEW Object()

? 'tokenizing'

RETURN toks && end of tokenize


PROCEDURE show_tokens(token_object)

? 'Displaying tokens'

RETURN && end of show_tokens


* end of ACTION_D.PRG
```

This version does nothing but pretend that it is tokenizing and displaying its work. I always start this way, to be sure that the program is working in the sequence that I intend. (This is the result of spending too much time trying to find a bug in a routine that was not, in fact, even called!)

Chapter 3 *Easing Into Objects -- Analysis*

Adding Properties

Next, let's have the tokenize() routine pretend to do its work, and the show_tokens() routine actually report results. For this we'll use both named and numbered object properties. This is easier to do than to explain, so I'll just show you how it's done. Listing 3-3 has tokenize() faking it and show_tokens() working.

Code Listing 3-3

```
FUNCTION tokenize(input)                                        16
LOCAL toks ; toks = NEW Object()                                17
                                                                18
toks.num_toks = 3                                               19
toks[1] = 'IF'                                                  20
toks[2] = 'expression'                                          21
toks[3] = 'EOS' && end of statement                             22
                                                                23
RETURN toks && end of tokenize                                  24
                                                                25
                                                                26
PROCEDURE show_tokens(token_object)                             27
                                                                28
FOR i = 1 TO token_object.num_toks                              29
   ? token_object[i]                                            30
ENDFOR                                                          31
                                                                32
RETURN && end of show_tokens                                    33
                                                                34
                                                                35
* end of ACTION_D.PRG                                           36
```

At line 19 I use a named property, num_toks, to hold the number of tokens. The next three lines use numbered properties, in familiar subscript notation, to hold those tokens. Unlike an array, your numbers do not have any notion of sequence. You could assign toks[1000] and toks[-1000] if you like. The only ones that exist are the ones you assign.

If you haven't been using Clipper or Fox or BASIC, the FOR loop will be new to you. (dBASE was pretty slow in adding this one!) It starts and ends a counter, which you can use in the loop, as you see in lines 29-31. Either ENDFOR or its synonym, NEXT, can be used to close the FOR loop.

57

Back to the subject at hand, the tokenizer invents EOS as a token that means End Of Statement. The parser will need to know that a statement ends. For instance, the parser will be looking for one of these pairs:

- DO CASE
- DO WHILE
- DO name
- DO EOS

The last one, DO EOS (DO, end of statement, meaning nothing follows the DO) is the start of a DO/UNTIL loop.

Tokenizing

Now we're ready to actually break an input line into tokens. To do this, we'll need a list of keywords. We won't need a complete list, just those that control program blocks.

Getting the First Keyword

At this point, I'll skip some intermediate steps and suggest that you copy the next listing from the disk. I've added the line SET EXACT OFF near the beginning of the program. Then I've added the keyword list shown in Listing 3-4.

Code Listing 3-4

```
FUNCTION tokenize(input)                           18
STATIC keyword_list                                19
                                                   20
DECLARE keyword_list[21]                           21
                                                   22
keyword_list[1]  = 'IF'                            23
keyword_list[2]  = 'ELSE'                          24
keyword_list[3]  = 'ENDIF'                         25
keyword_list[4]  = 'DO'                            26
keyword_list[5]  = 'WHILE'                         27
```

Chapter 3 *Easing Into Objects -- Analysis*

```
keyword_list[6]  = 'LOOP'                                28
keyword_list[7]  = 'EXIT'                                29
keyword_list[8]  = 'ENDDO'                               30
keyword_list[9]  = 'UNTIL'                               31
keyword_list[10] = 'FOR'                                 32
keyword_list[11] = 'ENDFOR'                              33
keyword_list[12] = 'NEXT'                                34
keyword_list[13] = 'CASE'                                35
keyword_list[14] = 'OTHERWISE'                           36
keyword_list[15] = 'ENDCASE'                             37
keyword_list[16] = 'FUNCTION'                            38
keyword_list[17] = 'PROCEDURE'                           39
keyword_list[18] = 'CLASS'                               40
keyword_list[19] = 'ENDCLASS'                            41
keyword_list[20] = 'RETURN'                              42
keyword_list[21] = 'ON'                                  43
                                                         44
LOCAL toks ; toks = NEW Object()                         45
                                                         46
toks.num_toks = 1                                        47
                                                         48
toks[1] = matches(input, keyword_list)                   49
RETURN toks                                              50
                                                         51
                                                         52
FUNCTION matches(line, list)                             53
                                                         54
w = UPPER( first_word(line) )                            55
                                                         56
* RETURN 'OTHER' if null input                           57
  IF EMPTY(w)                                            58
     RETURN 'OTHER'                                      59
  ENDIF                                                  60
                                                         61
* RETURN keyword if match                                62
  LOCAL i                                                63
                                                         64
  FOR i = 1 TO ALEN(list)                                65
                                                         66
     IF LEN(w) >= 4                                      67
        IF list[i] = w                                   68
           RETURN list[i]                                69
```

59

```
         ENDIF
      ELSE
        IF list[i] == w
           RETURN list[i]
        ENDIF
     ENDIF

  ENDFOR

* RETURN 'OTHER' if no match
   RETURN 'OTHER'

* end of matches


FUNCTION first_word(line)
LOCAL ln ; ln = LTRIM(line)

IF EMPTY(ln)
   RETURN ''
ENDIF

IF ln = '*'
   RETURN ''
ENDIF

IF ln = '&'+'&'
   RETURN ''
ENDIF

LOCAL i, stop

FOR i = 1 TO LEN( RTRIM(ln) )
   IF .NOT. ISALPHA( SUBSTR(ln,i,1) )
      stop = i-1
      EXIT
   ENDIF
   stop = i
ENDFOR

RETURN LEFT(ln,stop)
```

Chapter 3   ***Easing Into Objects -- Analysis***

From the top, the tokenize routine adds a STATIC list of keywords. It then calls the matches routine, which returns either the keyword matched at the start of the input line or the token OTHER. You can test this by running it and typing various lines that start with keywords or abbreviated keywords.

If you're being sharp-eyed, you've noticed that the keyword list is incomplete, even for block statements. There's no TEXT/ENDTEXT block, but that's because I think Crystal Reports handles that need so much better than TEXT/ENDTEXT that you'll never write another one.

You may think that SCAN/ENDSCAN deserve a place in your action diagrammer. (If you've never seen these, look at the SCAN documentation in the online help — it's a genuinely useful construct.) Go ahead and add them if you like. It's your code, not mine.

This lexer will always return just one token, but that is a detail we'll tend to next.

The matches() routine, from lines 53 to 82, calls first_word() to pick off the first word (any string of consecutive alphabetic characters) and then matches that against the keyword list. It does an inexact match if the input word is four or more characters long (matching WHIL to WHILE) but does an exact match if the word is less than four characters (not matching FO to FOR).

There's an ambiguity introduced with the ENDCLASS keyword, which matches ENDCASE in its first four letters. Visual dBASE matches ENDC to ENDCASE only, which is also what matches() does.

The first_word() routine, from 85 to 110, begins by making a copy of its input parameter. The parameter string is passed by reference, so changes in this routine could make unwanted changes in the value in the calling routine — bad software engineering. Working on a copy prevents this.

First_word() returns a null on null or comment lines. There's a bug in the Visual dBASE tokenizer, which I worked around at line 96:

```
IF ln = '&'+'&'    && this works
IF ln = '&&'       && this fails!
```

The second version shows that the dBASE tokenizer searches for double ampersand characters before it checks for open quotes. It reports an "open quote" error, which we know isn't the case. (We would be grateful if all bugs were this unimportant.)

61

The Rest of the Tokenizer

We want to know if the line following a DO continues with a WHILE, something else or nothing at all. We don't really care about too much else that we haven't handled by picking off keywords at the beginning of each line. So what we need to do is to slap an EOS on the end of each line that doesn't start with DO.

Most of our lines will be handed to the parser as OTHER EOS. This might be a comment, an assignment statement or a command like USE or SET. Our action diagrammer will handle them all the same way.

What we need to do is terminate every statement other than ones that start with DO with an EOS token. Then we'll do some more work on the DO lines. For the DO lines, we have to check to see if the statement is the start of a DO/UNTIL loop (nothing but a comment can follow the DO). If anything follows the DO, we want to know if it's the keyword CASE, WHILE or something else. Our existing routine matches() will work just fine for checking this.

Listing 3-5 shows the new code to add to your tokenize() routine.

Code Listing 3-5

```
toks[1] = matches(input, keyword_list)                    49
                                                          50
IF toks[1] <> 'DO'                                        51
   toks.num_toks = 2                                      52
   toks[2] = 'EOS'                                        53
 ELSE                                                     54
   LOCAL inp; inp = LTRIM(input) && chop leading blanks   55
   inp = RIGHT(inp, LEN(inp)-2) && chop off the DO        56
   inp = LTRIM(inp)                                       57
   IF LEN(inp) = 0 .OR. ;                                 58
      inp = '&'+'&'                                       59
      toks.num_toks = 2                                   60
      toks[2] = 'EOS'                                     61
    ELSE                                                  62
      toks.num_toks = 3                                   63
      toks[2] = matches(inp, keyword_list)                64
      toks[3] = 'EOS'                                     65
   ENDIF                                                  66
ENDIF                                                     67
                                                          68
RETURN toks                                               69
```

As you can see, we start by checking for the DO keyword. If we've got anything else, we'll just slap an EOS on as the second token and be done with it.

For DO (the ELSE branch, starting at line 54) we create a LOCAL variable inp so that we can chop the unwanted parts off the input line. Again, that line was passed by reference so changes to the variable input would change the value in the calling routine — a potential source of errors.

The first thing we do to inp is chop off the leading blanks. Next, we chop off two more characters on the left, which must be the word DO since we're working on a DO token. Then we chop off any leading blanks in what's left.

If there's nothing left or if what's left starts with two ampersands (inline comment), our DO is the start of a DO/UNTIL loop, so we put an EOS token on as the second and last token.

If there is more to the line, we call matches() again to find out what we've got. It might tell us that we've got a CASE, a WHILE, or an OTHER, or some other keyword. (We don't really care about any other keywords, but we'll let matches() do its work, anyway.)

Whatever matches() tells us is part of the rest of the line, we add that token as the second and put an EOS as the third and final token.

That's all the tokenizer has to do.

Implementing the Parser

If we were writing a compiler, we'd put together a formal description of our language in a form that a tool called a *parser generator* could understand. Then we'd let the parser generator write the parser. The best known parser generator is the UNIX-based tool, YACC.

YACC stands for Yet Another Compiler Compiler (some people thought of the parser as the compiler). As you can guess from the name, YACC was not the first of its breed, nor was it the last. Most UNIX-based languages originate with a YACC-written parser.

I'm permitting myself this digression into the background of parsers, since ours is so trivial that it hardly merits the name. It does, however, serve exactly the purpose that parsers do in other compilers: it analyzes the tokens that the lexer feeds in and prepares an output that the generator can act on.

As it turns out, our generator will find the tokens sufficient except in the case of the DO token. This takes just a tiny bit of additional analysis (although I don't want you running around telling everyone else how little analysis we're doing!).

We'll analyze the tokens that follow the DO and return a pseudo-keyword for the actions it might initiate:

- DO_CASE — start of DO CASE switch
- DO_UNTIL — start of DO/UNTIL loop
- DO_WHILE — start of DO WHILE loop
- DO_SUBR — call a sub-program

The Parser Output

Our generation machinery will want to know what type of program statement it's dealing with, but nothing else. All we'll have to give it is the keyword that starts the line (including our pseudo keywords for DO statements and OTHER for everything that we don't worry about).

So our job is to emit only a single word, given the input from the lexer. This means we can use a function that takes the lexer's object and reduces it to a single string. Let's start with the trivial version that just returns the first token.

Code Listing 3-6

```
* ACTION_D.PRG -- Action Diagrammer for dBWin Code      1
* copyright 1995, Martin L. Rinehart                    2
                                                        3
SET EXACT OFF                                           4
                                                        5
x = ''                                                  6
DO                                                      7
                                                        8
   ACCEPT 'line: ' TO x                                 9
   ? parse( tokenize(x) )                              10
                                                      11
UNTIL x = 'quit'                                       12
                                                      13
* end of action_d mainline                             14
```

```
                                                             15
                                                             16
FUNCTION parse( tok_obj )                                    17
                                                             18
RETURN tok_obj[1] && end of parse                            19
```

As you can see in Listing 3-6, the mainline is even simpler than it was, and the parse() function is trivial. Make these changes to your version, and use Ctrl+D to test them in the Command Window. Test several versions of DO, just to see the contrast after we fix up the parser.

Completing the Parser

Now let's finish parse(). We'll need to look at the next token when we come to a DO. Listing 3-7 shows the finished routine.

Code Listing 3-7

```
FUNCTION parse( tok_obj )                                    17
                                                             18
DO CASE                                                      19
   CASE tok_obj[1] <> 'DO'                                   20
      RETURN tok_obj[1]                                      21
                                                             22
   CASE tok_obj[2] = 'CASE'                                  23
      RETURN 'DO_CASE'                                       24
                                                             25
   CASE tok_obj[2] = 'WHILE'                                 26
      RETURN 'DO_WHILE'                                      27
                                                             28
   CASE tok_obj[2] = 'EOS'                                   29
      RETURN 'DO_UNTIL'                                      30
                                                             31
   OTHERWISE                                                 32
      RETURN 'DO_SUBR'                                       33
                                                             34
ENDCASE && end of parse()                                    35
```

The CASE at line 20 handles everything except the lines that start with DO. The rest of the CASEs handle, in order, DO CASE, DO WHILE, DO (in DO/UNTIL), and DO <name>.

Again, test this by pressing Ctrl+D and then running all the DO examples you can think of, as well as any other samples you wish. You should quit when you are satisfied that your tokenizer and parser are doing a solid job of analyzing the input lines.

Summary

In this chapter we began work on a program analysis utility that reads our code and writes action diagrams. We're building it compiler-style, so that it will be extensible in the future.

Along the way, we've broken the task down into the components of a compiler (the most common class of program analysis software). We've written a tokenizer, or lexer (short for lexical analysis), that picks out the relevant parts of the program input stream and passes them on to the parser in a form that's simple for the parser to handle.

We've written a parser, too. (It's trivially simple, but we won't tell anyone, will we?) Interestingly, the lexer hands the parser an object that encapsulates the token stream. (Again, the vocabulary is more complex than the code. Better this way than the other way around!)

In Chapter 4, we'll go on to build the generation machinery, including some stack machinery to handle nesting. We'll create our first class in Chapter 4. You'll be surprised at how simple the new object syntax makes this task.

Chapter 4

Easing Into Objects — Generation

In this chapter we're going to build the generation machinery for our action-diagramming utility. Our most important innovation here will be the creation of our first class.

The action diagrammer has to be able to handle arbitrarily deep nesting of code structures. This is a job well-suited to a stack. We'll create a special-purpose stack class designed to support just this application. You'll see that this class is elegantly simple to program and use.

To back up, our design was a lexer that would break the input line into tokens, coupled to a parser that would decide what each token meant. We built and tested them using manual input in the Command Window.

Our next job was to add file input and then build the stack machinery. We're going to build a temporary display so that we can watch the stack work as it handles real input.

Finally, we're going to create the output machinery that uses this stack to produce the actual action diagrams.

File Input in the Mainline

We'll begin with the file input. We'll use GETFILE(), exactly as we did in Chapter 2 when we wrote LISTER.

I've modified ACTION_D's mainline loop, changing the DO/UNTIL to a DO WHILE, and I've modified the output so that it writes the results of parse() to the Command Window's results pane. If parse() returns OTHER I don't write it out. This lets you focus on the main point.

The code is in Listing 4-1.

Code Listing 4-1

```
* ACTION_D.PRG -- Action Diagrammer for dBWin Code        1
* copyright 1995, Martin L. Rinehart                      2
                                                          3
SET EXACT OFF                                             4
                                                          5
LOCAL fname; fname = GETFILE('*.prg','Program to Analyze')
                                                          7
IF EMPTY(fname)                                           8
  RETURN                                                  9
ENDIF                                                    10
                                                         11
in_handle = FOPEN(fname)                                 12
                                                         13
LOCAL prog_line                                          14
                                                         15
DO WHILE .NOT. FEOF(in_handle)                           16
                                                         17
   prog_line = FGETS(in_handle)                          18
                                                         19
   y = parse( tokenize(prog_line) )                      20
   IF y <> 'OTHER'                                       21
      ? y                                                22
```

`    ENDIF`	23
	24
`ENDDO`	25
	26
`FCLOSE(in_handle)`	27
	28
`* end of action_d mainline`	29

When you add these changes, pressing Ctrl+D lets you select a .PRG and run, getting a simulation of real output. With this improvement, we're ready to go on to the generation phase.

By the way, doesn't this make you wonder where GETFILE() has been all your life? It's amazing how quickly that routine becomes an absolutely indispensable part of your programming repertoire.

The Stack Machinery

With the file input available, it's time to build the stack machinery. This is what it should do.

As we meet control-construct-starting tokens, like IF and DO_WHILE, we'll push them onto a stack. When we meet control-construct-ending keywords, like ENDIF and ENDDO, we'll pop them off the stack. If each token and its overhead takes 50 bytes (in practice they don't need that much) our stack could handle nesting up to 20 levels deep in 1K, or 200 levels deep in 10K. This means that we can handle a level of nesting that is not limited in any practical way by our software.

Here's how the stack will work. Assume that our input file has control structures like this:

```
IF                      1
ENDIF                   2
DO WHILE                3
   IF                   4
      IF                5
      ENDIF             6
      FOR               7
         IF             8
         ENDIF          9
      ENDFOR           10
   ENDIF               11
ENDDO                  12
```

When we initialize the stack, it will be zero elements deep (step 0 in the next block of code). With the base of the stack on the left, this is what the stack would look like as we push and pop for that input:

```
                                    0
IF                                  1
                                    2
DO WHILE                            3
DO WHILE, IF                        4
DO WHILE, IF, IF                    5
DO WHILE, IF                        6
DO WHILE, IF, FOR                   7
DO WHILE, IF, FOR, IF               8
DO WHILE, IF, FOR                   9
DO WHILE, IF                       10
DO WHILE                           11
                                   12
```

For the stack machine, we'll build a stack class and create a stack object. You'll see that this leads to an incredibly compact, simple way of building this machinery. The only downside is that it will take a lot more explanation than we've been using before this, because all the concepts and syntax will be new.

While you read through this section, keep one eye on the amount of code we actually use to implement our concepts. You'll see that it is incredibly small.

A Stack Class

The syntax for defining a class is

```
CLASS <name> OF <parent class>
  * constructor code
  * methods
ENDCLASS
```

Class Inheritance

Every class must *inherit* from a parent class. In the process, the new class immediately gains access to all the properties and methods of the parent. In our case, we're going to create a stack class that has almost nothing in common with the other Visual dBASE built-in classes, so we'll use the Object class as a parent.

Objects just know how to create themselves and to free themselves when they are no longer wanted. It's up to us to assign all their properties and methods. Here's the syntax we'll use to create a stack class from the Object class:

```
CLASS stack OF Object
```

Note that I'm using all_lower capitalization for my own class names, but following the Borland convention of using UpperLower case names for the built-in objects and properties. That's why stack is not capitalized but Object is capitalized, since it's a Borland class.

Constructor Code

The constructor code is any code that we want to execute to create an object (or an instance of the class). Within the constructor, the automatic variable This refers to the object being created. To add properties to your object, use this syntax:

```
This.<propname> = <value>
```

You can actually add properties anytime to your object. The Constructor code doesn't have to anticipate every property you might ever want to use.

For our stack class, we'll want to keep track of the number of elements on the stack, so we'll add a property like this:

```
This.stack_size = 0
```

Class Methods

Methods should really be called method properties, to distinguish them from data properties. The convention is to use the name *properties* to refer to data properties and the name *methods* to refer to method properties.

Methods are the subroutines that each object in your class can perform. Like other subroutines, they accept parameters in parentheses. Also like other subroutines, methods can either be procedures that do not return a value or functions that do return a value.

71

Visual dBASE now allows procedures to return values. It does not allow functions to not return values. I still use the procedure declaration when I don't intend to return a value, just to keep my conventions a little more meaningful.

Here are three methods that should come in handy in a stack class:

```
PROCEDURE push(element)

FUNCTION pop
RETURN element

FUNCTION look
RETURN element
```

The push() procedure will take the element parameter and add it to the stack.

The pop() function doesn't need a parameter. It will pop off and return the top element from the stack. (You could write a more sophisticated pop that took, as a parameter, the number of elements to pop. We won't need that here, so I've not done it.)

The look() function returns the top element of the stack, without popping it. By using a look() function, we get all access to the stack through the stack methods. This lets us re-write the internals of the stack class without impacting the programs that use the stack class. This is called encapsulation, and it is a key to good object-oriented programming.

At least, that's what you're supposed to say. In truth the stack class is so simple that I just write one whenever I need one. Let's take a look at the whole class, with the methods filled in.

A Stack Implementation

Listing 4-2 shows the stack class I've added at the end of my ACTION_D routine.

Code Listing 4-2

```
CLASS stack of Object                                         176
  This.stack_size = 0                                         177
                                                              178
  PROCEDURE push(elem)                                        179
  This.stack_size = This.stack_size + 1                       180
  This[This.stack_size] = elem   && end of stack::push        181
```

```
                                                                   182
    FUNCTION pop                                                   183
    This.stack_size = This.stack_size-1                            184
    RETURN This[This.stack_size+1]   && end of stack::pop          185
                                                                   186
    FUNCTION look                                                  187
    RETURN This[This.stack_size]   && end of stack::look           188
                                                                   189
ENDCLASS && stack                                                  190
```

If you are thinking about this code (you are, aren't you?) you see that I've not done any checking. You can pop from an empty stack and you will get a subscript error, for example. I leave it up to the calling routine to check the stack's size before popping.

Purists will object that there is no method that returns the stack's size. The program using the object will have to take a look at the stack_size property. All properties, the purists assert, should be accessed through methods.

I'm not a purist. If we create a method, say, how_big() then our calling code is slowed down. The counter argument is that we can change stack_size to something else, without bothering the calling routine. That's true, but it's just moved the problem: you can't change how_big(). If you've got to leave something constant, why not do it the simplest, fastest way available?

Testing the Stack Class

I tested my stack class in the Command Window, for starters. Here's a sample dialog:

```
set proc to action_d
foo = new stack()
foo.push(1)
foo.push('fred')
? foo.look()
? foo.pop()
? foo.pop()
set proc to
```

Figure 4-1 shows this Command Window session.

```
Command
clear
set proc to action_d
foo = new stack()
foo.push(1)
foo.push('fred')
? foo.look()
? foo.pop()
? foo.pop()
set proc to
```

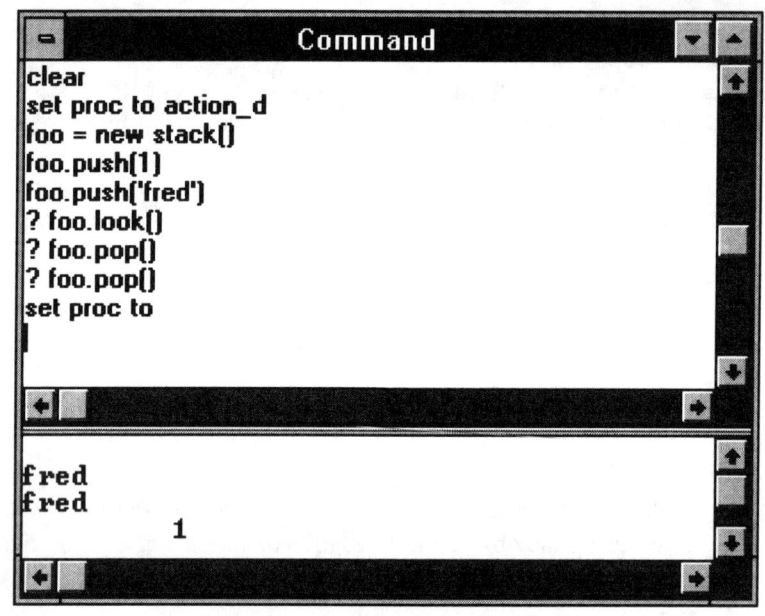

```
fred
fred
       1
```

Figure 4-1: Testing the stack class

The first line opens ACTION_D as a code library. The second creates a new stack, named foo. Then I push a couple values onto the stack. This shows the syntax for calling a method:

`<object>.<method>([params])`

As you can see, the parentheses are mandatory, whether or not you have parameters. They let Visual dBASE know that you are referring to a method, not a data property.

After pushing a couple of values, I look at the top of the stack, and then pop the two elements I pushed.

Finally, this dialog clears the set proc.

Using the Stack Class

What we want to do now is to use this class to stack, examine and pop the control structures that we meet in our code. I'll start by setting up the superstructure, and then making just IF and ENDIF do some work, to see if this thing is built sensibly.

Chapter 4 — Easing Into Objects -- Generation

Listing 4-3 shows the revised mainline.

Code Listing 4-3

```
in_handle = FOPEN(fname)                            12
                                                    13
LOCAL token, prog_line, control_stack               14
                                                    15
control_stack = NEW stack()                         16
                                                    17
DO WHILE .NOT. FEOF(in_handle)                      18
                                                    19
  prog_line = FGETS(in_handle)                      20
                                                    21
  token = parse( tokenize(prog_line) )              22
  IF token <> 'OTHER'                               23
                                                    24
     stack_em(token, control_stack)                 25
     show_stack(control_stack)                      26
                                                    27
  ENDIF                                             28
                                                    29
ENDDO                                               30
```

Since this is permanent code, I've started using LOCAL variables with meaningful names — it's good style to separate this code from the quick-and-dirty variables we had before.

At line 16 I built a new stack object. Then I use that object on lines 25 and 26, passing it first to the stack_em routine that actually does the work of stacking and popping, and to the show_stack routine that will let us look at what's happening.

The Stack_em() Routine

The long routine here is stack_em(), which will handle (or choose to ignore) each keyword excepting OTHER, which the mainline handles.

I started stack_em by swiping the list of keywords from the tokenize() routine. I replaced the DO keyword with the four new pseudo-keywords that the parser returns as tokens. When I had this list ready, I saved the ACTION_D.PRG file and used Alt+Tab to pop over to my favorite editor, where I built a macro that converted this list into CASE statements.

Learn Visual dBASE Programming

As you see in Listing 4-4, this routine is doing almost nothing, except with the IF and ENDIF keywords. It has no error checking, so we had better only use it with running code. (On disk, this code is also in L04-03.PRG.)

Code Listing 4-4

```
PROCEDURE stack_em(tok, cntrls)                37
                                               38
DO CASE                                        39
                                               40
  CASE tok = 'IF'                              41
     cntrls.push(tok)                          42
                                               43
  CASE tok = 'ELSE'                            44
                                               45
  CASE tok = 'ENDIF'                           46
     cntrls.pop()                              47
                                               48
  CASE tok = 'DO_CASE'                         49
                                               50
  CASE tok = 'DO_WHILE'                        51
                                               52
  CASE tok = 'DO_UNTIL'                        53
                                               54
  CASE tok = 'DO_SUBR'                         55
                                               56
  CASE tok = 'WHILE'                           57
                                               58
  CASE tok = 'LOOP'                            59
                                               60
  CASE tok = 'EXIT'                            61
                                               62
  CASE tok = 'ENDDO'                           63
                                               64
  CASE tok = 'UNTIL'                           65
                                               66
  CASE tok = 'FOR'                             67
                                               68
  CASE tok = 'ENDFOR'                          69
                                               70
  CASE tok = 'NEXT'                            71
                                               72
  CASE tok = 'CASE'                            73
```

Chapter 4 — Easing Into Objects -- Generation

```
                                                        74
    CASE tok = 'OTHERWISE'                              75
                                                        76
    CASE tok = 'ENDCASE'                                77
                                                        78
    CASE tok = 'FUNCTION'                               79
                                                        80
    CASE tok = 'PROCEDURE'                              81
                                                        82
    CASE tok = 'CLASS'                                  83
                                                        84
    CASE tok = 'ENDCLASS'                               85
                                                        86
    CASE tok = 'RETURN'                                 87
                                                        88
    CASE tok = 'ON'                                     89
                                                        90
ENDCASE && end of stack_em                              91
```

The Show_stack() Routine

The final routine I've added is the test display, show_stack(). It abandons any pretense of using the stack object as a standalone object, diving right into its internals. This might be unacceptable in a finished routine, but this is just for testing, so I've allowed myself the liberty.

To get ahead (and to offend the purists!) I'm going to commit this same sin with the finished code. Doing this will mean that the stack class here is not at all general, but is totally bound to this program. It is not reusable.

This doesn't bother me in the least. As you'll see in the following chapters, I pay plenty of attention to reuse possibilities in my more complex classes. This stack class is a trivial little thing that I can recreate anytime I want. It's so short that I'll type up a new one rather than looking around for some code to copy.

Would a reusable stack be nice? Maybe. Object-oriented code tends to get fat and slow, because every program carries a freight of general-purpose, all-things-to-all-people objects.

Fire up Borland's C++ and build a "Hello, world!" window using OWL (Object Windows Library) or do the same with Microsoft's C++ and MFC (Microsoft Foundation Classes). Either one will take a minute or so to compile and link hundreds of kilobytes of code. (Think about this the next time you press Ctrl+D!)

People blame object-oriented coding for this bloat. I disagree.

The problem is that O-O coders get so lost in the possibilities of object reuse that they forget that tiny little objects, used once only, can be very effective. Our little stack here is an excellent example. It's a nice, little object, and it won't complain if we violate the privacy of its internals.

Listing 4-5 shows the code that violates the object's privacy. (On disk, the code is in L04-03.PRG.)

Code Listing 4-5

```
PROCEDURE show_stack(cntrls)                          94
                                                      95
LOCAL i                                               96
                                                      97
?                                                     98
FOR i= 1 TO cntrls.stack_size                         99
                                                      100
   ?? cntrls[i]+' '                                   101
                                                      102
ENDFOR && end of show_stack                           103
```

Run this code against a program that you know has balanced IFs and ENDIFs. Make a test routine if you like. I used ACTION_D itself. To be sure you don't have nesting errors, pre-compile the program, In the Command Window:

```
compile action_d
```

When you run ACTION_D with these additions, you'll see the IFs in the stack vary from zero to two deep. You have to watch the results pane as the program runs, or you'll miss them all.

Adding the Other Tokens

To handle all the possible tokens, both right and wrong, we're going to need to improve our Look() method so that it will not generate an error if we ask it to look at an empty stack, and we're going to need a general-purpose error reporter.

Chapter 4 — Easing Into Objects -- Generation

Improving the Look() Method

The easy way to improve the Look() method is to add another token which it can return in the case of an empty stack. I've used "EMPTY" as the token.

This way our checking routines will all be simplified. For example, when we get an ELSE token, we'll want to check that there is an IF token on top of the stack. Any other token means that the ELSE is an error. By using an EMPTY token, we'll not need to write two checks — one to check that the stack has at least one token and another to check that the top token is an IF.

Listing 4-6 shows the improved code.

Code Listing 4-6

```
FUNCTION look                                   305
 IF This.stack_size > 0                         306
    RETURN This[This.stack_size]                307
 ELSE                                           308
    RETURN 'EMPTY'                              309
 ENDIF   && end of stack::look                  310
                                                311
ENDCLASS && stack                               312
```

This is easy to check from the Command Window:

```
set proc to action_d
foo = new stack()
? foo.look()            && reports EMPTY
set proc to
```

The Error_on() Procedure

To handle errors, we'll write a simple routine that shows us what token we are trying to handle, and what the top of the stack is. The problem with error handling in all code analysis routines is that one error tends to explode into a long list of errors.

What we need is to modify the mainline so that we can keep an error count. If an error is isolated, we'll just report it and keep on working. But if it triggers a chain of errors, we'll not want to go on for very long.

Listing 4-7 shows the modifications to the mainline that support this handling.

Learn Visual dBASE Programming

Code Listing 4-7

```
* ACTION_D.PRG -- Action Diagrammer for dBWin Code      1
* copyright 1995, Martin L. Rinehart                    2
                                                        3
#define MAX_ERRORS 3                                    4
                                                        5
PRIVATE error_count; error_count = 0                    6
                                                        7
SET EXACT OFF                                           8
                                                        9
LOCAL fname; fname = GETFILE('*.prg','Program to Analyze')  10
                                                        11
IF EMPTY(fname)                                         12
   RETURN                                               13
ENDIF                                                   14
                                                        15
in_handle = FOPEN(fname)                                16
                                                        17
LOCAL token, prog_line, control_stack                   18
                                                        19
control_stack = NEW stack()                             20
                                                        21
DO WHILE ( .NOT. FEOF(in_handle) ) .AND. ;              22
       ( error_count < MAX_ERRORS )                     23
                                                        24
```

With the error handling in the mainline, we'll need to add some token handling that actually calls our error routine in the stack_em() code. Listing 4-8 shows this routine with some tokens correctly handled. (This code is in L04-07.PRG on disk.)

Code Listing 4-8

```
PROCEDURE stack_em(tok, cntrls)                         42
LOCAL top                                               43
                                                        44
DO CASE                                                 45
                                                        46
   CASE tok = 'IF'                                      47
      cntrls.push(tok)                                  48
                                                        49
   CASE tok = 'ELSE'                                    50
```

```
   top = cntrls.look()
   IF top = 'IF'
      cntrls.pop()
      cntrls.push(tok)
    ELSE
      error_on('IF', cntrls)
    ENDIF

CASE tok = 'ENDIF'
   top = cntrls.look()
   IF top = 'IF' .OR. ;
      top = 'ELSE'
      cntrls.pop()
    ELSE
      error_on('IF', cntrls)
    ENDIF

CASE tok = 'DO_CASE'
   cntrls.push(tok)

CASE tok = 'DO_WHILE'
   cntrls.push(tok)

CASE tok = 'DO_UNTIL'
   cntrls.push(tok)

CASE tok = 'DO_SUBR'

CASE tok = 'WHILE'

CASE tok = 'LOOP'

CASE tok = 'EXIT'

CASE tok = 'ENDDO'
   top = cntrls.look()
   IF top = 'DO_WHILE'
      cntrls.pop()
    ELSE
      error_on('DO_WHILE', cntrls)
    ENDIF
```

```
      CASE tok = 'UNTIL'                               93
         top = cntrls.look()                           94
         IF top = 'DO_UNTIL'                           95
            cntrls.pop()                               96
         ELSE                                          97
            error_on('DO_WHILE', cntrls)               98
         ENDIF                                         99
                                                      100
      CASE tok = 'FOR'                                101
         cntrls.push(tok)                             102
                                                      103
      CASE tok = 'ENDFOR'                             104
         cntrls.pop()                                 105
                                                      106
      CASE tok = 'NEXT'                               107
         cntrls.pop()                                 108
                                                      109
      CASE tok = 'CASE'                               110
                                                      111
      CASE tok = 'OTHERWISE'                          112
                                                      113
      CASE tok = 'ENDCASE'                            114
         cntrls.pop()                                 115
                                                      116
      CASE tok = 'FUNCTION'                           117
                                                      118
      CASE tok = 'PROCEDURE'                          119
                                                      120
      CASE tok = 'CLASS'                              121
         cntrls.push(tok)                             122
                                                      123
      CASE tok = 'ENDCLASS'                           124
         cntrls.pop()                                 125
                                                      126
      CASE tok = 'RETURN'                             127
                                                      128
      CASE tok = 'ON'                                 129
                                                      130
ENDCASE && end of stack_em                            131
```

This routine now handles IF/ELSE/ENDIF correctly. Since an IF is possible anywhere, it just pushes an IF token onto the stack. An ELSE is only allowed when

Chapter 4　　　　　　　　　　　　　　　　　*Easing Into Objects -- Generation*

an IF token is on top of the stack, so we look() at the stack to be sure. (The look() could return an EMPTY token or some other token, such as DO_WHILE to trigger this error.)

Our final addition is to write the error_on() routine itself. This is quite simple, as you can see in Listing 4-9. (On disk, this code is also in L04-07.PRG.)

Code Listing 4-9

```
PROCEDURE error_on(bad_tok, stack)                                134
                                                                  135
* error_count is global here                                      136
error_count = error_count + 1                                     137
                                                                  138
? '*** Error: token '+bad_tok                                     139
? '    stack top: '+ stack.look()                                 140
?                                                                 141
                                                                  142
RETURN && end of error_on()                                       143
```

I've tested my code by running the deliberate bug file shown in Listing 4-10.

Code Listing 4-10

```
IF .t.
* nothing
ELSE
* nothing
ELSE
* nothing
ENDIF
```

When this works for you, try running ACTION_D against itself. If you have any errors, don't pick the Fix option. You'll have ACTION_D.PRG open as the input file to ACTION_D.PRO, the compiled and running program, so you won't be able to save ACTION_D.PRG from the Program Editor. Cancel and give the CLOSE ALL command in the Command Window. Then fix the problem in the Program Editor and start again.

83

CLASS/ENDCLASS

Let's get the CLASS construct handled correctly. A CLASS declaration cannot be nested in another block. For our action diagrammer, this means that the control stack must be empty when we come to a CLASS token.

Listing 4-11 shows the CLASS and ENDCLASS correctly handled.

Code Listing 4-11

```
CASE tok = 'CLASS'                          121
   IF cntrls.look() = 'EMPTY'               122
      cntrls.push(tok)                      123
   ELSE                                     124
      error_on(tok, cntrls)                 125
   ENDIF                                    126
                                            127
CASE tok = 'ENDCLASS'                       128
   IF cntrls.look() = 'CLASS'               129
      cntrls.pop()                          130
   ELSE                                     131
      error_on(tok, cntrls)                 132
   ENDIF                                    133
                                            134
```

Listing 4-12 shows a test file that has both a correct CLASS/ENDCLASS construct and an incorrect one.

Code Listing 4-12

```
IF
ENDIF

CLASS
   DO WHILE
   ENDDO
ENDCLASS

IF
   CLASS
   ENDCLASS
ENDIF
```

Chapter 4   *Easing Into Objects -- Generation*

For processing by our ACTION_D, you can just use keywords since the lexer and parser both quit reading your code after the first word (except for DO, when they read another word).

Figure 4-2 shows my result running the improved ACTION_D against this test file.

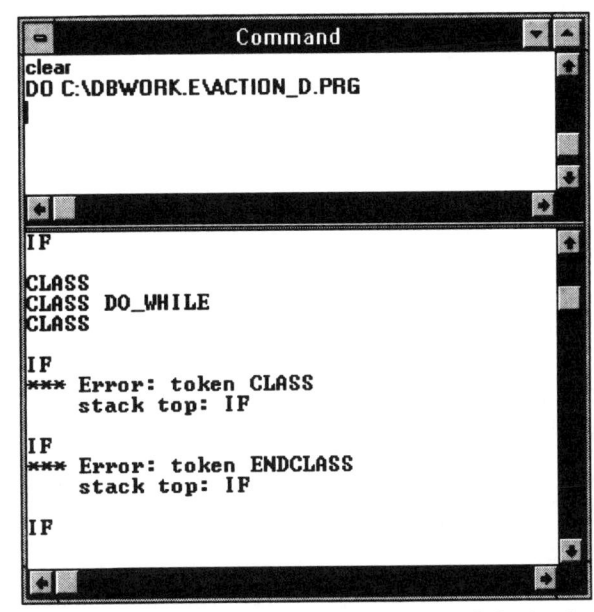

Figure 4-2: Running good and bad CLASS declarations

PROCEDUREs and FUNCTIONs

In spite of what Borland's documentation says, neither a PROCEDURE nor a function has to end with a RETURN. In fact, the only way dBASE knows that a subroutine has ended is that another one starts, a CLASS starts or you come to the end of the file. For example, this is a perfectly well-written function:

```
FUNCTION foo

IF DOW( DATE()-1 ) > 5
   RETURN 'weekend'
ELSE
   RETURN 'weekday'
ENDIF
```

85

Learn Visual dBASE Programming

Like CLASS declarations, FUNCTION and PROCEDURE statements cannot be nested in other control blocks, except that both are legal within a CLASS declaration.

A RETURN statement is legal anywhere any dBASE command can be given, and as the above example shows, it proves absolutely nothing about where a subroutine ends.

Listing 4-13 shows the code that implements this.

Code Listing 4-13

```
   CASE tok = 'ENDCASE'                              114
      cntrls.pop()                                   115
                                                     116
   CASE tok = 'FUNCTION' .OR. ;                      117
      tok = 'PROCEDURE'                              118
                                                     119
      top = cntrls.look()                            120
      IF top = 'EMPTY' .OR. ;                        121
         top = 'CLASS'                               122
         * ok, but do nothing                        123
      ELSE                                           124
         error_on(tok, cntrls)                       125
      ENDIF                                          126
                                                     127
   CASE tok = 'CLASS'                                128
      IF cntrls.look() = 'EMPTY'                     129
         cntrls.push(tok)                            130
      ELSE                                           131
         error_on(tok, cntrls)                       132
      ENDIF                                          133
                                                     134
   CASE tok = 'ENDCLASS'                             135
      IF cntrls.look() = 'CLASS'                     136
         cntrls.pop()                                137
      ELSE                                           138
         error_on(tok, cntrls)                       139
      ENDIF                                          140
                                                     141
   CASE tok = 'RETURN'                               142
```

```
                  * do nothing                             143
                                                          144
         CASE tok = 'ON'                                   145
```

I tested this code against the test routine shown in Listing 4-14.

Code Listing 4-14

```
PROCEDURE

FUNCTION

CLASS

  PROCEDURE

  FUNCTION

    DO WHILE
        PROCEDURE
        FUNCTION
    ENDDO

ENDCLASS
```

Figure 4-3 shows the result of a test run.

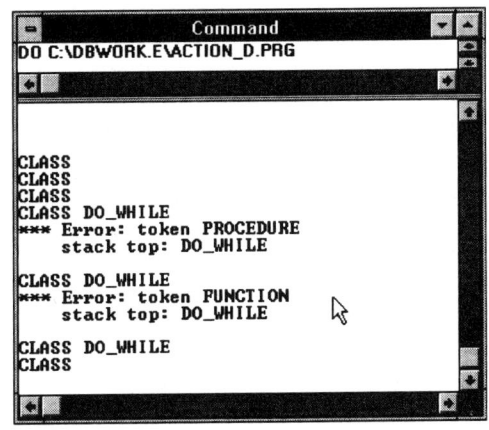

```
DO C:\DBWORK.E\ACTION_D.PRG

CLASS
CLASS
CLASS
CLASS DO_WHILE
*** Error: token PROCEDURE
    stack top: DO_WHILE

CLASS DO_WHILE
*** Error: token FUNCTION
    stack top: DO_WHILE

CLASS DO_WHILE
CLASS
```

Figure 4-3: Legal and illegal subroutine declarations

Fixing Up FOR Loops

The FOR loop can end with a NEXT or an ENDFOR statement. They are identical to dBASE. Many compiler/interpreter writers would reduce both to a single token. We haven't done this, because it can be a problem.

Suppose that you hand the lexer return token to your error routine (for example, a NEXT token for either a NEXT or an ENDFOR). Your error routine might report that it was trying to close, perhaps, a DO_WHILE with a NEXT. If you had written an ENDFOR, you would look in your code forever trying to find the errant NEXT.

It's much better for error handling to preserve the original input, even if this adds a bit of complexity to the generation code. As you can see in Listing 4-15, it doesn't add much complexity.

Code Listing 4-15

```
CASE tok = 'FOR'                                        101
    cntrls.push(tok)                                    102
                                                        103
CASE tok = 'ENDFOR' .OR. ;                              104
     tok = 'NEXT'                                       105
    IF cntrls.look() = 'FOR'                            106
       cntrls.pop()                                     107
    ELSE                                                108
       error_on(tok, cntrls)                            109
    ENDIF                                               110
                                                        111
CASE tok = 'CASE'                                       112
```

Listing 4-16 shows the test routine I used to check both good and bad FOR loops.

Code Listing 4-16

```
FOR
NEXT

FOR
ENDFOR
```

```
IF
NEXT

ENDFOR
```

Figure 4-4 shows the results I got running ACTION_D against this test file.

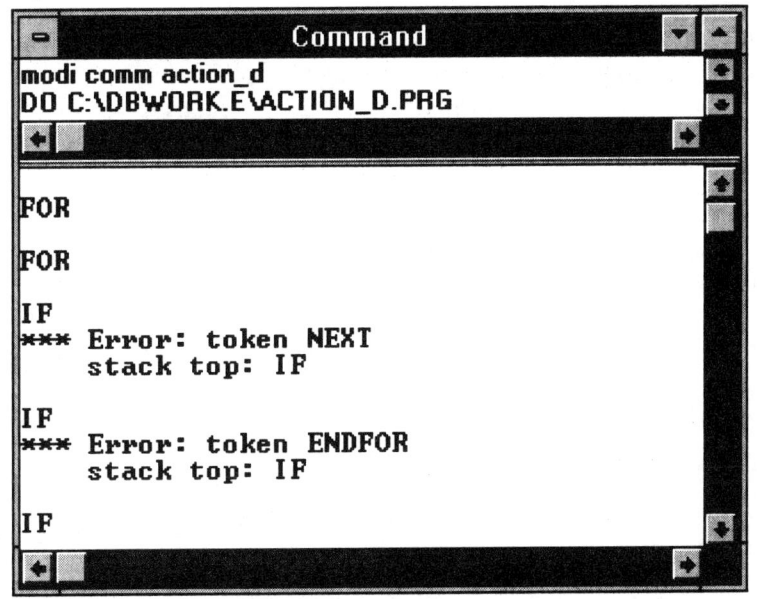

```
Command
modi comm action_d
DO C:\DBWORK.E\ACTION_D.PRG

FOR

FOR

IF
*** Error: token NEXT
    stack top: IF

IF
*** Error: token ENDFOR
    stack top: IF

IF
```

Figure 4-4: Errors on bad ENDFOR and NEXT statements

We haven't handled every construct — the DO_CASE token is the most notable absence — but let's take what we've got and try to do some output.

The Output Machinery

Our stack machinery is in place and working. It stacks and pops tokens quickly and easily and is smart enough to recognize errors for most control constructs. As you've seen, it's trivial coding to get our stack_em() routine to handle new control constructs.

Now it's time to actually do some action diagramming. For this, we'll need to prepare an output line prefix which draws appropriate "lines" between block starts and ends. Then we'll write the code itself.

Let's begin by doing something trivial, just to get our structure right.

Simple Output

For starters, let's fix up the mainline to handle output and write a routine that does output of both the program lines and our drawing prefix. For the moment, we'll just draw a line of vertical bars down the left border to get this to work. Listing 4-17 shows the new code.

Code Listing 4-17

```
* ACTION_D.PRG -- Action Diagrammer for dBWin Code          1
* copyright 1995, Martin L. Rinehart                        2
                                                            3
#define MAX_ERRORS 3                                        4
                                                            5
PRIVATE error_count; error_count = 0                        6
PRIVATE out_prefix; out_prefix = '|'                        7
PRIVATE out_handle                                          8
                                                            9
SET EXACT OFF                                              10
                                                           11
LOCAL fname; fname = GETFILE('*.prg','Program to Analyze') 12
                                                           13
IF EMPTY(fname)                                            14
   RETURN                                                  15
ENDIF                                                      16
                                                           17
in_handle = FOPEN(fname)                                   18
                                                           19
oname = LEFT( fname, RAT('.',fname) ) + 'TMP'              20
                                                           21
out_handle = FCREATE(oname)                                22
                                                           23
LOCAL token, prog_line, control_stack                      24
                                                           25
control_stack = NEW stack()                                26
                                                           27
```

```
DO WHILE ( .NOT. FEOF(in_handle) ) .AND. ;         28
        ( error_count < MAX_ERRORS )                29
                                                    30
   prog_line = FGETS(in_handle)                     31
                                                    32
   token = parse( tokenize(prog_line) )             33
   IF token <> 'OTHER'                              34
      stack_em(token, control_stack)                35
   ENDIF                                            36
                                                    37
   write_line(prog_line)                            38
                                                    39
ENDDO                                               40
                                                    41
FCLOSE(in_handle)                                   42
FCLOSE(out_handle)                                  43
                                                    44
* end of action_d mainline                          45
                                                    46
                                                    47
PROCEDURE write_line(line)                          48
                                                    49
FPUTS(out_handle, out_prefix + line)                50
                                                    51
RETURN && end of write_line                         52
                                                    53
```

The additions here are very similar to the code we wrote in Chapter 2 for LISTER. You should be sure to delete the old show_stack() call (it would have been line 35.5).

When I run this routine against the dummy input file in Listing 4-16, (T.PRG) it writes a T.TMP that looks like this:

```
|FOR
|NEXT
|
|FOR
|ENDFOR
|
```

```
|IF
|NEXT
|
|ENDFOR
|
```

This shows that we can write simple output, adding a prefix to our code lines. Now the job is to use our stack to build a sensible prefix.

Building the Prefix

I draw my lines using good old ASCII characters. This is highly portable, working on almost all equipment. Sticking to alphanumeric characters means that I don't have to worry about code pages and language drivers.

On the other hand, my output is quite old-fashioned in our modern, graphical world. I hope that one of you will get inspired to do something more elegant. I'm going to keep it simple.

Choosing the Prefix Characters

I'm going to use Y and N for the IF/ELSE/ENDIF construct. I'll run Ys down the page for the true part (before the ELSE) and Ns for the false part (after the ELSE). (If you wanted to use T and F for the true and false parts, you would have to pick something other than F for the FOR loop.)

For our three loops, DO WHILE, DO/UNTIL and FOR, I'll use W, U and F, respectively.

I'll outline DO CASE switches with Cs and use the double letter CL for CLASS definitions. (CLASS definitions always are on the left side of the page, not nested.) I'll separate the CASEs with digits, 1 for the first CASE, 2 for the second and so on. I'll use 0 (zero) for the OTHERWISE case (which means you don't need to care if it looks like the letter O).

Now we have to build our prefix as we push elements onto the stack and trim it as we pop elements off the stack.

A New Mainline

I want my action diagrams to look like this:

Chapter 4   *Easing Into Objects -- Generation*

```
IF
Y    * do this
Y    * and that
 ELSE
N    * do the
N    * other
ENDIF
```

If you think about it, there are four things that happen here. When we get to an IF (or other block start), we want to put a Y onto our output prefix, but not on the line with the IF. It goes onto the next line.

With the intervening lines (all comments, in the above example) you just print the code following the prefix.

The ENDIF shortens the prefix (here it blanks it, but there could be other open control structures) and prints, after shortening the output prefix.

Finally, the ELSE shortens the prefix, prints itself and then lengthens the prefix for the subsequent print lines.

This means that we have to be able to adjust the prefix either before or after (or both) printing the current line. The mainline changes shown in Listing 4-18 establish the communication we need to do this, through global variables.

Code Listing 4-18

```
control_stack = NEW stack()                                   27
                                                              28
PRIVATE change_prefix, new_prefix                             29
change_prefix = .F.                                           30
new_prefix = ''                                               31
                                                              32
DO WHILE ( .NOT. FEOF(in_handle) ) .AND. ;                    33
     ( error_count < MAX_ERRORS )                             34
                                                              35
  prog_line = FGETS(in_handle)                                36
                                                              37
  token = parse( tokenize(prog_line) )                        38
  IF token <> 'OTHER'                                         39
     stack_em(token, control_stack)                           40
  ENDIF                                                       41
                                                              42
  write_line(prog_line)                                       43
                                                              44
```

93

```
  IF change_prefix                                    45
     out_prefix = new_prefix                          46
     change_prefix = .F.                              47
  ENDIF                                               48
                                                      49
ENDDO                                                 50
```

The write_line() routine is going to write out_prefix followed by the program line. So if stack_em wants to change the output prefix before writing the current line, it just changes the prefix.

On the other hand, if stack_em() decides to change the output prefix after printing the current line, it puts the new prefix in the variable new_prefix and turns the change_prefix flag on.

Now that we can handle this, we need new routines to push and pop the stack.

New Pop and Push Routines

The pop code needs a simple change. It first trims the output prefix by three characters, and then does the real pop. I've added this to the mainline:

```
#define INDENT 3
```

This constant could, with some more work, be made to vary the amount of indent spacing. I haven't used it, though, for adding to the output prefix stack, so it's not completely implemented.

The pushing code is a bit more complicated, since it has to first decide what to push (based on what token it sees) and then push the new token through the new_prefix variable.

Listing 4-19 shows both routines.

Code Listing 4-19

```
                                                              175
PROCEDURE popper(stack)                                       176
                                                              177
out_prefix = LEFT( out_prefix, LEN(out_prefix) - INDENT )
stack.pop()                                                   179
                                                              180
RETURN && end of popper                                       181
                                                              182
```

```
PROCEDURE pusher(stack, token)

* out_prefix, new_prefix and change_prefix
* are PRIVATEs declared in the mainline

DO CASE
  CASE token = 'IF'
     new_prefix = out_prefix + 'Y '

  CASE token = 'ELSE'
     new_prefix = out_prefix + 'N '

  CASE token = 'DO_WHILE'
     new_prefix = out_prefix + 'W '

  CASE token = 'DO_UNTIL'
     new_prefix = out_prefix + 'U '

  CASE token = 'DO_CASE'
     new_prefix = out_prefix + 'C '

  CASE token = 'FOR'
     new_prefix = out_prefix + 'F '

  CASE token = 'CLASS'
     new_prefix = 'CL '

ENDCASE

change_prefix = .T.
stack.push(token)

RETURN && end of pusher
```

To use those routines, change all occurences of "cntrls.push(tok)" to "pusher(cntrls,tok)" and change all occurences of "cntrls.pop()" to "popper(cntrls)". Finally, make the initial value of out_prefix an empty string.

Testing and Fixing

With those modifications in place, we're ready to test.

The First Test

After trying a couple of the little .PRGs, I've run my ACTION_D against itself for its first real test. A small part of the results are shown in the following:

```
DO WHILE ( .NOT. FEOF(in_handle) ) .AND. ;
W             ( error_count < MAX_ERRORS )
W
W       prog_line = FGETS(in_handle)
W
W       token = parse( tokenize(prog_line) )
W       IF token <> 'OTHER'
W   Y       stack_em(token, control_stack)
W       ENDIF
W
W       write_line(prog_line)
W
W       IF change_prefix
W   Y       out_prefix = new_prefix
W   Y       change_prefix = .F.
W       ENDIF
W
ENDDO
```

This isn't quite what I had in mind, but it's definitely got the general idea. First, I'd like the control structures moved over one space:

```
 DO WHILE
W    * leave the Ws
W    * just outside
W    * the loop, please
 ENDDO
```

Next, I don't want ACTION_D to indent via the output prefix and add its indenting to the indenting that I did when I wrote the code. It shouldn't double up here.

Implementing Fixes

The first of these two problems is trivial to fix. We'll just add a space between the output prefix and the program line in the write_line() routine. Listing 4-20 shows this fix. (It's not on disk. Add the space at the highlighted line to L04-19.PRG.)

Code Listing 4-20

```
PROCEDURE write_line(line)                                        58
                                                                  59
FPUTS(out_handle, out_prefix + ' ' + line)                        60
                                                                  61
RETURN && end of write_line                                       62
```

This little change gives me the following result:

```
  DO WHILE ( .NOT. FEOF(in_handle) ) .AND. ;
W             ( error_count < MAX_ERRORS )
W
W       prog_line = FGETS(in_handle)
W
W       token = parse( tokenize(prog_line) )
W       IF token <> 'OTHER'
W   Y         stack_em(token, control_stack)
W       ENDIF
W
W       write_line(prog_line)
W
W       IF change_prefix
W   Y         out_prefix = new_prefix
W   Y         change_prefix = .F.
W       ENDIF
W
  ENDDO
```

That's a bit closer to what I wanted. Now let's address that double-indent problem. What I want to do is to replace however many spaces in the source code with the prefix. If the prefix is nine characters long, I want to replace the first nine characters of the input line, provided those characters are all blanks.

Of course, before trying to chop nine characters from the left side of the input line, we'd better be sure that there are nine characters there to chop off. (It could be just a blank line or a short comment or whatever.)

Listing 4-21 has the improved write_line code that handles this.

Code Listing 4-21

```
PROCEDURE write_line(line)                              58
LOCAL ln; ln = line                                     59
                                                        60
IF LEN(ln) > LEN(out_prefix)                            61
                                                        62
   IF EMPTY( LEFT(ln,LEN(out_prefix)) )                 63
      ln = RIGHT( ln, LEN(ln)-LEN(out_prefix) )         64
   ENDIF                                                65
                                                        66
ENDIF                                                   67
                                                        68
FPUTS(out_handle, out_prefix + ' ' + ln)                69
                                                        70
RETURN && end of write_line                             71
```

With that change in place the action diagram looks like this:

```
  DO WHILE ( .NOT. FEOF(in_handle) ) .AND. ;
W             ( error_count < MAX_ERRORS )
W
W    prog_line = FGETS(in_handle)
W
W    token = parse( tokenize(prog_line) )
W    IF token <> 'OTHER'
W  Y    stack_em(token, control_stack)
W    ENDIF
W
W    write_line(prog_line)
W
W    IF change_prefix
W  Y    out_prefix = new_prefix
W  Y    change_prefix = .F.
W    ENDIF
W
  ENDDO
```

This is starting to be what I wanted.

Chapter 4 Easing Into Objects -- Generation

Fixing the Silence

ACTION_D has enough work to do that even a relatively small program, such as ACTION_D itself, takes a while to process. I don't like the fact that I'm sitting watching the disk light for confirmation that real work is going on, even if it's only for a few seconds.

Let's put in a line counter and a status message that we can display. The status bar is a good location for these messages. (The Command Window is fine for messages, too, but only if it is open and not buried under another window.)

My improvements are shown in Listing 4-22.

Code Listing 4-22

```
                                                              32
LOCAL line_no; line_no = 0                                    33
                                                              34
DO WHILE ( .NOT. FEOF(in_handle) ) .AND. ;                    35
       ( error_count < MAX_ERRORS )                           36
                                                              37
  prog_line = FGETS(in_handle)                                38
  line_no = line_no + 1                                       39
  IF MOD(line_no,15) = 0                                      40
     SET MESSAGE TO 'Lines processed: ' + ;                   41
                 LTRIM( STR(line_no) )                        42
  ENDIF                                                       43
                                                              44
  token = parse( tokenize(prog_line) )                        45
  IF token <> 'OTHER'                                         46
     stack_em(token, control_stack)                           47
  ENDIF                                                       48
                                                              49
  write_line(prog_line)                                       50
                                                              51
  IF change_prefix                                            52
     out_prefix = new_prefix                                  53
     change_prefix = .F.                                      54
  ENDIF                                                       55
                                                              56
ENDDO                                                         57
                                                              58
```

```
FCLOSE(in_handle)                                             59
FCLOSE(out_handle)                                            60
SET MESSAGE TO                                                61
                                                              62
* end of action_d mainline                                    63
```

As you can see, I've created a new LOCAL variable and initialized it to zero in line 33. Lines 39 through 45 keep the count and print a message in the status bar every 15 lines. (My machine seems busy at 15 lines. The messages come too fast at 10 lines per message, but are too slow at 25 lines.)

One of the effects of this message is to make the process of writing the action diagram seem much faster. It's amazing what a little display will do to speed things up (or so it seems).

Finishing DO CASE Blocks

Let's go on to DO CASE switches, now that we're mostly running. DO CASE switches are interesting because what I want to do is number the cases. The interesting part is that DO CASE switches can nest, so the numberings can nest, too.

Our stack is general — you can push anything onto it that you like. We've been pushing our tokens (short character strings) but we could just as easily push numbers, dates, arrays, or other objects.

Actually, I'm using terms a little loosely. If you assign an array or an object to a variable, that variable just refers to the array or object, so it's correctly called an array or object reference variable. It is a reference to the array or object, unlike a string or date which actually contains the data value. When you push a string onto our stack, you push the string itself. When you push an object, you are really just pushing a reference to the object. That will become important later, but for our present purposes, we'll just pretend that the variable is an object or array.

Since our stack is general, we could push a DO_CASE token when we started the DO_CASE construct. Then we could push a numeric 1 when the first CASE token came around. At each subsequent CASE, we could pop the stack, add one, and push it back.

This would work fine for perfect input. However, it will crash on errors. When we process an ENDIF, for example, we look() at the top of the stack and compare it to IF or ELSE. We'll get a data type mismatch error if we try to compare a number to IF, which is what we'd get if an ENDIF erroneously followed a CASE.

Chapter 4 — Easing Into Objects -- Generation

To avoid this problem, we can create another stack. On this one, we'll record the last number used in each of however many nested DO CASE constructs we've got. Chances are that we'll never get more than two or three, but our stack will have room for a whole lot.

Modifying the Mainline

I made one unfortunate choice when I designed the mechanisms here. (Actually, I make lots of mistakes like this. The ones that are not informative, or are just too embarrassing, I edit out. I leave in a few that might help you, like this one.)

I used the token OTHER for lines that weren't one of our recognized keywords. ACTION_D uses:

```
IF token <> 'OTHER'
```

This let us handle our keyword lines, ignoring the others. Unfortunately, it boots out the keyword OTHERWISE along with the true OTHER token lines. The test should be:

```
IF token is_not_exactly_equal_to 'OTHER'
```

That's the first modification. We'll use the "==" comparison, which tests for exact equality, regardless of the setting of SET EXACT. Listing 4-23 shows this test.

Code Listing 4-23

```
token = parse( tokenize(prog_line) )            45
IF .NOT. (token == 'OTHER')                     46
    stack_em(token, control_stack)              47
ENDIF                                           48
```

The fix in Listing 4-23 lets OTHERWISE be processed, along with the other keyword tokens.

Adding the New Stack

Adding the new stack is more trouble to talk about than to do. Line 85, in Listing 4-24 shows how this is done. (On disk it's in Listing 4-23.PRG.)

101

Learn Visual dBASE Programming

Code Listing 4-24

```
PROCEDURE stack_em(tok, cntrls)                              82
LOCAL top                                                    83
                                                             84
STATIC case_counts = NEW stack()                             85
                                                             86
DO CASE                                                      87
```

Note that I've used a STATIC variable. Assignments like this to a STATIC are done just the first time the subroutine is called, which is exactly what we want.

Handling the Keywords in Stack_em()

Listing 4-25 (also in L04-23.PRG on disk) shows the new handlers added for DO_CASE, CASE, OTHERWISE, and ENDCASE keywords. The only tricky bits come because you must remember that either OTHERWISE or ENDCASE might immediately follow a DO_CASE. If you were writing top down, you might start your switch this way:

```
DO CASE
   * when I get to it, this switch
   * will handle the ...
   OTHERWISE
   * the default will be ...
ENDCASE
```

This is legal code, and can be quite sensible as you are writing. Get the main points, then fill in the details later.

Code Listing 4-25

```
CASE tok = 'DO_CASE'                                        110
   pusher(cntrls, tok)                                      111
   case_counts.push(0)                                      112
   ...                                                      113

CASE tok = 'CASE'                                           155
   top = cntrls.look()                                      156
   IF top = 'DO_CASE' .OR. ;                                157
      top = 'CASE'                                          158
      LOCAL n; n = case_counts.pop()+1                      159
      case_counts.push(n)                                   160
```

```
         IF n > 1                                  161
            popper(cntrls)                         162
         ENDIF                                     163
         pusher(cntrls, tok, n)                    164
      ELSE                                         165
         error_on(tok, cntrls)                     166
      ENDIF                                        167
                                                   168
CASE tok = 'OTHERWISE'                             169
   top = cntrls.look()                             170
   ? 'got other'                                   171
   IF top = 'CASE' .OR. ;                          172
      top = 'DO_CASE'                              173
      n = case_counts.pop()                        174
      case_counts.push(0)                          175
      IF n > 0                                     176
         popper(cntrls)                            177
      ENDIF                                        178
      pusher(cntrls, tok, 0)                       179
    ELSE                                           180
       error_on(tok, cntrls)                       181
    ENDIF                                          182
                                                   183
CASE tok = 'ENDCASE'                               184
   top = cntrls.look()                             185
   IF top = 'CASE' .OR. ;                          186
      top = 'OTHERWISE' .OR. ;                     187
      top = 'DO_CASE'                              188
      popper(cntrls)                               189
      IF top <> 'DO_CASE'                          190
         popper(cntrls)                            191
      ENDIF                                        192
      case_counts.pop()                            193
    ELSE                                           194
       error_on(tok, cntrls)                       195
    ENDIF                                          196
   ...                                             197
```

Learn Visual dBASE Programming

Adding the Pushy Words to Pusher()

The last changes are the additions to pusher(), which handle the three keywords that can push new values onto the stack. These are shown in Listing 4-26 (also in L04-23.PRG on disk).

Code Listing 4-26

```
PROCEDURE pusher(stack, token, case_num)                    239
...
   CASE token = 'DO_UNTIL'                                  255
      new_prefix = out_prefix + 'U '                        256
                                                            257
   CASE token = 'DO_CASE'                                   258
      new_prefix = out_prefix + 'C '                        259
                                                            260
   CASE token = 'CASE'                                      261
      new_prefix = out_prefix + ;                           262
              LEFT( LTRIM( STR(case_num,3) )+' ', 3 )
                                                            264
   CASE token = 'OTHERWISE'                                 265
      new_prefix = out_prefix + 'O '                        266
                                                            267
   CASE token = 'FOR'                                       268
```

Testing the Finished Product

Listing 4-27 is a file that I used to test handling of nested DO CASEs.

Code Listing 4-27

```
do case

   case

   case

   do case
      case

      case

      case
```

```
        case

           other

        endcase

        case

        otherwise

endcase
```

When I run this T.PRG through ACTION_D, I get this result in T.TMP:

```
do case
C
C     case
C  1
C     case
C  2
C  2        do case
C  2  C        case
C  2  C  1
C  2  C        case
C  2  C  2
C  2  C        case
C  2  C  3
C  2  C        case
C  2  C  4
C  2  C        other
C  2  C  0
C  2        endcase
C  2
C     case
C  3
C     otherwise
C  0
endcase
```

This is exactly what I wanted.

On Your Own

What about SCAN/ENDSCAN? If you've come from a different Xbase, this control block lets you process all the records in a table without a loop.

Some time back, Clipper added the ELSEIF statement, and now it's here in dBASE. Instead of writing this way:

```
IF cond_1
  * do thing 1
ELSE
  IF cond_2
     * do thing 2
  ELSE
     * do thing 3
  ENDIF
ENDIF
```

You can now write it this way:

```
IF cond_1
  * do thing 1
ELSEIF cond_2
  * do thing 2
ELSE
  * do thing 3
ENDIF
```

The ELSEIF eliminates a nesting level and a matched ENDIF every time you use it. You could use several in a single control construct, so this can mount up.

I haven't got around to ELSEIFs or SCAN/ENDSCANs yet. I hope that you pick the one that you're most likely to use (or both, if you're already using both) and add it (or them) to your ACTION_D routine.

Summary

In this chapter we've built the stack machinery and the generation machinery that complement the lexer and parser we built in Chapter 3. Together, these give us a complete action diagramming utility.

To build the stack machinery, we created our own class: the stack class. We used a stack object to hold our stack. Later, when we needed another stack for DO CASE numbers, it was trivially simple to create one.

We used a very simple class constructor, assigning just one property, the stack_size property. We created three methods, push(), pop() and look(), for our simple stack.

We didn't generalize our stack class to handle a lot of cases. Instead, we kept it small and simple to just meet our needs for this program. (In later chapters we'll build general-purpose classes. Both limited-purpose and general classes are valuable.)

The generation machinery was conceptually simple: we built a prefix and wrote it out in front of our lines of code. Handling such details as not double indenting code and making sure that we changed the prefix either before or after printing the current line kept our code from being as simple as we might want, but the world is like that.

Our last bit of coding involved adding another stack to handle the DO CASE construct. We saw that the second stack was trivially simple — we just asked for a NEW stack() and there it was.

In the next chapter, we're going to leave coding briefly and do some setup work before diving into the more advanced object-oriented user interface programming that we'll be starting in Chapter 6 and continuing through the rest of the book.

Chapter 5

We Get Set

Ready to start real object-oriented, event-driven Windows programming? Well, hold on.

In this chapter we're going to get ready to program. I'll show you how I set up Visual dBASE and explain how you can set up yours. If you're already a total WinMeister, you'll get to skip much of this short chapter. If you're a typical mouse clicker, you'll learn more keyboard tricks as we get our setup right.

We'll write a three-line program to help find out how much space is available in our Program Editor, but otherwise, this chapter is about using Windows and the Visual dBASE development environment.

Learn Visual dBASE Programming

Are you a total WinMeister? Answer this question and you're qualified: What's the difference in the Program Manager between pressing Alt, then Enter and pressing Alt+Enter?

If you got it right, take the WinMeister shortcut when I point it out. Making a guess, even if you guess right, doesn't count. That exit is for those who *know* the answer. If you're not a WinMeister, you'll find the answer to this question and lots more helpful hints here.

Setup

I'll go through my Visual dBASE setup, and I'll discuss my reasons for doing it the way I do it. Of course, this is a personal matter and I'm sure that you'll be trying to please yourself, not me. Try it my way to see how that works. Then change it to fit your own habits.

Windows

The first choice is which resolution to run.

If you're running a normal 14- or 15-inch monitor, you can't really drive Visual dBASE at any resolution higher than 640x480. At that resolution, the SpeedBar icons, for one example, are barely legible. Key texts, such as in the object Inspectors, are also pretty small. If you go to 800x600, you'll lose a lot, though you may find this acceptable after you really know the product. (At 1024x768 you'll need binoculars.) Visual dBASE is pretty well tuned for driving at 640x480.

Of course, if you're running a big, 21-inch monitor, you've got more choices. The rest of us will be jealous.

After you pick a resolution, get your access speeded up. I set up Ctrl+Alt+D as my hot key that starts Visual dBASE from the Program Manager. To do this, single click the Visual dBASE icon in the Program Manager, and then choose Files/Properties. (You can see on the Files menu that pressing Ctrl+Enter would have gotten you there immediately, without going through the menus.) Tab down, or click on the Shortcut key item, and press Ctrl+Alt+D (or whatever you choose).

Tip: Alt+F will get you to the Files menu. Either F10 or Alt by itself will switch you to the menus, landing you on the first one, which is always Files. So plain Alt, or F10, followed by Enter is good enough to get to the Files menu. Alt+Enter gets you immediately to Files/Properties.

Chapter 5 — We Get Set

Warning: Whenever I say something absolute, like *always*, you'd better be on guard. File is the first menu choice, but if you have a maximized MDI child window active, Alt gets you to its system menu button, to the left of File.

With your shortcut key established, go on to the File Manager (or DOS, if you're a crusty old-timer like me) for the next step.

DBASEWIN.INI

All the settings we'll make are automatically recorded in your startup file, DBASEWIN.INI. By default, Visual dBASE places this file in the same directory as the executables. If you didn't change things too much, that is \VISUALDB\BIN.

But Visual dBASE first looks for DBASEWIN.INI in your working directory. So copy \VISUALDB\BIN\DBASEWIN.INI into your \DBWORK directory. All our changes will be made here. If you really muck things up, you can always just delete \DBWORK\DBASEWIN.INI, and Visual dBASE will go back to reading the old one.

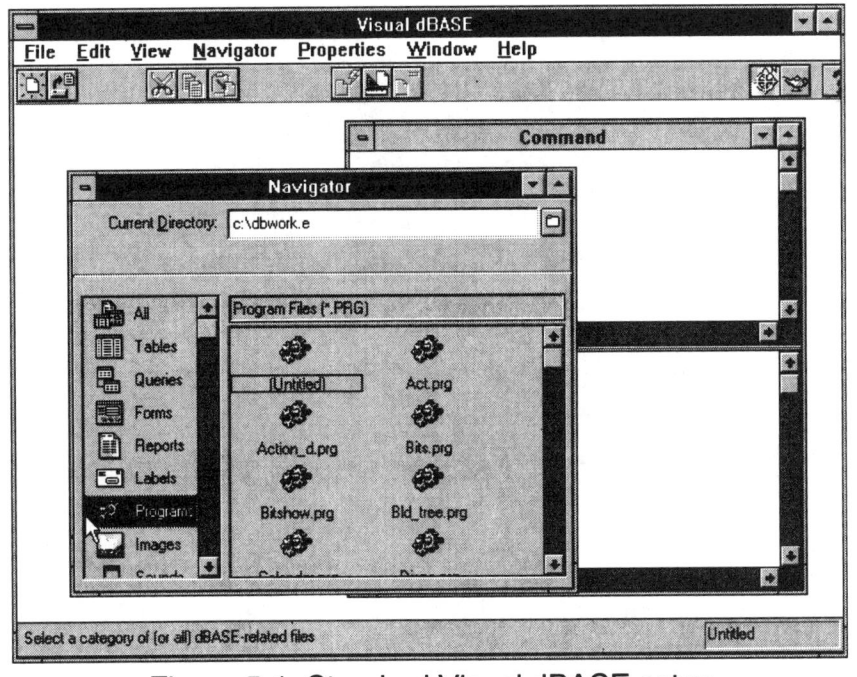

Figure 5-1: Standard Visual dBASE setup

111

The Navigator

With the .INI in your work directory, press your shortcut key and Visual dBASE will start up. A starting setup is shown in Figure 5-1.

The Navigator is the control tool that end users prefer. The Command Window is the control tool that programmers prefer. Being in the latter class, I suggest that you should not ignore the Navigator, since it can be very useful. When your hand is already on the mouse (when you're in the Form Designer, for instance) you can keep your hand on the mouse and use the Navigator.

Start by clicking on a file type where you have some files in your working directory. Figure 5-1 shows my Program collection. Now let's make this useful.

First, those big gear icons are, in my opinion, a senseless waste of real estate. Choose the View menu and click Details (it's one of the bottom three choices). This gives you the Navigator shown in Figure 5-2.

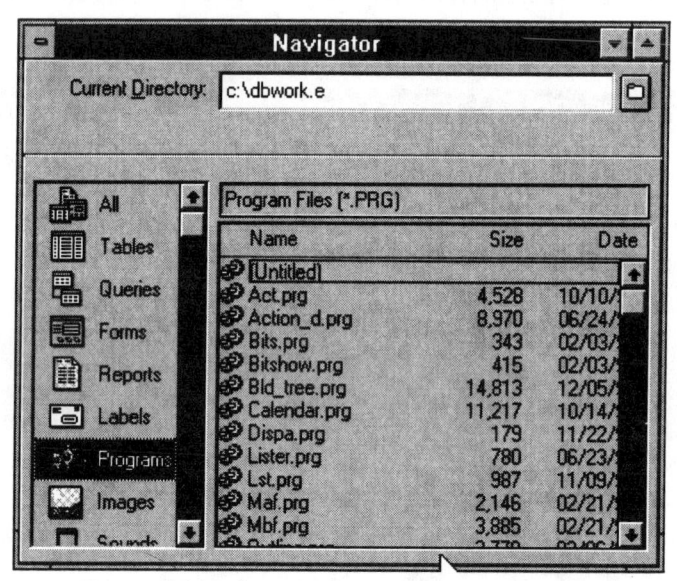

Figure 5-2: File Details replacing icons

Return to the View menu and choose the Sort option. From the cascading menu, choose the sort order you want for your files. I choose Name, since most files in a group already have the same extension.

The SpeedBar

I don't like that SpeedBar at the top. Vertical real estate is precious. It's going to determine how many lines of code you can see at once in the Program Editor. So choose Properties/Desktop and then click on the Application tab.

Choose either the right or the left side of your screen for the SpeedBar. Then exit to take a look. My setup is shown in Figure 5-3.

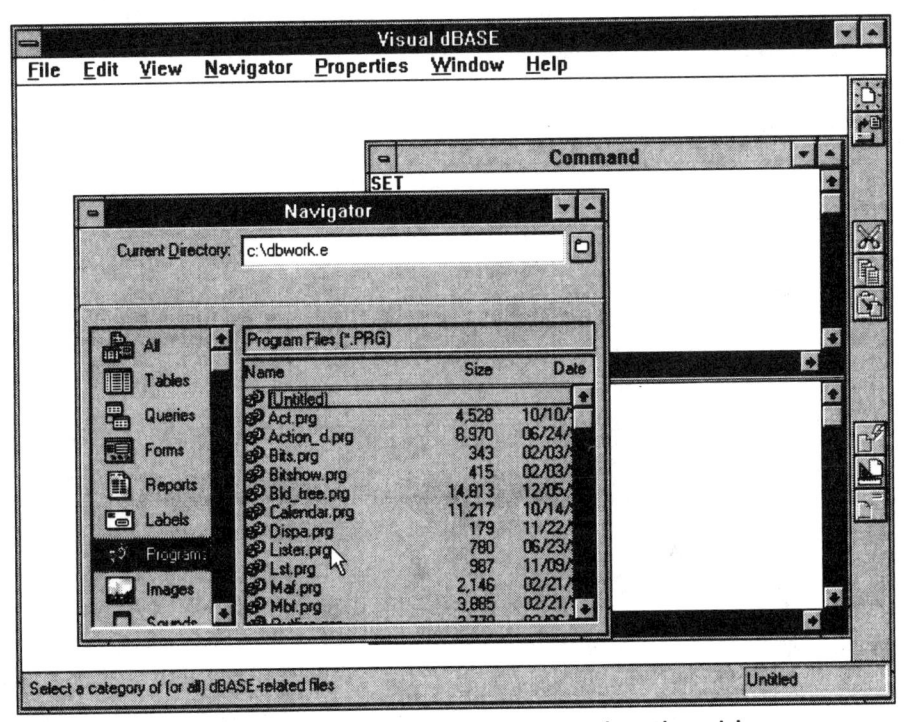

Figure 5-3: The SpeedBar moved to the side

Warning: Borland's SpeedBar buttons aren't very bright. If they don't fit, they'll not make any effort to slide back into view.

Running the SpeedBar vertically will cost you the right-hand icons. You may miss the icons for the Navigator and the Command Window. However, these are always available through the Window menu as Window/1 and Window/2 respectively.

Tip: The SpeedBar location is stored in DBASEWIN.INI. Ignore the documentation's advice about not editing this file — it's a plain text file and Notepad or any other editor can change it. For one example, you could change the SpeedBar line to "SpeedBarStyle = 2", for the left-hand side, or "SpeedBarStyle = 3", for the right.

Now you WinMeisters (those of you who answered the Alt/Enter question right, before you read the answer here) turn forward to Figure 5-7. Set up your Visual dBASE to look *exactly* like that. The rest of us will get there one step at a time, with lot's of hints along the way.

The Command Window

If you're here, you're not a total WinWonk. That's good. It means you've got a life. I worry about those other folks. (I had to check the answer to that question, myself.)

Let's get started arranging Visual dBASE. As you see in Figure 5-4, I set up my Command Window across the top of the screen. There are some tricks here.

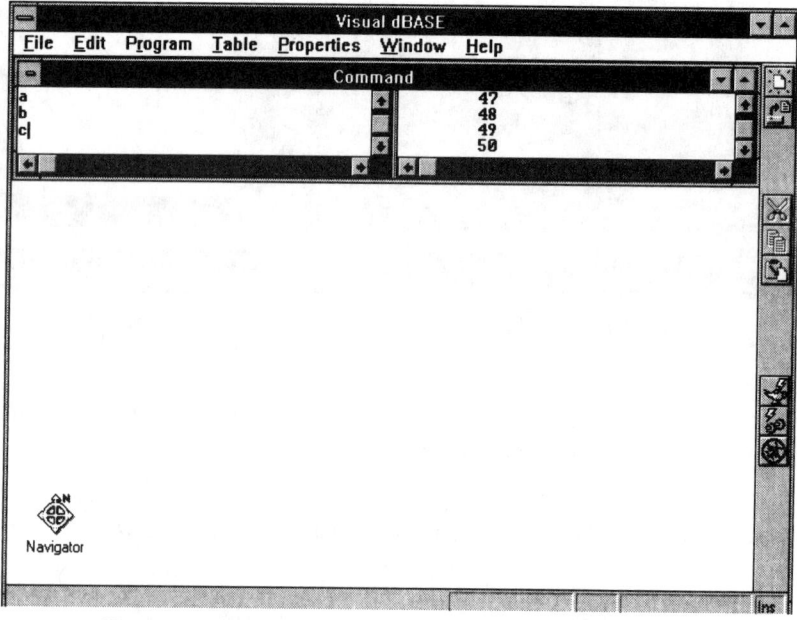

Figure 5-4: Command Window across the top

Chapter 5 *We Get Set*

First, close your Navigator and select the Command Window. (You could minimize your Navigator for the same effect. Both the Navigator and the Command Window are always available as windows or icons.) When you choose Properties with the Command Window active, you'll have the Command Window as a menu choice.

I put the input pane on the left. For fonts, I use the defaults. Click the Reset Fonts button to get the defaults.

Set your Command Window up, and then try this trick. I don't like to waste vertical space, so I chop off the title line that says Command Window. (I know it's the Command Window, even without the title.) With the Command Window selected, drag the corners until it takes the full width of the Visual dBASE client area and gives you about four lines of commands and results. Then drag the title bar into position at the exact top of your client area.

After your Command Window is positioned in the client area, press Alt+hyphen to get the Command Window's System Menu. Choose Move and tap the up arrow exactly three times. Press Enter to complete the move. You should now have neatly decapitated the Command Window title bar, but left the up arrow buttons on the elevators (which is all you'll need, anyway). Figure 5-5 shows you what it should look like.

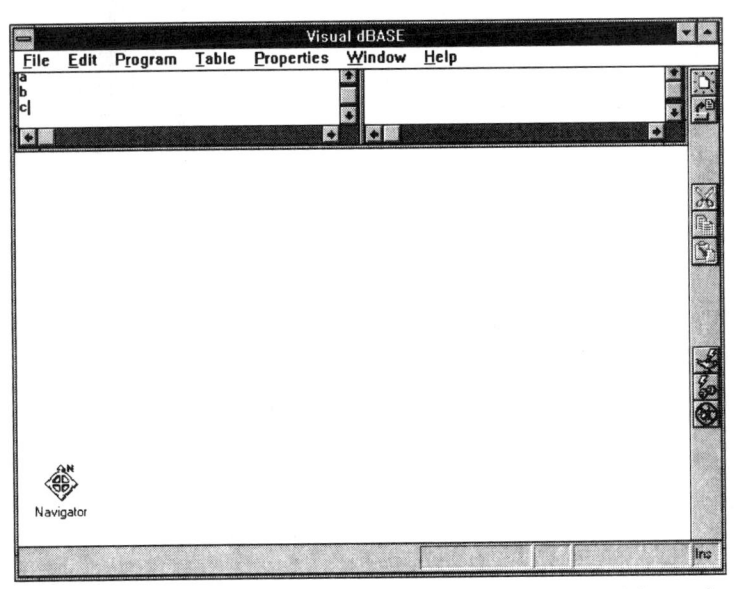

Figure 5-5: Command Window properly positioned

115

Tip: Alt+hyphen gets the system menu of the active child window. (Alt+spacebar gets a parent's system menu, or the system menu of a modal window.) x and n, as in Maximize and Minimize, let you resize from the keyboard. If you are either maximized or minimized, the Restore option is available. It's the first in the system menu, so it is the default. Alt+hyphen, then Enter restores from the keyboard.

The Program Editor

My last setup step is to size the Program Editor. To get the Program Editor on your desktop, type "modi comm t" in the Command Window. Figure 5-6 shows my Program Editor in a preliminary position.

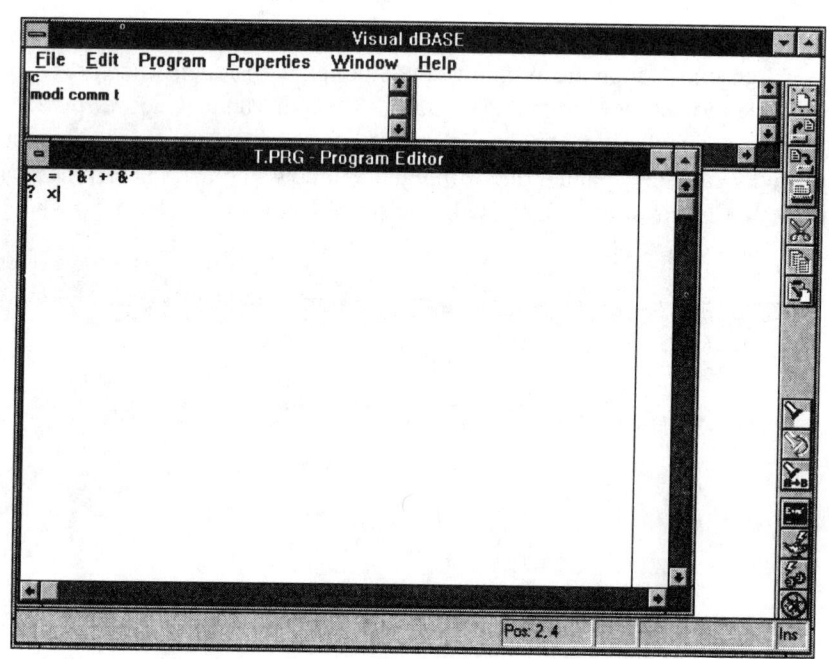

Figure 5-6: Program Editor, partly positioned

If you notice the vertical line on the right side of my Program Editor, that's because I'm writing this book. If you turn word wrap on, that line will appear marking your selected right margin. (Choose Properties/Program Editor when the Program Editor is active.) In the Program Editor dialog, you'll probably prefer the default settings, word wrap off, auto-colors and auto-indent on.

Chapter 5 ___We Get Set___

Give your Program Editor about the width shown here. When you start editing multiple files, you'll see that each one is launched a bit to the right of the last, so having space on the right helps you grab the one you want.

As you see in Figure 5-6, overlap the title of the Program Editor window on top of the Command Window's horizontal scroll bars. (When you choose the Command Window, it will automatically bring those elevators up, overlaying the Program Editor title.) Bring the bottom down to the bottom of your screen.

To get the maximum lines on the screen, I make the Program Editor's horizontal elevator disappear off the bottom of the screen.

If you can live without horizontal scroll, press Alt+hyphen and select Size. Press the down arrow four times and then press Enter to end the size process. You'll lose the elevator and the last line of the editor. The Program Editor always creates an extra blank line at the bottom, so you can't use the very last line on the screen. No harm in sending it off the edge of the earth. You should be left with about half the vertical elevator's down arrow showing — just enough to click on.

Tip: I don't use long lines when I program, so I don't need the horizontal elevator. If you limit your listings to 60 characters wide, you can print your code listings in 7-point type, two columns per page, with over one hundred lines per column. Saving paper is nice, but the big advantage is that you can see 1,000 lines of code at once if your physical desktop can hold five sheets of paper.

You could get more vertical real estate by turning the status bar off. I can live without the status bar, but I leave it on. Why? Because the programs we write will probably be for end users for whom the status bar is very helpful. We'll want to use the status bar in our programs. It's hard to program the status bar if you don't leave it turned on.

With the vertical setup right, we're ready for the final fine-tuning. Choose Properties/Program Editor on the menu. Select it and you'll be able to set the Program Editor font to your liking. Choosing the right font is important. I use 9-point Terminal, regular. Pick a font and weight that you like.

The bigger the font, the easier it is to read, but the fewer lines you'll see. If you use a proportional font, you'll get more characters per line but it won't be as easy to neatly arrange your listings in vertical stacks, like this one:

```
top    = 5
left   = 15
height = 12
width  = 42
```

Learn Visual dBASE Programming

Stay away from serifs. They make for good reading on the printed page, but should be avoided, except for occasional decorative effects, on the screen.

Got it set? Good. Now return to the Program Editor and let's see how good our setup is. Enter the code in Listing 5-1.

Code Listing 5-1

```
set alternate to t.t
set alternate on
for i = 1 to 50
   ? i
endfor
set alternate off
set alternate to
```

When you see a listing that has no style, nothing capitalized, you'll know it's throwaway code. Write it fast, run it, then discard it.

You should have the numbers 1 through 50 on separate rows of a file T.T. You want these lines, not the program you just ran, in your Program Editor. The fast way to delete everything in T.PRG is to press Ctrl+Home to move the cursor to the top-left, then hold the Shift key down while you hold the down arrow key.

Holding the Shift key down while you use the arrows is one way of selecting text. The other is to drag the mouse over the lines you want. Whichever you prefer, when you have selected everything, press Del and it will disappear.

Now read in the file T.T you just created. Choose Edit/Insert from File and type T.T as the file name in the Open File dialog. The whole file will be read in. Again, Ctrl+Home will get you back to the top.

I clicked the down arrow on the vertical elevator just once, to make the starting line of T.T disappear (it's a blank line).

As you see in Figure 5-7, my setup gives me 28 lines.

Got it set up? Play with it until you're happy. Exit Visual dBASE and all this will be written into your DBASEWIN.INI file, so it will be there the next time you start Visual dBASE.

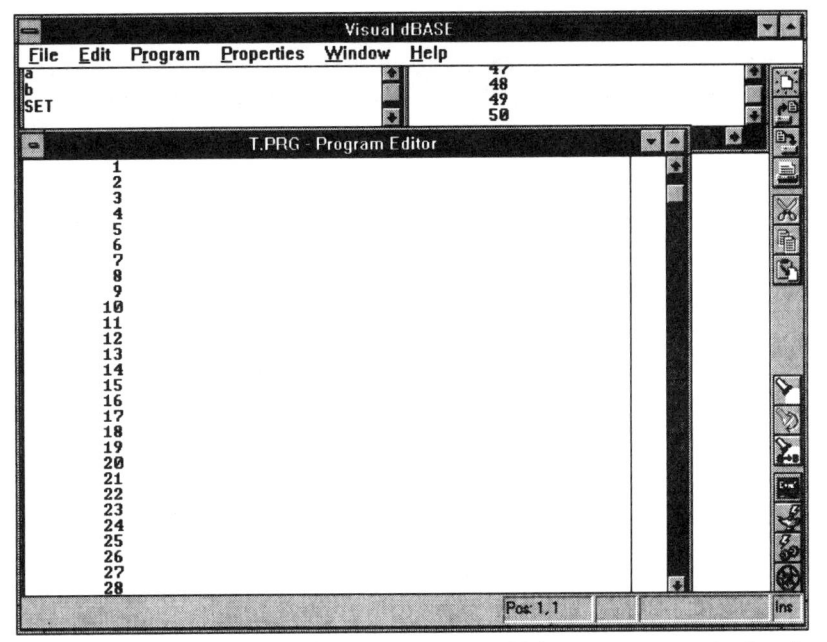

Figure 5-7: 28 lines in the Program Editor, not maximized

Summary

In this chapter, we've taken the time to get set up for the serious programming that's just ahead.

You assigned a shortcut key to get you rapidly into Visual dBASE from the Program Manager.

You put DBASEWIN.INI into your working directory, where it will override the copy in \VISUALDB\BIN.

Then we arranged Visual dBASE' Navigator, SpeedBar, Command Window, and Program Editor to get a usable programming setup.

We managed a setup that will give us 28 vertical lines in the Program Editor.

Before you go on to the next chapter, where we'll start serious work in object-oriented, event-driven programming, let me remind you that I keep my favorite text editor running in a separate Windows session.

Learn Visual dBASE Programming

I use 50 lines in text mode for my other editor. A quick press of Alt+Tab switches from Visual dBASE to my main editor, so I really have the best of both worlds: the integrated Visual dBASE environment, plus my favorite text editor.

Chapter 6

Object-Oriented and Event-Driven

In this chapter we're going to be having some fun tickling a form. Along the way, we'll be programming object properties and using event handlers to write event-driven code. In Chapter 7 we'll begin programming a calendar class. We'll be using the techniques shown here.

From Chapter 7 on, we'll be working on useful classes. For this chapter, we'll use a throwaway class to demonstrate lots of aspects of Visual dBASE object-oriented and event-driven programming.

Learn Visual dBASE Programming

In this chapter, you will:

- Launch a new form
- Create a new class and launch objects from it
- Study the functioning of constructor code
- Assign properties in the constructor code
- Build an event handler
- Assign properties in the event handler
- Use a STATIC variable in the event handler
- Meet and use function pointers
- Meet and use codeblocks
- Attach an object with its own event handler

Let's go right back to where we were in Chapter 1. We'll launch a form and then set some of its properties. After we've done that, we'll add some event-handling methods, and you'll get your first glimmer of how this new paradigm works. OK?

Form Basics

Let's get to work on T.PRG, where we'll write lots of test programs. Enter the code in Listing 6-1.

Code Listing 6-1
```
foo = new form()
foo.text = 'This is a new form'
foo.open()
```

When you run this code, you will be launching a window, as you see in Figure 6-1.

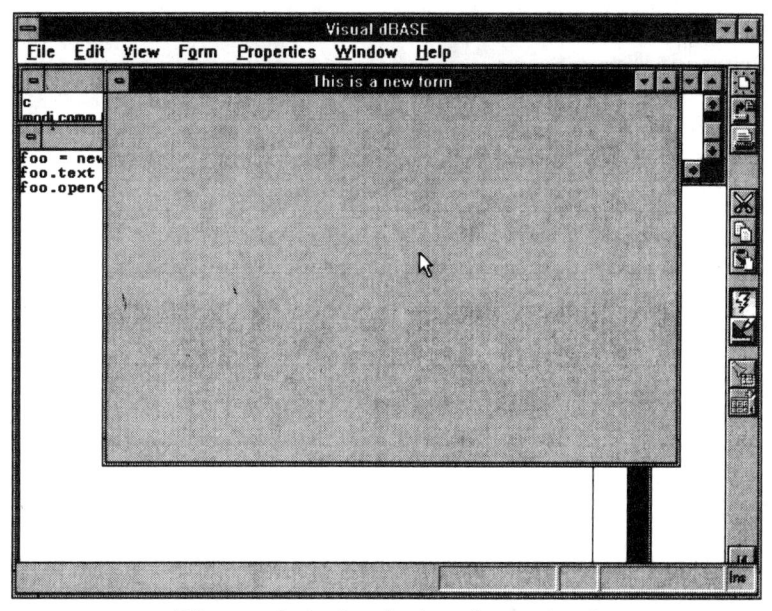

Figure 6-1: A window launched

An Intelligent Windows Window

Go ahead and move your window around, resize it and so on. When you are convinced that you have really built an educated, Windows-aware window, close it (Ctrl+F4 or double-click the system menu button). After you launch a new window, close it before you launch another one. I'll not bother saying this again.

As you saw in Chapter 1, your program has run to completion, but the window is alive and well. In fact, if you think of the window as the program, you'll be closer to the mark than if you continue to think about your mainline. The job of the mainline is to launch windows and then get out of the way.

Creating a New Class

Let's rebuild the program to define a new class and then launch an object that is a member of that class. Listing 6-2 shows the revised version.

Code Listing 6-2
```
foo = new my_class()
foo.open()
```

123

Learn Visual dBASE Programming

```
class my_class of form
  this.text = 'This is a class-based form'
endclass
```

Within a class definition, the keyword *this* refers to the object you are creating. Actually, that is true only in the constructor code, which is all the code preceding the first procedure or function definition in the class.

The Class Constructor

The constructor is a subroutine that runs when you use the NEW operator to create a new instance of a class. Make the changes shown in Listing 6-3 to see exactly what happens.

Code Listing 6-3

```
foo = new my_class()
wait
foo.open()

class my_class of form
  ? 'running the constructor'
  this.text = 'This is a class-based form'
endclass
```

When you run this program, it will pause, as you see in Figure 6-2.

As you see, your constructor code has run and the program is now waiting before the foo.open() line. When you press a key, the form will be launched.

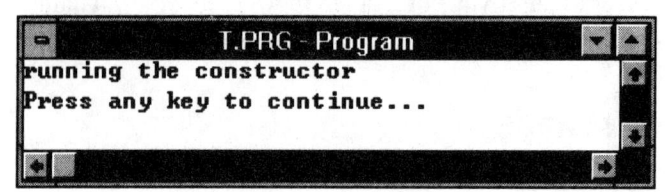

```
┌─────────────────────────────────────┐
│ ▫        T.PRG - Program        ▼▲ │
│running the constructor             │
│Press any key to continue...        │
│                                    │
│ ←                               →  │
└─────────────────────────────────────┘
```

Figure 6-2: The pause before launch

Chapter 6 Object-Oriented and Event-Driven

Assigning Properties in the Constructor

Let's use the constructor to put the window into the center of the screen, where we can see the Command Window. Delete the two lines you added in the last step, and add the ones shown in Listing 6-4.

Code Listing 6-4

```
foo = new my_class()
foo.open()

class my_class of form
   this.text = 'This is a class-based form'
   this.top = 5
   this.left = 25
   this.height = 15
   this.width = 50
endclass
```

With this code in place, when you run the program it should look like what I'm showing in Figure 6-3.

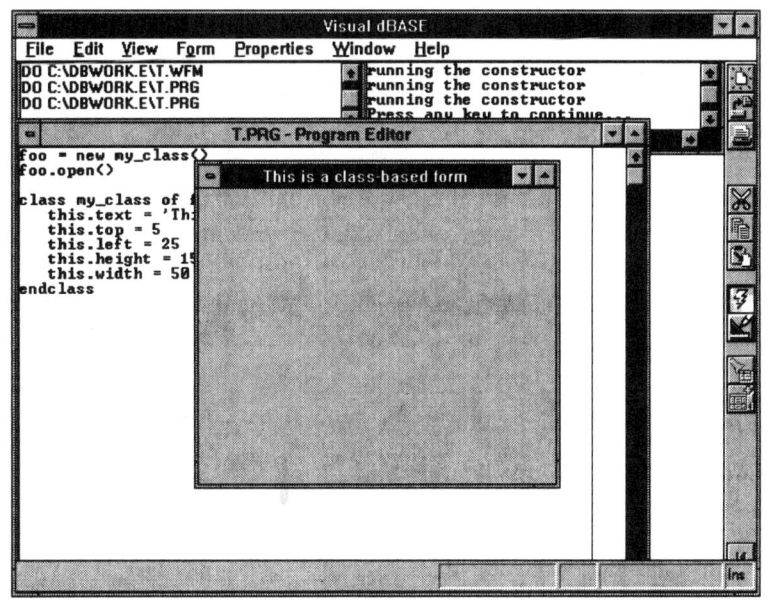

Figure 6-3: Relocating the my_class object

125

Writing Event Handlers

Now that we can see both our object and the Command Window, let's add a routine that handles an event. There are lots of different events to which a form can respond. One of them is being moved. For these events, Borland supplies built-in properties that we can use.

Responding to a Move Event

In Listing 6-5, I've added a reporting function for the built-in OnMove event.

Code Listing 6-5
```
foo = new my_class()
foo.open()

class my_class of form
...
  this.width = 50

  procedure OnMove
     ? 'moved to'+str(this.top)+str(this.left)

endclass
```

I've run this program, as you can see in Figure 6-4.

As you can also see, I've moved the object a few times, and I've also resized it. When you resize it (drag a corner or side) you don't trigger the OnMove event. On the other hand, when you move it (drag the title bar) you get the output in the Command Window, which shows that your event-handler is being called and is working.

Assigning Properties in the Event Handler

When you get that working, let's use our new knowledge to create an object with a little personality. The one in Listing 6-6 doesn't much enjoy being resized.

Chapter 6 *Object-Oriented and Event-Driven*

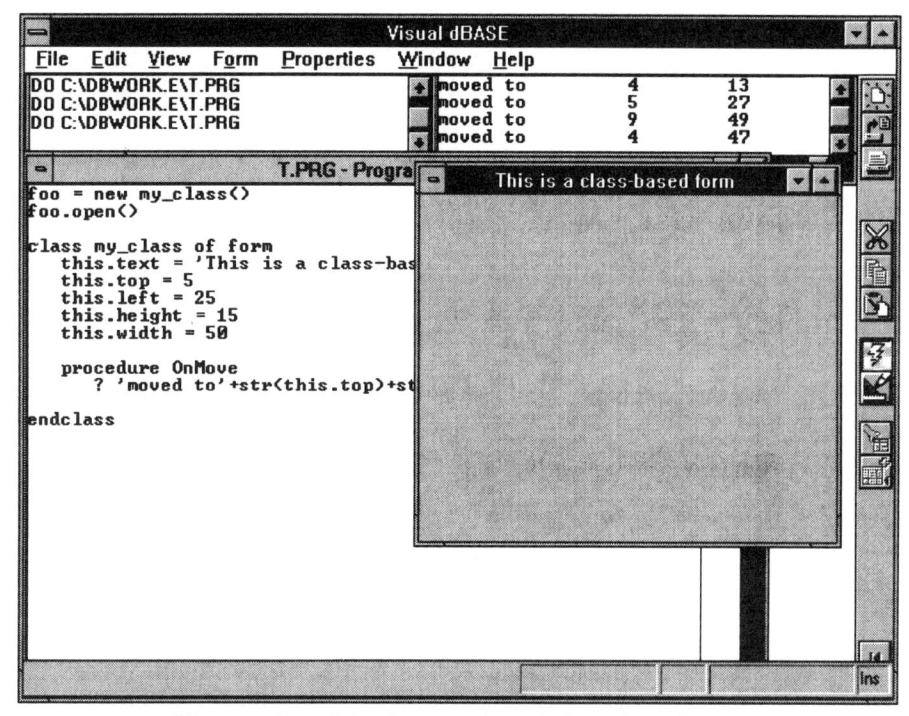

Figure 6-4: Moving and resizing the object

Code Listing 6-6

```
foo = new my_class()
foo.open()

class my_class of form
   this.text = 'This is a class-based form'
   this.top = 5
   this.left = 25
   this.height = 15
   this.width = 50

   procedure OnMove
      ? 'moved to'+str(this.top)+str(this.left)

   procedure OnSize
      ? 'Stop it!  That tickles!'
      this.height = 15
```

127

Learn Visual dBASE Programming

```
      this.width = 50
endclass
```

When you run that form, it complains in the Command Window and rejects any attempt to change its size. (I told you we'd add some personality, but I didn't claim that it would be a *nice* personality.)

For a complete list of events which you can program, try this in the command window:

```
help class form
```

By the way, if you're doing this work in the office, you might try some message like "OnSize event was triggered" or whatever. Trying to explain what I've put here when your boss drops in might be, well, a bit of a ticklish situation.

Using STATIC Variables in the Event Handler

Now let's do some counting to see how many times the form is tickled (or resized, if you prefer). Add the three lines shown in Listing 6-7 and think about them before you run the revised program. Do you think you know what will happen?

Code Listing 6-7

```
foo = new my_class()
foo.open()

class my_class of form
   this.text = 'This is a class-based form'
   this.top = 5
   this.left = 25
   this.height = 15
   this.width = 50

   procedure OnMove
      ? 'moved to'+str(this.top)+str(this.left)

   procedure OnSize
      ? 'Stop it!  That tickles!'

   static resize_tries_count=0
```

128

Chapter 6 — Object-Oriented and Event-Driven

```
   resize_tries_count = resize_tries_count+1
   ?? resize_tries_count

this.height = 15
this.width = 50
endclass
```

When you run the program, you're in for a bit of a surprise. Every time you attempt to resize your form, you'll get two or three repeats of the tickle message. What's going on?

STATIC Finds Recursion in the Event Handler

The answer is simple. The OnSize handler is triggering calls to itself. When it assigns a new height or width, it is resizing the form, so it triggers the OnSize event.

Luckily, we are setting the size to constant values, so we don't fall into an infinite loop. Setting the height to 15 doesn't trigger the OnSize event if the height is already 15. If we had done something like this:

```
* DON'T DO THIS!
this.height = this.height + 1
```

We would have an infinite loop that would grow the form until we crashed Windows. (At least I think that's what would happen. I'm not about to risk my computer by actually testing this. Don't try this on any computer you're not ready to discard.)

STATIC Scope in the Event Handler

Ready for another surprise? Close your form and then run the program again. Got it? That's right, the variable is not set to zero when you run the program again. STATIC variables have their values written into the .PRO at compile time. The run-time value is retained for your entire dBASE session (or until you recompile).

Ready for another surprise? Leave your form on the screen and run your program again. Resize your new form and then resize your old form. Got it? Both forms share a single variable. Unlike PRIVATE or LOCAL variables, the STATIC is created at compile time and then used by whatever objects call the subroutine.

129

Tip: Since STATIC variables have a very long life, you have to be careful about naming them. If you use a common name, such as i, you're sure to get into trouble. Make it a habit to use something nice and long and completely descriptive, such as resize_tries_count. You want to pick a name that you can be sure won't be used for any other purpose.

Using Named Subroutines

STATIC variables are a powerful tool. Now let's leave STATICs while we go on to learn some more about Visual dBASE so that we can make the OnSize subroutine not call itself recursively.

How do you make an OnSize event-handler that won't call itself recursively? Start by changing the name, and then assign the function pointer to the event.

Using Subroutine Reference Variables

Did I say function pointer? Did we just stumble into the C language by mistake? No we didn't. You're about to meet a facility that is both immensely powerful and trivially simple.

In Visual dBASE, the name of a subroutine is a reference to the subroutine. Just as you can assign an object or array to a variable, a function or procedure is automatically assigned to a variable, whose name is the the name of the subroutine.

Open a second editor window for X.PRG and enter this code:

```
a = b
? a( )

function b
return "I'm Mister B"
```

You'll see the report, "I'm Mister B," in your Command Window's results pane. What happens? When you wrote the function named b, a subroutine reference was assigned to the variable b. Borland calls these function pointers, although they work for either functions or procedures and are really references, not pointers.

In the preceding little example, we assigned a the value in b. Since the value of b was a subroutine reference, a became another subroutine reference. Using the parentheses after a subroutine reference tells dBASE to execute the code, as always.

This is the secret to writing non-recursive OnSize events that resize a form. Start by rewriting your T.PRG as you see in Listing 6-8.

Code Listing 6-8

```
foo = new my_class()
foo.open()

class my_class of form
   this.text = 'This is a class-based form'
   this.top = 5
   this.left = 25
   this.height = 15
   this.width = 50

   this.OnSize = class::on_size

   procedure OnMove
      ? 'moved to'+str(this.top)+str(this.left)

   procedure on_size

      ? 'Stop it!  That tickles!'

      static resize_tries_count=0
      resize_tries_count = resize_tries_count+1
      ?? resize_tries_count

      this.height = 15
      this.width = 50

endclass
```

I used Borland's names for the built-in functions, with the UpperLower capitalization they use. For my own, I use all_lower names, with underscores. Here I'm calling Borland's built-in function OnSize and my own is on_size. (Bear in mind that dBASE is not case-sensitive. It's the underscore character that is the real difference.)

131

Using the Scope Resolution Operator

This assignment introduces new syntax:

```
this.OnSize = class::on_size
```

The double colon is called the scope resolution operator. It has the same meaning here as it does in C++. It's used to specify the source of a subroutine. If you had three classes, named Tom, Dick, and Harry, they could each have a method named paint. These would be the calls to the three different routines:

```
Tom::paint()
Dick::paint()
Harry::paint()
```

The Class Scope

Using the keyword *class* in front of the scope resolution operator tells dBASE that you mean the routine as defined in the current class definition.

What we have done here does not change the program's operation. You'll still get the recursive calls when you test this version. But it gives you the mechanism to fix that.

Codeblocks Add Another Subroutine Type

We'll need to use an empty codeblock to eliminate our recursion. (Actually, we won't absolutely need a codeblock, but the other solutions are inelegant.) Ready to meet codeblocks?

Expression Codeblocks

If you've used Clipper 5.x you're familiar with the simplest of Visual dBASE codeblock facilities. Again open a second Program Editor window for X.PRG and test this:

```
c = {||2+2}
? c()
```

The variable c contains a codeblock — a bit of compiled code that can be run just like any other subroutine. It's very important to bear in mind that codeblocks

Chapter 6 — Object-Oriented and Event-Driven

are compiled at compile time. (Unlike macros, which are compiled at run time, and are consequently very slow.)

Our sample codeblock is a simple expression. Let's add a parameter.

```
x = 3
twice = {|p| 2*p}
? twice(x)
```

When you run that, you'll find that twice(x) is 6. What you just wrote is almost identical to this:

```
x = 3
? twice(x)

function twice(p)
return 2*p
```

The only difference is that you write a codeblock in a line which can be anywhere, including in the middle of a subroutine. This means that you can write very readable code by putting the definition of the function right where you'll use it.

Now for you Clipperheads who are feeling just a wee bit condescending because you've been using codeblocks for a couple of years or more, we're going to leave Clipper behind.

Statement Codeblocks

So far we've been using the expression-type codeblock, which is analogous to a function. Now we'll expand to using the statement-type codeblock, which is analogous to a procedure. You can write as many statements as you want in a statement codeblock, separating them with semicolons. The only restriction is that you must put them all on one line. (Program lines are limited to 4K bytes, so this isn't very restrictive, unless you're writing a book restricted to 60-byte lines.)

Your statement(s) in a statement-type codeblock must each follow a semicolon. Here's an example:

```
c = {;? "I'm C!";? "And you're not me!"}
c()
```

133

You can also use parameters with statement-type codeblocks. Try entering these in your Command window:

```
c = {|p|;? "parameter is: ";?? p}
c(3)
c('fred')
```

You'll see your parameters duly reported in the Command window's results pane.

One typical reason for using a statement-type codeblock is to be able to use an IF test. Again, try this in the Command Window:

```
c = {|p|; IF p = 0; ? date(); ENDIF}
c(0)
c(1)
```

Warning: The ELSE statement did not work in a codeblock in dBASE 5.0. If you need compatibility with that version, use an IIF().

The only thing you cannot do is combine the two types of codeblock. If you have an expression before the first semicolon, the statements following the first semicolon will be ignored.

All of this is a lead-in to the simplest possible statement codeblock, the null codeblock.

Using a Null Codeblock

Our recursion avoidance strategy is to assign a null codeblock to the event handler when the otherwise recursive function begins. Then we'll do our work and, at the end, reassign the event handler.

Listing 6-9 shows how this works.

Code Listing 6-9

```
foo = new my_class()
foo.open()

class my_class of form
   this.text = 'This is a class-based form'
   this.top = 5
   this.left = 25
```

Chapter 6 — Object-Oriented and Event-Driven

```
   this.height = 15
   this.width = 50

   this.OnSize = class::on_size

procedure OnMove
   ? 'moved to'+str(this.top)+str(this.left)

procedure on_size

   this.OnSize = {;}

   ? 'Stop it!  That tickles!'

   static resize_tries_count=0
   resize_tries_count = resize_tries_count+1
   ?? resize_tries_count

   this.height = 15
   this.width = 50

   this.OnSize = class::on_size
endclass
```

As you can see, this was much more trouble to explain than it was to do. In on_size(), we start the routine by assigning a null codeblock to the OnSize event handler. That way, the assignment of new height and width properties will not call anything. When on_size() is done, we reassign the function pointer to the event, so it will be ready to work the next time it is needed.

When you run this version, you will see the STATIC count incremented exactly once, every time you resize your form.

Attaching Another Object

Among the most common events to program is the OnClick event of a Pushbutton object. Let's add one that will close our form. Listing 6-10 shows how a simple codeblock can program a Pushbutton object.

135

Code Listing 6-10

```
foo = new my_class()
foo.open()

class my_class of form
  this.text = 'This is a class-based form'
  this.top = 5
  this.left = 25
  this.height = 15
  this.width = 50

  this.OnSize = class::on_size

  this.close_button = NEW Pushbutton(this)

  this.close_button.top = this.height - 5
  this.close_button.left = this.width/2 - 5
  this.close_button.height = 2
  this.close_button.width = 10
  this.close_button.text = "Close"
  this.close_button.OnClick = { ;form.close() }

  procedure OnMove
     ? 'moved to'+str(this.top)+str(this.left)

  procedure on_size

     this.OnSize = {;}

     ? 'Stop it!  That tickles!'

     static resize_tries_count=0
     resize_tries_count = resize_tries_count+1
     ?? resize_tries_count

     this.height = 15
     this.width = 50

     this.OnSize = class::on_size

endclass
```

This new code attaches a pushbutton to the form. As you see, it is very similar to the code used for assigning properties, including the event property, to the form itself. You name, create and attach the object by saying:

```
this.close_button = NEW Pushbutton(this)
```

Close_button is a property of your form object, which you create with that line. It happens to be a Pushbutton object. (More exactly, it's an object reference variable, referring to a Pushbutton object.) Since it is an object, it can also have properties, such as:

```
this.close_button.top
this.close_button.OnClick
```

As with forms, the *Top* property of a Pushbutton is one of the four location properties (Top, Left, Height, and Width). The OnClick property is an event. Assigning a codeblock to the event gives Visual dBASE something to do when the event is triggered.

You probably guessed that the Form.Close() syntax calls a built-in method of the Form class, Close(). The Close() method, as you would expect, closes the form.

Tip: Note that I've positioned the Pushbutton object with dimensions taken from its parent form. This makes it easy to change the form's size at a later date and still have the Pushbutton stay in the same relative location.

When you run this form, you'll see that the Close Pushbutton gives you an easier way of closing the form. (It's about time this form did something polite, isn't it?)

Summary

I hope you've enjoyed this quick introduction to object-oriented, event-driven programming in Visual dBASE. You've met the techniques that we'll be using through the rest of this book as we build our classes.

In this chapter, you built a new class and launched objects from that class. You used the constructor code to assign properties to the object. We explored the constructor, showing how it is called by the NEW operator.

You wrote your first event handlers. You made a distinctly crabby little object that refused to be resized (which also showed you how to program object properties in an event handler). You used a STATIC variable in an event handler and explored its rather wide-ranging scope.

Then you went on to use function pointers and codeblocks to avoid recursion in the event handler. You met expression and statement codeblocks, on your way to using a simple, null codeblock.

Finally, you attached a Pushbutton object to your form, setting its properties and including a codeblock-based event handler.

I hope you had some fun along the way. Starting in Chapter 7, we'll be using these techniques to write classes that will show you how systems are built.

Chapter 7

On to the Calendar

Now that you've met object-oriented, event-driven programming, it's time to start some commercial-quality work, no? I know, one chapter doesn't make you a master, does it? Not to worry. Before we're done programming, you should have a lot of confidence in your ability.

We'll start with a calendar class, because that's totally visual and gives you instant feedback on your brilliant (and, perhaps, sometimes not so brilliant) work.

Learn Visual dBASE Programming

As we build the calendar, you will:

- Create a new calendar class
- Draw a grid using Line objects
- Program so that the user can resize the calendar
- Add day naming Text objects
- Add days as Text objects

Now let's start with a CALENDAR.PRG.

Creating a Calendar Class

In the Command window, type "modi comm calendar".

Then read in SKELETON.PRG (Alt+E for the Edit menu, then I for Insert from File and then type "SKELETON" or click on it). Use Ctrl+R to replace both SKELETONs with CALENDARs and add a comment on the top line. Mine is shown in Listing 7-1.

Code Listing 7-1

```
* CALENDAR.PRG -- The calendar class
* copyright 1995, Martin L. Rinehart

* end of CALENDAR.PRG
```

Our calendar class will be a special type of form that has a calendar on it. We'll display a month plus whatever spare days fit, and let the user click to select a day, or to turn the pages backward or forward a month or a year at a time. We'll also have keyboard-equivalent commands, so the calendar will be suitable for popping up when you are busy using the keyboard, such as for data entry.

Since the underlying behavior is that of a Form object, we'll inherit from the Form class. Our calendars will be standard, MDI-child windows.

Tip: Making the inheritance decision is fundamental to programming any class. Even when you are dead sure what object to inherit from, always pause for a minute and cross-examine yourself about the choice.

Chapter 7   **On to the Calendar**

Listing 7-2 shows the calendar class created in CALENDAR.PRG.

Code Listing 7-2

```
* CALENDAR.PRG -- The calendar class
* copyright 1995, Martin L. Rinehart

foo = new calendar("Test Calendar")
foo.open()

CLASS calendar(title) OF Form(title)

ENDCLASS

* end of CALENDAR.PRG
```

I've used a parameter after the class name. In this case, the parameter is the form's title. I pass this parameter along to the object from which we are inheriting. You can pass parameters to the constructor of an object, but they must be known at the time the constructor is called. This means that you can only use parameters passed to the derived class, constants and expressions built with parameters and constants. (Actually, you can sneak in some other things, like PUBLIC variables, but that's not good style.)

Here's another way to declare the calendar class, using a fixed title:

```
CLASS calendar OF Form("Calendar")
```

Tip: Think through your class parameters carefully. Don't use them unless you are confident that the parameter will almost always come in handy.

When you press Ctrl+D, your form, labeled Test Calendar, should pop up and stare at you, with a very blank expression. Our job is now to turn this dumb animal into a smart calendar animal. We'll start by adding a grid of seven days per week, by six weeks per month.

Adding a Grid of Line Objects

I know, there aren't six weeks in a month, are there? Still, that's how many weeks down the page you have to allow for the occasional month. Suppose you have a 31 day month that starts on Friday. In the first week, you'll have the first (Friday) and

141

second (Saturday). The next 28 days fill the next four weeks, completely. You've still got the 31st to handle, which will start one more week.

Let's draw a grid of lines that will enclose six rows of seven days each. This will take a grid of eight vertical lines and seven horizontal lines.

You draw lines on a form using objects of the Line class. I'm going to add the lines as numbered, not named, properties of the calendar object. This is an example of a numbered property:

```
foo = NEW Object()
foo[23] = 'The first property!'
```

The number 23 looks like a subscript in this example, but there is a very important difference between numbered properties and array elements. In this example, property 23 is the first and only property that the object has. The existence of property number 23 does *not* imply that there are properties 1, 2 and so on.

Borland's documentation calls these array numbers a *sparse array* notation. In fact, you can use this notation for sparse arrays, very easily. (A sparse array is one in which most elements do not have values.) These property numbers make implementing sparse arrays trivially simple, but they are useful for many other purposes.

Tip: Use numbered properties whenever you want to assign properties in a loop.

Drawing the Vertical Lines

I'm going to assign the vertical lines to properties 101 through 108. The horizontal lines will be properties 201 through 207. (You could use any numbers you like. I find these easy to remember.)

Listing 7-3 shows the new code.

Code Listing 7-3

```
* CALENDAR.PRG -- The calendar class
* copyright 1995, Martin L. Rinehart

foo = new calendar("Test Calendar")
foo.open()

CLASS calendar(title) OF Form(title)
```

Chapter 7 *On to the Calendar*

```
This.draw(This)

PROCEDURE draw(cal)
LOCAL i, lft, rgt, stp, tp, btm

lft = .5
rgt = cal.width - 5.5
stp = (rgt - lft) / 7

tp = 1.5
btm = cal.height - 2.25

FOR i = 101 TO 108
   cal[i] = NEW Line(cal)

   cal[i].Top = tp
   cal[i].Left = lft + (i-101)*stp
   cal[i].Bottom = btm
   cal[i].Right = cal[i].Left

ENDFOR

ENDCLASS

* end of CALENDAR.PRG
```

Figure 7-1 shows the result I get when I launch this calendar.

As you see, I don't add these properties as part of the constructor code. They are put in the draw() routine, which is called in the constructor. You can also see that the locations of the lines are calculated from the coordinates of the calendar object.

Warning: Every visual object is positioned and sized with Top, Left, Height, and Width coordinates, except for Lines. The Line class has Top, Left, Bottom, and Right coordinates. The Top and Left coordinates locate one end of a Line. The Bottom and Right coordinates locate the other end. The Top can be above or below the Bottom, and the Left can be on either side of the Right.

Tip: Lines also have a Width property, which defaults to 1 and is measured in pixels. Fat lines have rounded ends, centered around the nominal coordinates. This lets you draw all sorts of things with lines — even circles.

143

Learn Visual dBASE Programming

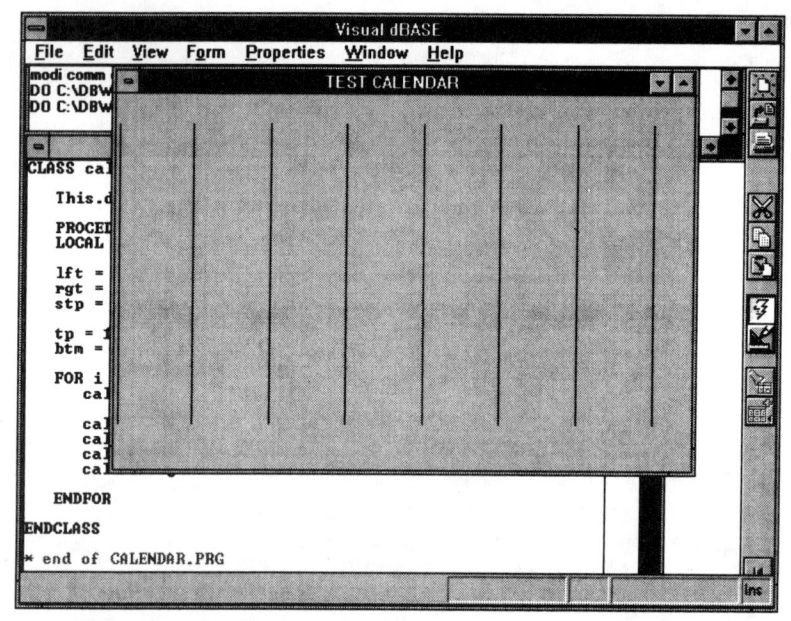

Figure 7-1: The vertical lines begin the calendar

The draw() routine is used because we'll want the user to be able to resize the calendar. When the calendar is resized, we'll want to redraw these lines (among other things) so that they fit in the new size.

You can also see that I've passed the calendar object as a parameter to the draw routine. I make a simple rule: only use *this* in constructor and event-handling routines. In fact, the variable *this* is also created in subroutines called one level down from these routines and would be available in the draw() subroutine. It would not be available in a routine called by draw().

Tip: I find it too much trouble to check that I am only one level down (and even worse trouble when I insert another routine above the one I first wrote). I let Visual dBASE pass *this* to routines that it calls, but I pass my objects explicitly to routines that I call.

Drawing the Horizontal Lines

Listing 7-4 shows the lines added to draw the horizontal lines.

Code Listing 7-4

```
ENDFOR                                          29
                                                30
stp = (btm-tp) / 6                              31
                                                32
FOR i = 201 TO 207                              33
   cal[i] = NEW Line(cal)                       34
                                                35
   cal[i].Top = tp + (i-201)*stp                36
   cal[i].Left = lft                            37
   cal[i].Bottom = cal[i].Top                   38
   cal[i].Right = rgt                           39
                                                40
ENDFOR                                          41
                                                42
ENDCLASS                                        43
```

The results of this code are shown in Figure 7-2.

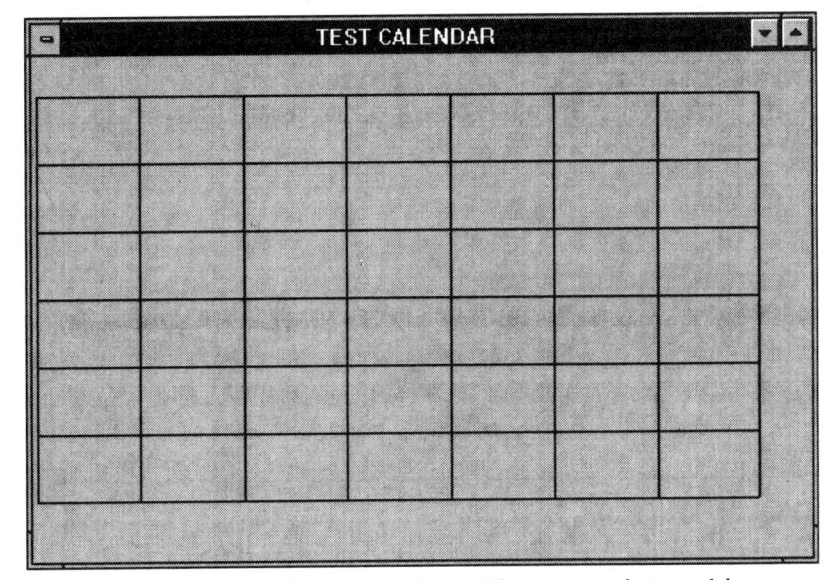

Figure 7-2: The calendar with a complete grid

Letting the User Resize the Calendar

Our next job is to redraw these lines when the user resizes the calendar. Listing 7-5 shows a line added to call the draw() routine in response to the OnSize event.

Code Listing 7-5

```
CLASS calendar(title) OF Form(title)                    7
                                                        8
  This.draw(This)                                       9
  This.OnSize = { ;This.draw(This) }                   10
                                                       11
  PROCEDURE draw(cal)                                  12
```

Unfortunately, this just doesn't work. Figure 7-3 shows the mess I made after several resizings.

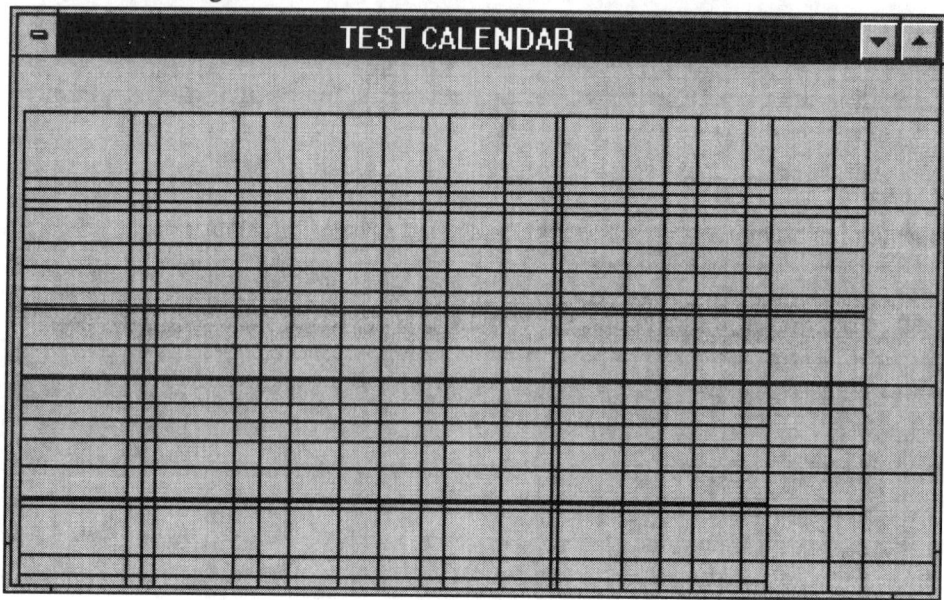

Figure 7-3: The calendar with a mess of grids

This isn't what we want. The problem is that we created the lines in the draw() routine, so every time draw() is called, it creates a new set of lines. What we need to do is create the lines in the constructor and use the draw routine to put them in their places. Listing 7-6 shows the corrected code.

146

Code Listing 7-6

```
* CALENDAR.PRG -- The calendar class                        1
* copyright 1995, Martin L. Rinehart                        2
                                                            3
foo = new calendar("Test Calendar")                         4
foo.open()                                                  5
                                                            6
CLASS calendar(title) OF Form(title)                        7
                                                            8
  * create the lines                                        9
    LOCAL i                                                10
                                                           11
    FOR i = 101 TO 108                                     12
        This[i] = NEW Line(This)                           13
    ENDFOR                                                 14
                                                           15
    FOR i = 201 TO 207                                     16
        This[i] = NEW Line(This)                           17
    ENDFOR                                                 18
                                                           19
This.draw(this)                                            20
This.OnSize = { ;This.draw(This) }                         21
                                                           22
PROCEDURE draw(cal)                                        23
LOCAL i, lft, rgt, stp, tp, btm                            24
                                                           25
lft = .5                                                   26
rgt = cal.width - 5.5                                      27
stp = (rgt - lft) / 7                                      28
                                                           29
tp = 1.5                                                   30
btm = cal.height - 2.25                                    31
                                                           32
FOR i = 101 TO 108                                         33
                                                           34
   cal[i].Top = tp                                         35
   cal[i].Left = lft + (i-101)*stp                         36
   cal[i].Bottom = btm                                     37
   cal[i].Right = cal[i].Left                              38
                                                           39
ENDFOR                                                     40
                                                           41
```

147

```
    stp = (btm-tp) / 6                                          42
                                                                43
    FOR i = 201 TO 207                                          44
                                                                45
        cal[i].Top = tp + (i-201)*stp                           46
        cal[i].Left = lft                                       47
        cal[i].Bottom = cal[i].Top                              48
        cal[i].Right = rgt                                      49
                                                                50
    ENDFOR                                                      51
                                                                52
ENDCLASS                                                        53
                                                                54
* end of CALENDAR.PRG                                           55
```

When you add the new lines to your CALENDAR.PRG, don't overlook the deletions at lines 34 and 45. Those were the lines that created the NEW lines, which are replaced by the code added to the constructor.

Tip: I often indent a group of lines under a comment, when the comment describes the job being done. It's one more way to get a small increment in readability. Since I'm the person most likely to have to maintain my own code, I take advantage of every opportunity to make my code more readable.

When you run this program, you get a calendar that is fun to resize.

Did I say calendar? Well, it's beginning to feel like it might become a calendar when it grows up. Let's add the labels for the days of the week, across the top.

Labeling the Days of the Week

Text is added to a form with the Text object. We'll add seven text objects in the constructor and position them in the draw() routine. These additions are shown in Listing 7-7.

Code Listing 7-7

```
CLASS calendar(title) OF Form(title)                            7
    STATIC day_names = "SunMonTueWedThrFriSat"                  8
                                                                9
...
                                                                20
```

```
* create the day labels                                     21
  FOR i = 301 to 307                                        22
     This[i] = NEW Text(This)                               23
     This[i].Text = SUBSTR(day_names, 1+3*(i-301), 3)
     This[i].Alignment = 4 && Centered                      25
     This[i].Top = .25                                      26
     This[i].Height = 1                                     27
  ENDFOR                                                    28
                                                            29
This.draw(This)                                             30
This.OnSize = { ;This.draw(This) }                          31
                                                            32
PROCEDURE draw(cal)                                         33
LOCAL i, lft, rgt, stp, tp, btm                             34
...
                                                            62
* Day labels                                                63
  LOCAL wdth; wdth = (rgt - lft) / 7                        64
  FOR i = 301 TO 307                                        65
     cal[i].Left = cal[i-200].Left                          66
     cal[i].Width = wdth                                    67
  ENDFOR                                                    68
                                                            69
ENDCLASS                                                    70
                                                            71
* end of CALENDAR.PRG                                       72
```

In Listing 7-7, ellipses show existing code that I've excluded from the listing.

As you see, a STATIC variable holds the source data that lists all the day names. (I presume that you are always alert for ways to improve my code. If English isn't your native language, I'm sure you'll substitute your own text in the day_names variable.)

Figure 7-4 shows the result of adding the names. Our object is starting to look like a calendar.

The Text property of a Text object is, of course, the character string that will be displayed. The Alignment property of a Text object ranges from 0 to 11. Values from 0 through 8 are top-left aligned (0), top-center aligned (1) and so on, through lower-right (8). The next three values specify word wrapping alignments on the left (9), center (10) and right (11).

Learn Visual dBASE Programming

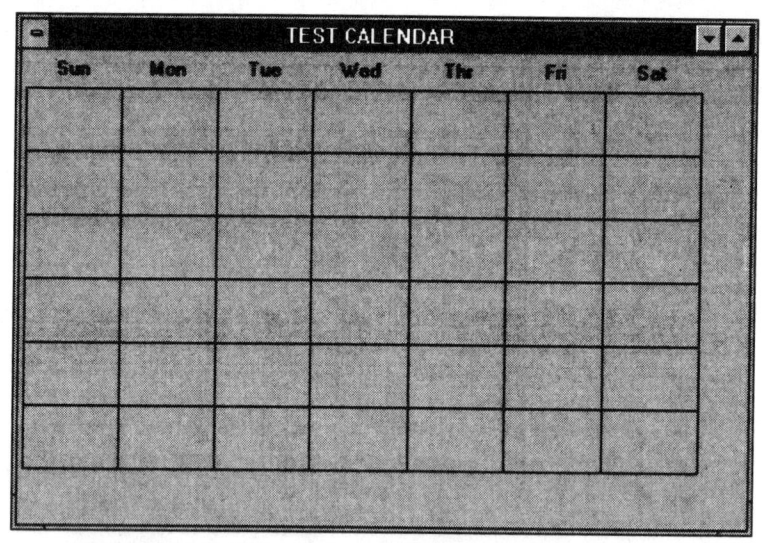

Figure 7-4: Day names added to our calendar

To get a definitive view of the properties and values of any object, create a form, attach the property, and then call the INSPECT() built-in function. In the Command window, try this:

```
foo = NEW Form( )
foobar = NEW Text(foo)
INSPECT(foobar)
```

Figure 7-5 shows the Command window and the object properties Inspector that I've launched to check the Alignment properties. A little menu of Alignment values pops up in response to a click on the arrow that appears in the right side of the Alignment property. Alignment is one of the Position Properties in the properties tab.

Warning: Don't use a variable name like bar. It's the same as the built-in function name BAR(). Unfortunately, dBASE frequently allows function names as variable names, too. Bar would work perfectly in the above example, for instance. It doesn't always distinguish them, however, so you can never be sure when your code will fail.

After you test variables in the Command window, you can free the resources they take by releasing them. The RELEASE ALL command will do a nice cleanup job.

Chapter 7   *On to the Calendar*

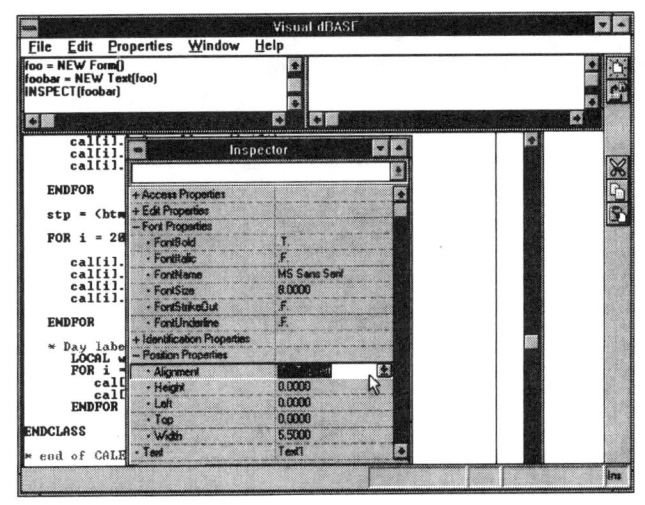

Figure 7-5: Inspecting Alignment properties

Adding Date Objects

Our next job is to add days in the interior of our calendar. We'll want to show each day's number. We'll also want to highlight the currently selected day and let the user click the mouse or use arrow keys to highlight a different day.

Adding Date Calculation Functions

Before we can add days, we'll need to add functions that choose the first date, given a selected date. Mine are shown in Listing 7-8.

Code Listing 7-8

```
ENDCLASS                                                          123
                                                                  124
                                                                  125
FUNCTION find_start(dt)                                           126
                                                                  127
* Given any date, this function returns a start date for a
* calendar's page. It assumes that the first of the month
* of the given date should be in the top line of the             130
* calendar.                                                       131
                                                                  132
LOCAL first                                                       133
```

151

```
first = make_date( MONTH(dt), 1, YEAR(dt) )           134
                                                      135
RETURN first - (DOW(first)-1)                         136
                                                      137
                                                      138
* end of find_start()                                 139
                                                      140
                                                      141
FUNCTION make_date(mo, da, yr)                        142
                                                      143
* This function returns a date when passed three numbers,
* representing the month, day, and year, respectively. 145
                                                      146
SET DATE TO MDY                                       147
                                                      148
RETURN CTOD( STR(mo,2) + '/' + ;                      149
             STR(da,2) + '/' + ;                      150
             STR(yr,4) )                              151
                                                      152
* end of make_date()                                  153
                                                      154
                                                      155
* end of CALENDAR.PRG                                 156
```

Note that I've added these functions outside the class definition. I chose this because these functions are not just methods of a calendar, but could be useful functions elsewhere, too.

The problem with functions such as this is testing. You don't want to use them in the calendar object without having tested them first. Fortunately, the Command window makes it simple. This shows how:

```
SET PROCEDURE TO calendar ADDITIVE
? make_date(1, 15, 95)
x = {1/15/95}
? find_start(x)
```

When you are done testing, clear the procedure file:

```
SET PROCEDURE TO
```

Chapter 7   **On to the Calendar**

As always, you can use all lowercase and abbreviate to four letters, which I always do in the Command window.

Calling with a Date Parameter

With these functions tested, we can add our days. To return to the beginning, we'll need to tell our calendar, when we first call it, what day we want highlighted. And we'll need to record this fact as a property of the calendar.

Listing 7-9 shows the modifications to the first few lines of CALENDAR.PRG. On disk, these changes are in L07-08.PRG, as are the rest of the listings in this chapter.

Code Listing 7-9

```
* CALENDAR.PRG -- The calendar class                  1
* copyright 1995, Martin L. Rinehart               2
                                                      3
foo = new calendar( "Test Calendar", date() )         4
foo.open()                                            5
                                                      6
CLASS calendar(title, sdate) OF Form(title)           7
   STATIC day_names = "SunMonTueWedThrFriSat"         8
```

The added parameter for the calendar object is not passed to the Form object's constructor. Forms don't know what to do with dates.

Creating Day Objects

With the selected date available, we can create the days. I chose to build days from Text objects. You'll see that Texts have the capabilities we'll need.

Listing 7-10 shows the new constructor code.

Code Listing 7-10

```
   ENDFOR                                            30
                                                     31
* add the days                                       32
   FOR i = 1 TO 42                                   33
      This[i] = NEW Text(This)                       34
      This[i].Alignment = 2 && Top, right            35
   ENDFOR                                            36
```

153

```
        This.set_days(This)                              37
                                                         38
This.draw(This)                                          39
This.OnSize = { ;This.draw(This) }                       40
                                                         41
* end of constructor                                     42
```

This creates 42 day objects and sets their Alignment property to the top right, which is where I like my numbers in a calendar. The set_days() method, which we'll come to next, takes the selected day, uses it to calculate the starting day, and then assign each day object its date. Among other uses, you need to know each day's date to get its text (the day number) assigned.

Setting the Day Objects

I've also added "* end of ..." comments throughout the file.

Listing 7-11 shows the set_days() routine.

Code Listing 7-11

```
* end of calendar::draw                                  105
                                                         106
                                                         107
PROCEDURE set_days(cal)                                  108
                                                         109
cal.start_date = find_start(cal.selected_date)           110
                                                         111
LOCAL dt; dt = cal.start_date                            112
                                                         113
FOR i = 1 TO 42                                          114
   cal[i].date = dt                                      115
   cal[i].Text = LTRIM( STR(DAY( dt )) )                 116
   dt = dt + 1                                           117
ENDFOR                                                   118
                                                         119
* end of calendar::set_days                              120
                                                         121
                                                         122
ENDCLASS                                                 123
```

Chapter 7   On to the Calendar

This routine uses the find_start() function to assign the starting date. Line 110 shows this date being assigned to a new property of the calendar object. Generally, I like to assign properties in the constructor, but this one fits naturally here. We'll make more use of this method when, for instance, we teach our calendar to go forward and backward a month at a time.

The two lines inside the FOR loop assign two properties to each day object. Cal[i], for i values from 1 to 42, started life as a Text object. Here I add a new property, date, so that the day will know something about itself. (This will become important when we start moving the highlighting around as the user changes from one day to another.) Then I assign the appropriate text for the day to display.

Drawing the Day Objects

Listing 7-12 shows the addition of days to the draw() routine.

Code Listing 7-12

```
* Days                                                          83
  LOCAL j, k, ht, wd                                            84
                                                                85
  ht = cal[202].Top  - cal[201].Top  - .2                       86
  wd = cal[102].Left - cal[101].Left - .4                       87
  k = 1                                                         88
                                                                89
  FOR i = 1 TO 6                                                90
                                                                91
                                                                92
     FOR j = 1 TO 7                                             93
        cal[k].Top    = cal[i+200].Top  + .1                    94
        cal[k].Height = ht                                      95
        cal[k].Left   = cal[j+100].Left + .2                    96
        cal[k].Width  = wd                                      97
        k = k + 1                                               98
     ENDFOR                                                     99
                                                                100
  ENDFOR                                                        101
```

Inside the nested FOR loops, the appropriate coordinates are assigned to each of the 42 days. I've calculated the coordinates by using the position of the lines, which we determined earlier in the draw() routine. Each day text object is sized to be just a bit smaller than the space between the lines.

Learn Visual dBASE Programming

Note that I've used increments that are twice as big horizontally as vertically. This is because our coordinates are measured in character units. Borland has named this unit the Turpin, after Bill Turpin, head of dBASE development.

The size of each Turpin is determined by the Form's scale font properties. By default, the ScaleFontName is MS Sans Serif and the ScaleFontSize is 8 points. This works out to a Turpin that is about twice as high as it is wide.

Once you have made these additions, you are ready to test. When you run your new calendar, it will have days displayed, as you see in Figure 7-6.

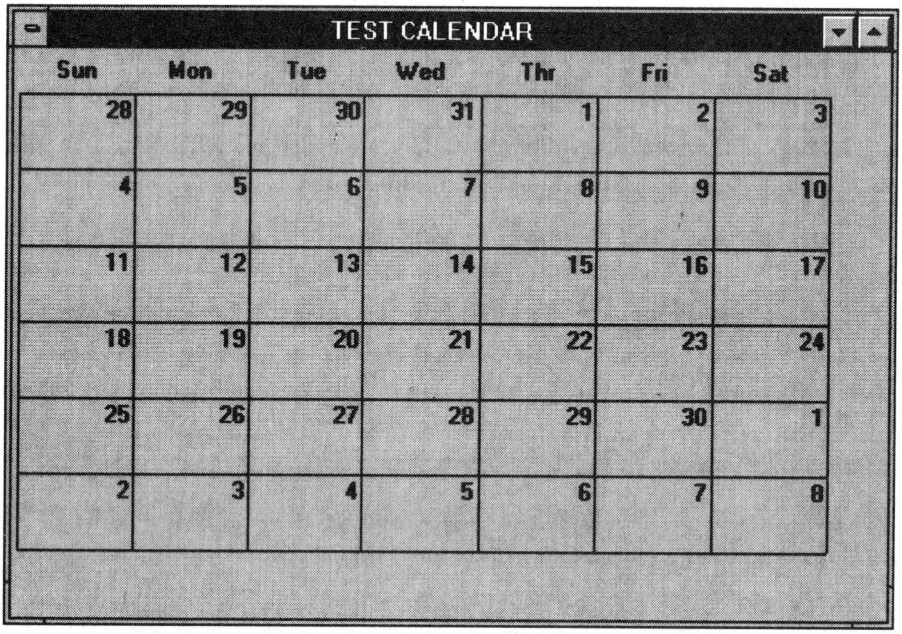

Figure 7-6: Day objects added to the calendar

Improving Performance

When you resize your calendar, you'll see that it is very clumsy and slow. The reason for this is that every time you change a visual property, Visual dBASE asks Windows to repaint the object. For each day, when you resize you assign four new position and size properties. This will trigger 42 times 4 repaints for just the days.

To speed this up, add the two lines shown in Listing 7-13.

Chapter 7   On to the Calendar

Code Listing 7-13

```
PROCEDURE draw(cal)                                         45
LOCAL i, lft, rgt, stp, tp, btm                             46
cal.Visible = .F.                                           47
                                                            48
...
                                                           102
cal.Visible = .T.                                          103
                                                           104
* end of calendar::draw                                    105
```

The very first thing in the draw() routine is to set the calendar's Visible property to False. As you would probably guess, this hides the calendar. When draw() has done all its work, Visible is turned back on, so the whole calendar is drawn at once. This speeds up the process wonderfully.

The Whole Calendar Class

For those of you who have borrowed this book from your library, long after someone removed the disk, Listing 7-14 shows the complete CALENDAR.PRG (L07-08.PRG on disk) to this point.

Code Listing 7-14

```
* CALENDAR.PRG -- The calendar class for WPIM              1
* copyright 1995, Martin L. Rinehart                       2
                                                           3
foo = new calendar( "Test Calendar", date() )              4
foo.open()                                                 5
                                                           6
CLASS calendar(title, sdate) OF Form(title)                7
  STATIC day_names = "SunMonTueWedThrFriSat"               8
                                                           9
  This.selected_date = sdate                              10
                                                          11
  * create the lines                                      12
    LOCAL i                                               13
                                                          14
    FOR i = 101 TO 108                                    15
       This[i] = NEW Line(This)                           16
    ENDFOR                                                17
```

157

```
      FOR i = 201 TO 207
         This[i] = NEW Line(This)
      ENDFOR

   * create the day labels
      FOR i = 301 to 307
         This[i] = NEW Text(This)
         This[i].Text = SUBSTR(day_names, 1+3*(i-301), 3)
         This[i].Alignment = 4 && Centered
         This[i].Top = .25
         This[i].Height = 1
      ENDFOR

   * add the days
      FOR i = 1 TO 42
         This[i] = NEW Text(This)
         This[i].Alignment = 2 && Top, right
      ENDFOR
      This.set_days(This)

This.draw(This)
This.OnSize = { ;This.draw(This) }

* end of constructor


PROCEDURE draw(cal)
LOCAL i, lft, rgt, stp, tp, btm
cal.Visible = .F.

lft = .5
rgt = cal.width - 5.5
stp = (rgt - lft) / 7

tp = 1.5
btm = cal.height - 2.25

FOR i = 101 TO 108

   cal[i].Top = tp
   cal[i].Left = lft + (i-101)*stp
```

```
   cal[i].Bottom = btm                              60
   cal[i].Right  = cal[i].Left                      61
                                                    62
ENDFOR                                              63
                                                    64
stp = (btm-tp) / 6                                  65
                                                    66
FOR i = 201 TO 207                                  67
                                                    68
   cal[i].Top    = tp + (i-201)*stp                 69
   cal[i].Left   = lft                              70
   cal[i].Bottom = cal[i].Top                       71
   cal[i].Right  = rgt                              72
                                                    73
ENDFOR                                              74
                                                    75
* Day labels                                        76
   LOCAL wdth; wdth = (rgt - lft) / 7               77
   FOR i = 301 TO 307                               78
      cal[i].Left  = cal[i-200].Left                79
      cal[i].Width = wdth                           80
   ENDFOR                                           81
                                                    82
* Days                                              83
   LOCAL j, k, ht, wd                               84
                                                    85
   ht = cal[202].Top  - cal[201].Top  - .2          86
   wd = cal[102].Left - cal[101].Left - .4          87
   k = 1                                            88
                                                    89
   FOR i = 1 TO 6                                   90
                                                    91
                                                    92
      FOR j = 1 TO 7                                93
         cal[k].Top    = cal[i+200].Top  + .1       94
         cal[k].Height = ht                         95
         cal[k].Left   = cal[j+100].Left + .2       96
         cal[k].Width  = wd                         97
         k = k + 1                                  98
      ENDFOR                                        99
                                                   100
   ENDFOR                                          101
```

```
    cal.Visible = .T.

* end of calendar::draw


  PROCEDURE set_days(cal)

  cal.start_date = find_start(cal.selected_date)

  LOCAL dt; dt = cal.start_date

  FOR i = 1 TO 42
     cal[i].date = dt
     cal[i].Text = LTRIM( STR(DAY( dt )) )
     dt = dt + 1
  ENDFOR

* end of calendar::set_days


ENDCLASS


FUNCTION find_start(dt)

* Given any date, this function returns a start date for a
* calendar's page. It assumes that the first of the month
* of the given date should be in the top line of the
* calendar.

LOCAL first

first = make_date( MONTH(dt), 1, YEAR(dt) )

RETURN first - (DOW(first)-1)

* end of find_start()


FUNCTION make_date(mo, da, yr)
```

```
* This function returns a date when passed three numbers,
* representing the month, day, and year, respectively.   145
                                                         146
SET DATE TO MDY                                          147
                                                         148
RETURN CTOD( STR(mo,2) + '/' + ;                         149
             STR(da,2) + '/' + ;                         150
             STR(yr,4) )                                 151
                                                         152
* end of make_date()                                     153
                                                         154
                                                         155
* end of CALENDAR.PRG                                    156
```

Summary

In this chapter, we've begun work on the calendar class. We started by creating a new class that inherited from the built-in Form class.

We used numbered properties to add horizontal and vertical lines. We drew lines with the Line object.

We put the line drawing code into a draw() procedure, which we could call when the OnSize event was triggered. This lets the user resize the calendar, and we respond by redrawing it appropriately.

We used Text objects to label the days of the week, across the top of the calendar.

Then we went on to use another set of Text objects as the days in the interior of the calendar. We added date handling functions outside the class definition to support the dates.

In the constructor code we created 42 day objects from Text objects. We wrote a routine that added a date property to each day, so that each day knows what day it represents. We used the built-in Text property to label each day, and the Alignment property to locate the label properly.

We added day objects to the draw() routine, so that these were also positioned and sized according to the form's size. Finally, we turned the display of the form off and then on by manipulating its Visible property.

We've got an inanimate calendar at this point. In Chapter 8, we're going to bring this calendar to life.

Chapter 8

The Calendar Comes Alive

In Chapter 7, we drew a calendar, but it was an inanimate object. In this chapter we're going to bring it alive. In this chapter you will:

- Highlight the selected date
- Move the highlighted date in response to mouse clicks
- Adjust the day objects for better appearance
- Display the month and year

- Add pushbuttons to change months
- Add pushbuttons to change years

Before we're done, we'll have a collection of objects on our form that will all respond to mouse clicks in an intelligent fashion. All their event-handling will be coordinated with the calendar, which will be the master, controlling object.

As you work through this chapter you'll be working in the new paradigm. You'll launch an object and let its event-handlers do your work and this paradigm should begin to come into focus.

Selecting Dates with the Mouse

We haven't highlighted the selected date yet, so we can't see it. That's our first job.

Highlighting the Selected Day

First, we'll define a selected color. By using a #define command we'll make it easy to change this later if we change our minds. Then we'll modify the set_days() routine to assign this color to the right day. My code is in Listing 8-1.

Code Listing 8-1

```
* CALENDAR.PRG -- The calendar class                        1
* copyright 1995, Martin L. Rinehart                        2
                                                            3
#define HIGH_COLOR '+W/N'                                   4
                                                            5
foo = new calendar( "Test Calendar", date() )               6
...
   PROCEDURE set_days(cal)                                110
                                                          111
   cal.start_date = find_start(cal.selected_date)         112
                                                          113
   LOCAL dt; dt = cal.start_date                          114
                                                          115
   FOR i = 1 TO 42                                        116
      cal[i].date = dt                                    117
      cal[i].Text = LTRIM( STR(DAY( dt )) )               118
                                                          119
```

Chapter 8 — The Calendar Comes Alive

```
    IF dt = cal.selected_date                          120
        cal[i].ColorNormal = HIGH_COLOR                121
    ENDIF                                              122
                                                       123
    dt = dt + 1                                        124
ENDFOR                                                 125
                                                       126
* end of calendar::set_days                            127
```

When I run this version, I get the calendar shown in Figure 8-1.

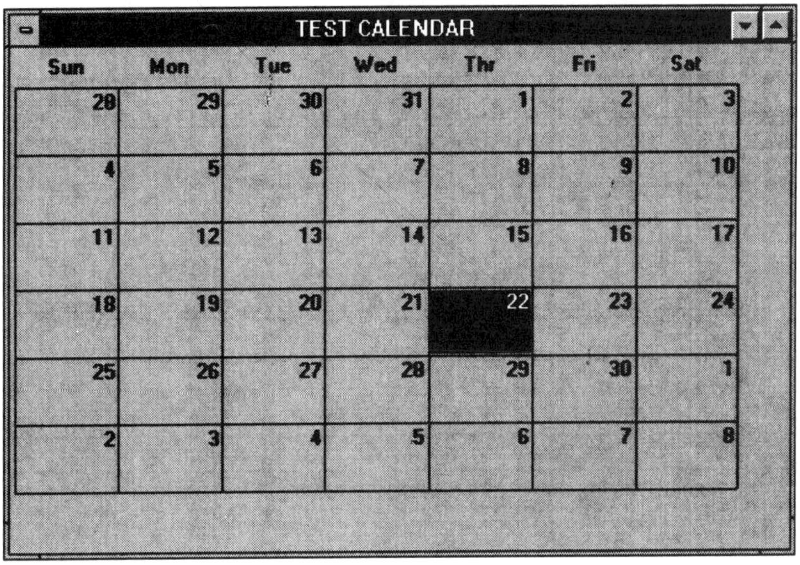

Figure 8-1: The selected day is highlighted.

With the day highlighted, we're ready to use the mouse to move the day around.

Moving the Selected Day

Text objects (our days are built from Texts) don't have an OnClick event property. They do have an OnLeftMouseDown event property that, as its name suggests, is triggered when the user presses the left mouse button. This makes a pretty good substitute for an OnClick.

165

Learn Visual dBASE Programming

We need to have the day select itself and deselect the former choice when it receives a click. We can do this by writing an event handler and attaching a codeblock to each day's OnLeftMouseDown. Listing 8-2 shows these additions.

Code Listing 8-2

```
* CALENDAR.PRG -- The calendar class                             1
* copyright 1995, Martin L. Rinehart                             2
                                                                 3
#define HIGH_COLOR   '+W/N'                                      4
#define PLAIN_COLOR  'N/W'                                       5
                                                                 6
...
                                                                34
   * add the days                                               35
      FOR i = 1 TO 42                                           36
         This[i] = NEW Text(This)                               37
         This[i].Alignment = 2 && Top, right                    38
         This[i].OnLeftMouseDown = { ;class::day_click() }
      ENDFOR                                                    40
      This.set_days(This)                                       41
                                                                42
This.draw(This)                                                 43
This.OnSize = { ;This.draw(This) }                              44
                                                                45
* end of constructor                                            46
                                                                47
                                                                48
PROCEDURE day_click                                             49
* This is the day (Text object) which was clicked.              50
                                                                51
* ignore clicks on the currently selected date                  52
   IF This.date = Form.selected_date                            53
      RETURN                                                    54
   ENDIF                                                        55
                                                                56
LOCAL dnum                                                      57
dnum = Form.selected_date - Form.start_date + 1                 58
                                                                59
```

Chapter 8
The Calendar Comes Alive

```
Form[dnum].ColorNormal = PLAIN_COLOR            60
This.ColorNormal = HIGH_COLOR                   61
Form.selected_date = This.date                  62
                                                63
RETURN && end of calendar::day_click            64
                                                65
```

I've added a PLAIN_COLOR constant at line 5. You need this to return the previously highlighted day to a non-highlighted color (done at line 60). Line 39 assigns a codeblock to each day, which will call the new event handler. Because you have assigned 42 separate codeblocks, the This variable in the event handler will be one of those 42 objects.

The event handler itself is straightforward. At lines 53 through 55 it checks to see if you have clicked the day that is already highlighted. If you did, it exits without doing anything. (This could be dispensed with, but it avoids annoying flicker when you double-click, for example.)

The dnum variable is used to calculate the number of the previously highlighted day so that its color can be reset (lines 57 through 60). Then the currently selected day is highlighted and its date is assigned to the calendar's selected_date property.

When you run the code with these improvements, you'll see that you have brought your calendar to life.

Improving the Day Spacing

One of the things that I learned by running this version was that the space I'd allowed around the border of individual days wasn't enough to guarantee that I'd get at least a pixel or two between the edge of my day and my calendar grid lines.

The space you get here will be a function of your equipment, chosen resolution, and calendar size. I suppose that a complex routine could carefully consider all these factors and calculate coordinates accordingly. (You'd first convert everything to pixels, then lay out the line grid so that it was on integral pixel boundaries.)

On the other hand, I'm more interested in getting to changing years and months, so I'll do a quick fix, putting in a fatter allowance. While I'm at it, I've converted to using another constant. Listing 8-3 shows these changes.

Learn Visual dBASE Programming

Code Listing 8-3

```
* CALENDAR.PRG -- The calendar class                          1
* copyright 1995, Martin L. Rinehart                          2
                                                              3
#define HIGH_COLOR   '+W/N'                                   4
#define PLAIN_COLOR  'N/W'                                    5
                                                              6
#define DAY_SPACE 0.4                                         7
                                                              8
...
   * Days                                                   107
     LOCAL j, k, ht, wd                                     108
                                                            109
     ht = cal[202].Top  - cal[201].Top  - DAY_SPACE         110
     wd = cal[102].Left - cal[101].Left - DAY_SPACE*2       111
     k = 1                                                  112
                                                            113
     FOR i = 1 TO 6                                         114
                                                            115
                                                            116
        FOR j = 1 TO 7                                      117
           cal[k].Top    = cal[i+200].Top  + DAY_SPACE/2
           cal[k].Height = ht                               119
           cal[k].Left   = cal[j+100].Left + DAY_SPACE      120
           cal[k].Width  = wd                               121
           k = k + 1                                        122
        ENDFOR                                              123
                                                            124
     ENDFOR                                                 125
                                                            126
cal.Visible = .T.                                           127
                                                            128
* end of calendar::draw                                     129
```

The constant DAY_SPACE specifies the space to waste, in Turpins, around each day object. I try to put half this space in the top and left; the other half goes on the bottom and right. Since each Turpin is about twice as high as it is wide, the horizontal spacing is made twice the size of the vertical spacing.

When you run this you should get a very acceptable spacing. It annoys me that it's not more perfect, but I keep reminding myself that I'm focusing on this issue right now. Later on I'll be focusing on just using the calendar, and it's very usable even with a small asymmetry in the spacing.

Adjusting the Month

What I want now is the ability to change months. For starters, I'd like the calendar to tell me what month it is reporting, and then I'd like to be able to use PgUp and PgDn to turn its pages. I'd also like this functionality on pushbuttons, so I can click with the mouse when my hands aren't on the keyboard.

Displaying the Month

Let's start by labeling the month that is being displayed. I've allowed border space on the right of the days, which we can use. Because we're displaying six weeks at a time, we'll always have the first of two months on the calendar. The top row has the first of the selected month and row 5 or 6 has the first of the following month. I'd like to label both of these.

I'll create two Text objects and assign them to new properties of the calendar: month_label1 and month_label2. Then I'll use another function to assign text values, such as July 1995 or Oct. 1996. We can use a string and let the left word-wrapping alignment take care of positioning this text in the object.

The only remaining problem is to have the draw routine decide where to place these. It can line the first one up with the first horizontal line, and the second one will be lined up with either the fifth or sixth horizontal line, depending on which one holds the start of the month.

To check on the start of the month we'll just check the date 34 days after the calendar's starting date (that's Saturday of the fifth week). If the DAY() of that date is 7 or less, the new month starts in the fifth row. Otherwise it starts in the sixth.

I'll use one trick here that depends on an undocumented feature. dBASE accepts the thirteenth month of the year as the first month of the following year. Listing 8-4 shows all the additions.

Code Listing 8-4

```
* CALENDAR.PRG -- The calendar class                                    1
* copyright 1995, Martin L. Rinehart                                    2
                                                                        3
#define HIGH_COLOR   '+W/N'                                             4
```

169

Learn Visual dBASE Programming

```
#define PLAIN_COLOR 'N/W'                                    5
                                                             6
#define DAY_SPACE    0.4                                     7
#define MONTH_WIDTH 5.5                                      8
                                                             9
foo = new calendar( "Test Calendar", date() )               10
foo.open()                                                  11
                                                            12
CLASS calendar(title, sdate) OF Form(title)                 13
   STATIC day_names = "SunMonTueWedThrFriSat"               14
                                                            15
   This.selected_date = sdate                               16
   This.month_label1 = NEW Text(This)                       17
   This.month_label2 = NEW Text(This)                       18
   STORE MONTH_WIDTH-.5 TO ;                                19
      This.month_label1.Width, ;                            20
      This.month_label2.Width                               21
   STORE 9 TO ;                         && Left wrap        22
      This.month_label1.Alignment, ;                        23
      This.month_label2.Alignment                           24
   STORE 2 TO ;                                             25
      This.month_label1.Height, ;                           26
      This.month_label2.Height                              27
                                                            28
...
   PROCEDURE draw(cal)                                      81
   LOCAL i, lft, rgt, stp, tp, btm                          82
   cal.Visible = .F.                                        83
                                                            84
   lft = .5                                                 85
   rgt = cal.width - MONTH_WIDTH                            86
   stp = (rgt - lft) / 7                                    87
...
   * Month labels                                          139
      STORE cal[108].Left + .25 TO ;                       140
         cal.month_label1.Left, cal.month_label2.Left      141

      cal.month_label1.Top = cal[201].Top                  142
      * start_date + 34 is Saturday, row 5                 143
      cal.month_label2.Top = ;                             144
         IIF( DAY(cal.start_date + 34) < 7, ;              145
            cal[205].Top, ;                                146
```

Chapter 8 — The Calendar Comes Alive

```
                    cal[206].Top )                      147
                                                        148
   cal.Visible = .T.                                    149
                                                        150
   * end of calendar::draw                              151
                                                        152
                                                        153
   PROCEDURE set_days(cal)                              154
   STATIC month_names = ;                               155
      'Jan.Feb.Mar.Apr.May JuneJulyAug.Sep.Oct.Nov.Dec.'
                                                        157
   cal.start_date = find_start(cal.selected_date)       158
                                                        159
   LOCAL dt; dt = cal.start_date                        160
                                                        161
   FOR i = 1 TO 42                                      162
      cal[i].date = dt                                  163
      cal[i].Text = LTRIM( STR(DAY( dt )) )             164
                                                        165
      IF dt = cal.selected_date                         166
         cal[i].ColorNormal = HIGH_COLOR                167
      ENDIF                                             168
                                                        169
      dt = dt + 1                                       170
   ENDFOR                                               171
                                                        172
   * set month labels                                   173
      dt = cal.start_date + 6  && Saturday, 1st row     174
      cal.month_label1.Text = month_id( dt )            175
      cal.month_label2.Text = month_id( ;               176
         make_date( MONTH(dt)+1, 1, YEAR(dt) ) )
                                                        178
   * end of calendar::set_days                          179
                                                        180
                                                        181
ENDCLASS                                                182
...
FUNCTION month_id(dt)                                   215
                                                        216
* returns 9 character string: "Mmmm YYYY"               217
                                                        218
STATIC month_names = ;                                  219
```

171

```
    'Jan.Feb.Mar.Apr.May JuneJulyAug.Sep.Oct.Nov.Dec.'         220
                                                               221
LOCAL mo; mo = MONTH(dt)                                       222
                                                               223
RETURN SUBSTR(month_names, mo*4 - 3, 4) + ;                    224
    ' ' + LEFT( DTOS(dt), 4 )                                  225
                                                               226
* end of month_id()                                            227
                                                               228
                                                               229
* end of CALENDAR.PRG                                          230
```

At line 8, I've added a new constant, MONTH_WIDTH, so that we could adjust the space to the right of the days if we needed to use more or less. This was the constant 5.5 at line 86. I've also used it at line 19 to define the month_label objects' widths.

The code from lines 17 through 27 defines the new objects and assigns their constant properties: height, width, and alignment.

The code from lines 139 through 147 is added to the draw() routine. First, it positions the left side of our month_label objects at a quarter of a Turpin to the right of the last vertical line. Then it lines the first label up with the first horizontal line. The second label is lined up with the fifth or sixth horizontal line, depending on whether the fifth Saturday in the month is a day greater than 7.

The actual text of these labels is assigned in lines 174 through 178. The month_id() function is called for the first Saturday on the calendar and for the date one month later. (This is where I let dBASE figure out that 13/1/94 is the same as 1/1/95, for instance.)

The month_id() function, lines 215 through 227, returns the string that will wrap to fit in our Text label objects. It uses a STATIC string where each month is abbreviated to four characters or spelled out, if it fits in four characters. For the year, it uses the DTOS() built-in function, which always returns a string in the YYYYMMDD form, regardless of the setting of CENTURY.

When you build this functionality, you might want to add the month_id() code first. Again, you can test this in the Command window, with dialog like this:

```
set proc to calendar addi
? month_id( {12/1/94} )
? month_id( {13/1/95} )
```

Chapter 8 — The Calendar Comes Alive

```
? month_id( {1/1/95} )
set proc to
```

Don't bother putting the text into the calendar until you have tested this function and are sure it will work. Then make the other changes. My labeled calendar is shown in Figure 8-2.

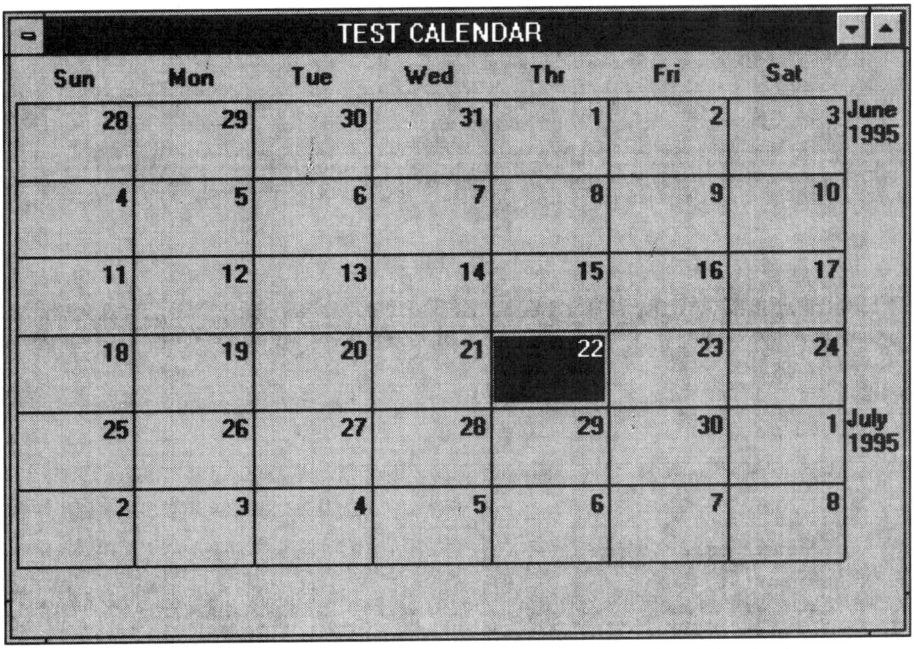

Figure 8-2: The calendar with the months labeled

Changing Months

Our next job is to actually teach the calendar to go from one month to the next. We can add a pair of pushbuttons, labeled PgUp and PgDn, and have clicks on these buttons turn the calendar's pages.

As an aside, I labeled my first calendar buttons this way to remind myself to program the keystrokes. I intended to rename the buttons after I had hooked up the keystrokes. Somehow I never got around to it. These may be somewhat silly names at first, but once you click on PgUp, for example, you see what it does. You also get a definite suggestion that tapping the PgUp key will probably do the same thing. I'm beginning to think that these button names weren't so temporary, after all.

173

Learn Visual dBASE Programming

Adding Pushbuttons

Before we hook actual functionality to our pushbuttons, let's put them on our calendar and have them report to us in the Command window when they are clicked.

As with our other objects, we'll create pushbuttons in the constructor code and position them in the draw() method. Listing 8-5 shows the new code.

Code Listing 8-5

```
                                                                  28
* Add pgup/pgdn pushbuttons                                       29
  This.pgup_button = NEW pushbutton(This)                         30
  This.pgdn_button = NEW pushbutton(This)                         31
  This.pgup_button.Text = "PgUp"                                  32
  This.pgdn_button.Text = "PgDn"                                  33
  STORE 1.5 TO ;                                                  34
     This.pgup_button.Height, ;                                   35
     This.pgdn_button.Height                                      36
  This.pgup_button.OnClick = { ;? 'Page Up!'}                     37
  This.pgdn_button.OnClick = { ;? 'Page Down!'}                   38
                                                                  39
...
                                                                 159
* PgUp/Dn buttons                                                160
  STORE cal[207].Top + .25 TO ;                                  161
     cal.pgup_button.Top, ;                                      162
     cal.pgdn_button.Top                                         163
                                                                 164
  LOCAL wid; wid = cal[102].Left - cal[101].Left                 165
  cal.pgup_button.Left = cal[101].Left + 1.5*wid                 166
  cal.pgdn_button.Left = cal[108].Left - 3*wid                   167
  STORE wid * 1.25 TO ;                                          168
     cal.pgup_button.Width, ;                                    169
     cal.pgdn_button.Width                                       170
                                                                 171
```

In Listing 8-5, the first block of lines are the ones to add to the constructor, to create pushbuttons. The second group are lines added to the draw() method.

I've located the pushbuttons quickly, based on the width of each day. When we get our full set of buttons, we'll have to fiddle with the locations to get it to look just right. For the moment, this gives you buttons that you can click, as shown in Figure 8-3.

Chapter 8 The Calendar Comes Alive

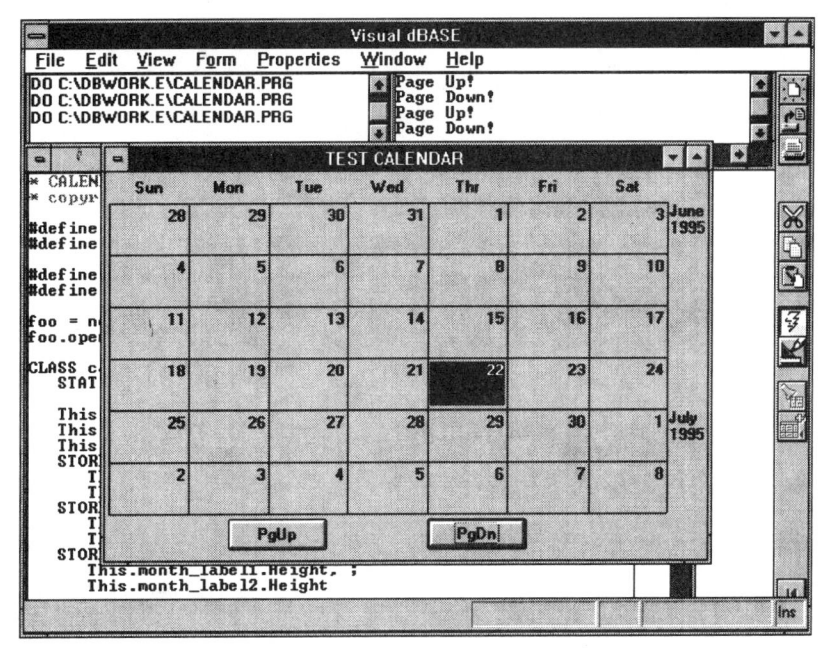

Figure 8-3: Calendar with pushbuttons being clicked

As you see in the Command window (drag the calendar by its title bar to uncover the Command window's results pane) these buttons are happily reporting each time you click them. Now what we need to do is actually change months.

Really Changing Months

Luckily for us, we're structured in a way that makes changing the months dead simple. All we have to do is pick a new selected_date and call the set_days() routine. Or at least that's almost true.

Listing 8-6 shows the code I've added as a first cut.

Code Listing 8-6

```
         This.pgdn_button.Height                              36
      This.pgup_button.OnClick = { ; class::next_month(-1) }
      This.pgdn_button.OnClick = { ; class::next_month(1) }
                                                              39
...
   PROCEDURE next_month( months_to_add )                     205
                                                             206
```

175

```
LOCAL dt; dt = Form.selected_date                    207
LOCAL mo; mo = MONTH(dt) + months_to_add             208
LOCAL yr; yr = YEAR(dt)                              209
                                                     210
IF mo > 12                                           211
   mo = mo - 12                                      212
   yr = yr + 1                                       213
ELSEIF mo < 1                                        214
   mo = mo + 12                                      215
   yr = yr - 1                                       216
ENDIF                                                217
                                                     218
Form.selected_date = make_date( mo, DAY(dt), yr )    219
                                                     220
Form.set_days(Form)                                  221
                                                     222
* end of calendar::next_month                        223
                                                     224
                                                     225
ENDCLASS                                             226
```

At lines 37 and 38, I've changed the codeblocks to call the next_month() method. This method is shown in lines 205 through 223.

Next_month is programmed to take any positive or negative number of months as a parameter and adjust the selected date by the specified amount. (Actually, it will only work correctly in the range +12 to -12, but that's all we'll use.) After picking the new date, it calls the set_days() method.

My first test drive with this code is shown in Figure 8-4. As you can see, we've left a small detail out of our routine.

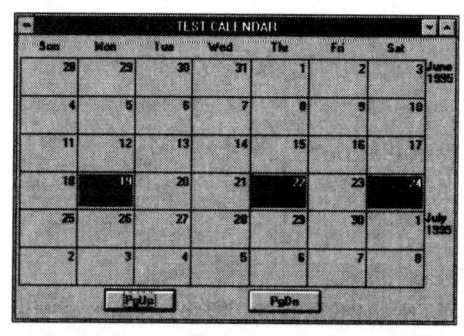

Figure 8-4: A small detail was overlooked.

Chapter 8   The Calendar Comes Alive

The obvious problem is that we didn't tell the next_month() method that a day was already highlighted. The days being just dumb Text objects don't know how to change colors. We have to tell them. Computers are like that.

This is simple to fix, fortunately, because the next problem we'll face is not so simple. Listing 8-7 has the needed addition to the next_month() routine.

Code Listing 8-7

```
PROCEDURE next_month( months_to_add )                    205
                                                         206
LOCAL dt; dt = Form.selected_date                        207
LOCAL mo; mo = MONTH(dt) + months_to_add                 208
LOCAL yr; yr = YEAR(dt)                                  209
                                                         210
IF mo > 12                                               211
   mo = mo - 12                                          212
   yr = yr + 1                                           213
ELSEIF mo < 1                                            214
   mo = mo + 12                                          215
   yr = yr - 1                                           216
ENDIF                                                    217
                                                         218
LOCAL dnum                                               219
dnum = Form.selected_date - Form.start_date + 1          220
Form[dnum].ColorNormal = PLAIN_COLOR                     221
                                                         222
Form.selected_date = make_date( mo, DAY(dt), yr )        223
                                                         224
Form.set_days(Form)                                      225
                                                         226
* end of calendar::next_month                            227
```

With this addition, your calendar is very much alive and well. At least it is until you do something a little bit difficult. Try selecting March 31 and clicking PgUp, for example. That will flip you back to March 2 or 3 (dBASE's replacements for the date you really chose: February 31).

Alternatively, you could try to go forward a month from January 31. Again, dBASE will get you into March, which is what February 31 means to it.

177

Really Changing Months Correctly

I'll bet you're thinking that this was the kind of thing that happened all the time in your old procedural coding days. Well, writing the event handlers that objects use is procedural coding. It hooks together differently, but the logic is subject to all the same problems when you meet messy, real-world situations, like dates.

Fortunately, there is a way to fix this problem that takes very little code. The problem only occurs when you go from a longer month into a shorter one, asking for the 30th of February or the 31st of November, for examples. The result is always a date that is in the next month.

All you need to do is to see if the date that you've built is in the month you had intended. If it is, you're in luck. If not, step backwards a day at a time until you get into the month you wanted. Listing 8-8 shows this addition to the next_month() method.

Code Listing 8-8

```
PROCEDURE next_month( months_to_add )                    205
                                                         206
LOCAL dt; dt = Form.selected_date                        207
LOCAL mo; mo = MONTH(dt) + months_to_add                 208
LOCAL yr; yr = YEAR(dt)                                  209
                                                         210
IF mo > 12                                               211
   mo = mo - 12                                          212
   yr = yr + 1                                           213
ELSEIF mo < 1                                            214
   mo = mo + 12                                          215
   yr = yr - 1                                           216
ENDIF                                                    217
                                                         218
LOCAL dnum                                               219
dnum = Form.selected_date - Form.start_date + 1          220
Form[dnum].ColorNormal = PLAIN_COLOR                     221
                                                         222
Form.selected_date = make_date( mo, DAY(dt), yr )        223
                                                         224
DO WHILE MONTH(Form.selected_date) > mo                  225
   Form.selected_date = Form.selected_date - 1           226
ENDDO                                                    227
                                                         228
Form.set_days(Form)                                      229
```

Chapter 8   The Calendar Comes Alive

```
                                                             230
  * end of calendar::next_month                              231
```

This fix may not be the fastest possible, especially if you have backed up from March 31 to March 3, looking for February 28. But I believe that it takes a lot less code than any other method.

With this code in place, our calendar is now completely month-savvy. It can flip forward or backward and it's happy to report the month and year.

For fast changes over longer times, let's get our calendar to move a year at a time.

Adjusting the Year

I use the Home and End keys to flip to the beginning or end of the current year. If we're already at the end of the year on an End press, for example, I flip forward another full year. This means that no date is very many clicks or keypresses away.

At least not for my purposes. I do scheduling of software and book projects, which never takes me out more than a few years. If your application is tracking the history of the Middle Ages, you'll want to add a spinbutton or some other way of making very long jumps. I'll leave that to you.

Again, let's use pushbutton objects before we get to programming keystroke event handlers.

Adding Home and End Pushbuttons

Listing 8-9 shows the added code that provides the two new pushbuttons. Again, this is primarily a matter of adding new constructor code to create the buttons, draw() code to position the buttons, and then a pair of simple routines to perform the actual work.

Code Listing 8-9

```
                                                             39
  * Add home/end pushbuttons                                 40
    This.home_button = NEW pushbutton(This)                  41
    This.end_button = NEW pushbutton(This)                   42
    This.home_button.Text = "Home"                           43
    This.end_button.Text = "End"                             44
    STORE 1.5 TO ;                                           45
```

179

```
              This.home_button.Height, ;                           46
              This.end_button.Height                               47
     This.home_button.OnClick = { ; class::go_home() }             48
     This.end_button.OnClick = { ; class::go_end() }               49
                                                                   50
...
                                                                  183
   * Home/End buttons                                             184
     STORE cal.pgup_button.Top TO ;                               185
        cal.home_button.Top, ;                                    186
        cal.end_button.Top                                        187
                                                                  188
     cal.home_button.Left = cal[101].Left                         189
     cal.end_button.Left = cal[108].Left - 1.5*wid                190
     STORE wid * 1.25 TO ;                                        191
        cal.home_button.Width, ;                                  192
        cal.end_button.Width                                      193
                                                                  194
   cal.Visible = .T.                                              195
                                                                  196
   * end of calendar::draw                                        197
...
   PROCEDURE go_end                                               200
                                                                  201
   Form.lolight_date(Form)                                        202
                                                                  203
   LOCAL dt; dt = Form.selected_date                              204
                                                                  205
   IF (MONTH(dt) < 12) .OR. (DAY(dt) < 31)                        206
      Form.selected_date = make_date( 12, 31, YEAR(dt) )
     ELSE                                                         208
      Form.selected_date = make_date( 12, 31, YEAR(dt)+1 )
   ENDIF                                                          210
                                                                  211
   Form.set_days(Form)                                            212
                                                                  213
   * end of calendar::go_end                                      214
                                                                  215
                                                                  216
   PROCEDURE go_home                                              217
                                                                  218
   Form.lolight_date(Form)                                        219
```

Chapter 8   The Calendar Comes Alive

```
   LOCAL dt;  dt = Form.selected_date                         220
                                                              221
                                                              222
   IF (MONTH(dt) > 1) .OR. (DAY(dt) > 1)                      223
      Form.selected_date = make_date( 1, 1, YEAR(dt) )        224
    ELSE                                                      225
      Form.selected_date = make_date( 1, 1, YEAR(dt)-1 )
   ENDIF                                                      227
                                                              228
   Form.set_days(Form)                                        229
                                                              230
* end of calendar::go_home                                    231
                                                              232
                                                              233
   PROCEDURE lolight_date(cal)                                234
                                                              235
   LOCAL dnum                                                 236
   dnum = cal.selected_date - cal.start_date + 1              237
   cal[dnum].ColorNormal = PLAIN_COLOR                        238
                                                              239
* end of lolight_date                                         240
                                                              241
```

    The constructor code and the draw() code are very similar to the same code for the first pair of buttons we added. All that is different are details such as the labels of the buttons and their positions.

    Again, I chose the button names as a temporary measure prior to arriving at something more sensible. After I ran my first calendar for a while, I found that these names fit their functions admirably and encouraged users to try the corresponding keyboard buttons. So they've stayed. You're welcome to choose better names, if you can think of better ones.

    I've also added a routine called lolight_date (lines 233-240) which reverses the setting of the currently highlighted date. I leave it to you to retrofit a call to this routine in the two other places where we've already added similar code.

    My working calendar is shown in Figure 8-5.

    We've really brought our calendar to life. It's responding to our clicks and looking like a real calendar. We haven't hooked up keystrokes and we still need to work on the buttons, but we're certainly in business with a working calendar.

Learn Visual dBASE Programming

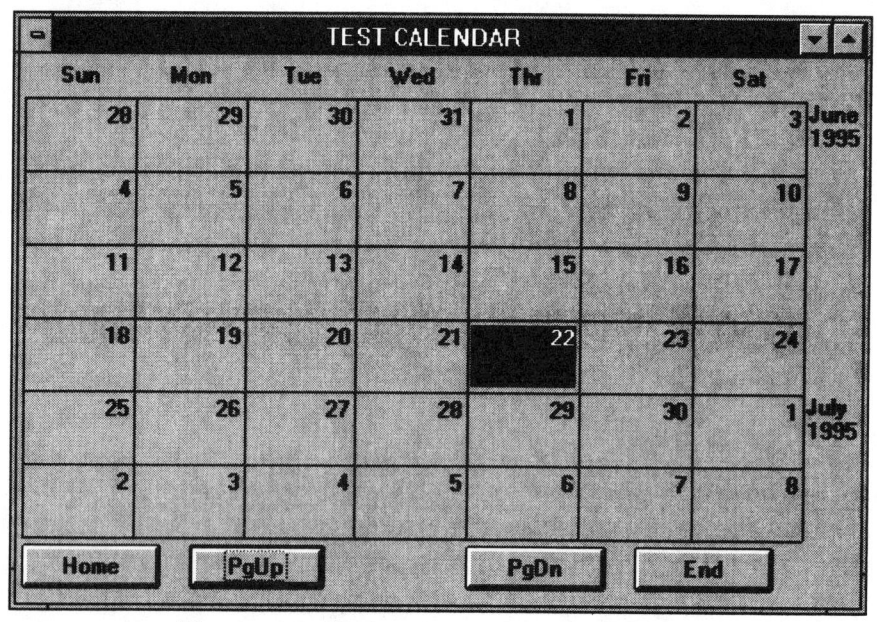

Figure 8-5: Calendar with pushbuttons

The Full Listing

For those who don't have access to the disk, Listing 8-10 shows the code found in L08-09.PRG.

Code Listing 8-10

```
* CALENDAR.PRG -- The calendar class
* copyright 1995, Martin L. Rinehart

#define HIGH_COLOR   '+W/N'
#define PLAIN_COLOR  'N/W'

#define DAY_SPACE    0.4
#define MONTH_WIDTH  5.5

foo = new calendar( "Test Calendar", date() )
foo.open()
```

182

```
CLASS calendar(title, sdate) OF Form(title)
   STATIC day_names = "SunMonTueWedThrFriSat"

   This.selected_date = sdate
   This.month_label1 = NEW Text(This)
   This.month_label2 = NEW Text(This)
   STORE MONTH_WIDTH-.5 TO ;
      This.month_label1.Width, ;
      This.month_label2.Width
   STORE 9 TO ;                          && Left wrap
      This.month_label1.Alignment, ;
      This.month_label2.Alignment
   STORE 2 TO ;
      This.month_label1.Height, ;
      This.month_label2.Height

   * Add pgup/pgdn pushbuttons
   This.pgup_button = NEW pushbutton(This)
   This.pgdn_button = NEW pushbutton(This)
   This.pgup_button.Text = "PgUp"
   This.pgdn_button.Text = "PgDn"
   STORE 1.5 TO ;
       This.pgup_button.Height, ;
       This.pgdn_button.Height
   This.pgup_button.OnClick = { ; class::next_month(-1) }
   This.pgdn_button.OnClick = { ; class::next_month(1) }

   * Add home/end pushbuttons
   This.home_button = NEW pushbutton(This)
   This.end_button = NEW pushbutton(This)
   This.home_button.Text = "Home"
   This.end_button.Text = "End"
   STORE 1.5 TO ;
       This.home_button.Height, ;
       This.end_button.Height
   This.home_button.OnClick = { ; class::go_home() }
   This.end_button.OnClick = { ; class::go_end() }

   * create the lines
     LOCAL i

     FOR i = 101 TO 108
```

```
         This[i] = NEW Line(This)
      ENDFOR

      FOR i = 201 TO 207
         This[i] = NEW Line(This)
      ENDFOR

   * create the day labels
      FOR i = 301 to 307
         This[i] = NEW Text(This)
         This[i].Text = SUBSTR(day_names, 1+3*(i-301), 3)
         This[i].Alignment = 4 && Centered
         This[i].Top = .25
         This[i].Height = 1
      ENDFOR

   * add the days
      FOR i = 1 TO 42
         This[i] = NEW Text(This)
         This[i].Alignment = 2 && Top, right
         This[i].OnLeftMouseDown = { ;class::day_click() }
      ENDFOR
      This.set_days(This)

This.draw(This)
This.OnSize = { ;This.draw(This) }

* end of constructor


PROCEDURE day_click
* This is the day (Text object) which was clicked.

* ignore clicks on the currently selected date
   IF This.date = Form.selected_date
      RETURN
   ENDIF

LOCAL dnum
dnum = Form.selected_date - Form.start_date + 1

Form[dnum].ColorNormal = PLAIN_COLOR
```

Chapter 8 *The Calendar Comes Alive*

```
This.ColorNormal = HIGH_COLOR
Form.selected_date = This.date

RETURN && end of calendar::day_click



PROCEDURE draw(cal)
LOCAL i, lft, rgt, stp, tp, btm
cal.Visible = .F.

lft = .5
rgt = cal.width - MONTH_WIDTH
stp = (rgt - lft) / 7

tp = 1.5
btm = cal.height - 2.25

FOR i = 101 TO 108

   cal[i].Top = tp
   cal[i].Left = lft + (i-101)*stp
   cal[i].Bottom = btm
   cal[i].Right = cal[i].Left

ENDFOR

stp = (btm-tp) / 6

FOR i = 201 TO 207

   cal[i].Top = tp + (i-201)*stp
   cal[i].Left = lft
   cal[i].Bottom = cal[i].Top
   cal[i].Right = rgt

ENDFOR

* Day labels
   LOCAL wdth; wdth = (rgt - lft) / 7
   FOR i = 301 TO 307
      cal[i].Left = cal[i-200].Left
      cal[i].Width = wdth
```

```
    ENDFOR

* Days
  LOCAL j, k, ht, wd

  ht = cal[202].Top  - cal[201].Top  - DAY_SPACE
  wd = cal[102].Left - cal[101].Left - DAY_SPACE*2
  k = 1

  FOR i = 1 TO 6

     FOR j = 1 TO 7
        cal[k].Top    = cal[i+200].Top + DAY_SPACE/2
        cal[k].Height = ht
        cal[k].Left   = cal[j+100].Left + DAY_SPACE
        cal[k].Width  = wd
        k = k + 1
     ENDFOR

  ENDFOR

* Month labels
  STORE cal[108].Left + .25 TO ;
     cal.month_label1.Left, cal.month_label2.Left
  cal.month_label1.Top = cal[201].Top
  * start_date + 34 is Saturday, row 5
  cal.month_label2.Top = ;
       IIF( DAY(cal.start_date + 34) < 7, ;
            cal[205].Top, ;
            cal[206].Top )

* PgUp/Dn buttons
  STORE cal[207].Top + .25 TO ;
     cal.pgup_button.Top, ;
     cal.pgdn_button.Top

  LOCAL wid; wid = cal[102].Left - cal[101].Left
  cal.pgup_button.Left = cal[101].Left + 1.5*wid
  cal.pgdn_button.Left = cal[108].Left - 3*wid
  STORE wid * 1.25 TO ;
     cal.pgup_button.Width, ;
```

```
            cal.pgdn_button.Width

* Home/End buttons
   STORE cal.pgup_button.Top TO ;
      cal.home_button.Top, ;
      cal.end_button.Top

   cal.home_button.Left = cal[101].Left
   cal.end_button.Left = cal[108].Left - 1.5*wid
   STORE wid * 1.25 TO ;
      cal.home_button.Width, ;
      cal.end_button.Width

cal.Visible = .T.

* end of calendar::draw



PROCEDURE go_end

Form.lolight_date(Form)

LOCAL dt; dt = Form.selected_date

IF (MONTH(dt) < 12) .OR. (DAY(dt) < 31)
   Form.selected_date = make_date( 12, 31, YEAR(dt) )
 ELSE
   Form.selected_date = make_date( 12, 31, YEAR(dt)+1 )
ENDIF

Form.set_days(Form)

* end of calendar::go_end



PROCEDURE go_home

Form.lolight_date(Form)

LOCAL dt; dt = Form.selected_date

IF (MONTH(dt) > 1) .OR. (DAY(dt) > 1)
```

Learn Visual dBASE Programming

```
      Form.selected_date = make_date( 1, 1, YEAR(dt) )
   ELSE
      Form.selected_date = make_date( 1, 1, YEAR(dt)-1 )
   ENDIF

Form.set_days(Form)

* end of calendar::go_home


PROCEDURE lolight_date(cal)

LOCAL dnum
dnum = cal.selected_date - cal.start_date + 1
cal[dnum].ColorNormal = PLAIN_COLOR

* end of lolight_date

PROCEDURE set_days(cal)
STATIC month_names = ;
   'Jan.Feb.Mar.Apr.May JuneJulyAug.Sep.Oct.Nov.Dec.'

cal.start_date = find_start(cal.selected_date)

LOCAL dt; dt = cal.start_date

FOR i = 1 TO 42
   cal[i].date = dt
   cal[i].Text = LTRIM( STR(DAY( dt )) )

   IF dt = cal.selected_date
      cal[i].ColorNormal = HIGH_COLOR
   ENDIF

   dt = dt + 1
ENDFOR

* set month labels
   dt = cal.start_date + 6 && Saturday, 1st row
   cal.month_label1.Text = month_id( dt )
   cal.month_label2.Text = month_id( ;
         make_date( MONTH(dt)+1, 1, YEAR(dt) ) )
```

Chapter 8   *The Calendar Comes Alive*

```
    * end of calendar::set_days


    PROCEDURE next_month( months_to_add )

    LOCAL dt; dt = Form.selected_date
    LOCAL mo; mo = MONTH(dt) + months_to_add
    LOCAL yr; yr = YEAR(dt)

    IF mo > 12
       mo = mo - 12
       yr = yr + 1
    ELSEIF mo < 1
       mo = mo + 12
       yr = yr - 1
    ENDIF

    LOCAL dnum
    dnum = Form.selected_date - Form.start_date + 1
    Form[dnum].ColorNormal = PLAIN_COLOR

    Form.selected_date = make_date( mo, DAY(dt), yr )

    DO WHILE MONTH(Form.selected_date) > mo
       Form.selected_date = Form.selected_date - 1
    ENDDO

    Form.set_days(Form)

    * end of calendar::next_month

ENDCLASS


FUNCTION find_start(dt)

* Given any date, this function returns a start date for a
* calendar's page.  It assumes that the first of the month
* of the given date should be in the top line of the
* calendar.
```

189

```
LOCAL first

first = make_date( MONTH(dt), 1, YEAR(dt) )

RETURN first - (DOW(first)-1)

* end of find_start()


FUNCTION make_date(mo, da, yr)

* This function returns a date when passed three numbers,
* representing the month, day, and year, respectively.

SET DATE TO MDY

RETURN CTOD( STR(mo,2) + '/' + ;
             STR(da,2) + '/' + ;
             STR(yr,4) )

* end of make_date()


FUNCTION month_id(dt)

* returns 9 character string: "Mmmm YYYY"

STATIC month_names = ;
   'Jan.Feb.Mar.Apr.May JuneJulyAug.Sep.Oct.Nov.Dec.'

LOCAL mo; mo = MONTH(dt)

RETURN SUBSTR(month_names, mo*4 - 3, 4) + ;
       ' ' + LEFT( DTOS(dt), 4 )

* end of month_id()


* end of CALENDAR.PRG
```

Chapter 8   *The Calendar Comes Alive*

Summary

At this point, our calendar is highly functional. I want to do two things before we call it complete. First, the keystroke handlers should be hooked up and second, the pushbuttons should be positioned to allow OK and Esc buttons in the middle of the bottom line.

But we've certainly come a long way, and I'm pretty sure that if anyone were looking over your shoulder at the calendar you've built this far, they'd be convinced that you are a real Windows programmer, doing real object-oriented work.

We've built a calendar by inheriting from the Form class. A grid of Line objects drew the calendar, and between the lines we added a grid of Text objects which serve as our days.

In this chapter, we hooked the days (Texts) OnLeftMouseDown events to the action (moving the highlighted day) that the calendar's user probably expects.

In addition to clicking on the day we want, we've provided pushbuttons that turn the calendars pages by month and by year.

In the next chapter, we're going to complete the calendar by adding keyboard operations and the finishing touches to the pushbuttons.

Chapter 9

Finishing the Calendar

In Chapter 8 you brought your calendar to life. It showed a selected day and let you click on the days on the calendar to change the selected day. You also hooked the month and year to pushbuttons that let you turn the pages.

In this chapter, we're going to continue to make this calendar work. Our first job will be to add keyboard manipulation capability, since a good GUI program can be driven from either the keyboard or with the pointing device.

Along the way, we'll look closely at some of the finer points about these topics:

- The This parameter
- The scope resolution operator
- ON KEY event handlers for keyboard events

Finally, we're going to provide a classic pair of dBASE exits — one that saves your new date and the other which discards your input, restoring the original value. We'll add pushbuttons so you can use your mouse for these functions and we'll have keyboard equivalents.

Keystroke Events

In Visual dBASE there is a very nice Key event available for Entryfield objects, which would do just what we want if it were more widely supported. Unfortunately, it's not. We'll need to revert to dBASE IV-style ON KEY handlers. They aren't as friendly to us as programmers, but the users will never know the difference.

Let's begin with some strategy. There are lots of ways we could make keystroke handlers work. I make it a rule that any object that wants to handle keystrokes has to be independent of any other object that may also want to handle keystrokes.

Many objects use common keystrokes as part of their built-in functionality. For example, the Ctrl+U keystroke is frequently used to delete records. The Left and Right arrow keys are frequently used to navigate within a field.

What I do is have my custom objects, such as the calendar, clear all keystroke handling and establish their own whenever they get focus. The Open() method triggers the OnGotFocus event. OnGotFocus is also triggered when you open a minimized window, or when you switch from one open window to another. So this event is ideal for defining keystrokes.

Given that strategy, the actual coding is very simple. After all, all we have to do is call the routines we've already written from ON KEY assignments.

How Not to Handle Keystrokes

Well, as I said, the coding is very simple. What I forgot to mention is that there is a rich supply of ways to do it wrong, and a short supply of techniques that work. There are some complications here.

How Not to Use This

First, let me tell you what you want to do to handle, for example, the PgUp keypress. You want to call the next_month() method with a parameter of -1, just as we did in the codeblock attached to our pgup_button's OnClick handler. We'll assign the call in a set_keys() routine that will be called on every OnGotFocus event in the parent calendar.

In Visual dBASE, you don't even need the keyword DO in front of a subroutine call. So here's our first example of code that won't work:

```
* THIS CODE DOESN'T WORK!

PROCEDURE set_keys

* 'This' is the parent calendar

ON KEY LABEL PgUp This.next_month(-1)
...
```

If you do this, Visual dBASE will tell you that it doesn't know what This is as soon as you press the PgUp key. What gives?

In object-oriented, event-driven programming, as in so much of life, timing is everything. Consider the times at which these routines run. When the calendar object gets focus (is launched, restored from an icon, or switched to by clicking on it, or by cycling to it with Ctrl+Tab, or whatever) the set_keys() routine will be called. That's done by this codeblock assigned to the event:

```
This.OnGotFocus = { ; This.set_keys() }
```

This code is in the constructor function for the calendar, so This is the calendar. The This in the codeblock is not defined at the time the assignment is made. However, at runtime, when the calendar gets focus, it will call the codeblock, passing a reference to itself as This. So the codeblock will run the calendar's own set_keys() method, again, passing it a reference to itself as This.

Now let's think about the set_keys() routine. When it is called, Visual dBASE creates the This parameter automatically. It's like any other parameter. When the routine in which it is used terminates, it is released. So This in the set_keys() routine appears when set_keys() is called and disappears when set_keys() terminates.

Set_keys() leaves the statement This.next_month(-1) — that's the same as DO This.next_month(-1) — attached to the PgDn key. When that key is pressed, it will call that statement, just as the calendar calls the set_keys() routine when it gets focus.

Unfortunately, the PgDn key has no idea who This is. It never did assign a This parameter, and if it were to start now, the only thing it could reasonably assign as This is itself, a key.

That's not an object; it's a hardware key. The one on your keyboard. It has no idea what is happening on your screen. All it knows is that you pushed it. Internally the software knows that a routine should be executed, so it tries. But it has no way of knowing what This is.

To repeat, Visual dBASE automatically creates the This parameter when it calls constructor functions and when it calls event handlers. It also passes This to the routines called by the constructor and event handlers, but it stops after the first level of call. ON KEY handlers are nowhere near this definition.

How Not to Use Calendar

Since the keystroke doesn't know who This is, perhaps we can get around the problem with code like:

```
* THIS CODE CRASHES!

PROCEDURE set_keys

* 'This' is the parent calendar

ON KEY LABEL PgUp calendar::next_month(-1)
...
```

That assignment uses the scope resolution operator to tell Visual dBASE that it wants the next_month() method for the calendar class. There is still a problem with this code.

The problem is that it's not enough to know that we want the calendar class's next_month() routine. We need to know which calendar we are talking about. After all, the user might have launched two or three or twenty calendars on the screen at once. They are all separate objects of the calendar class. A method must know which object it is working for.

In dBASE 5, this error triggered a serious crash, launching the "dBASE may have become unstable" dialog.

GPFs and Other Crashes

The GPF (Windows General Protection Fault) is an error triggered when one Windows program is caught (by Windows) trying to read or write to another program's assigned memory. Windows returns a "you can't do that" message to the offending program.

Visual dBASE traps that response and returns its "dBASE may have become unstable" message to you or your user. A more sincere (although less friendly) message would be, "I've gotten lost, and you'd better close down fast!"

Borland's simple GPFs, the ones caused when a programmer types the wrong thing in a line of code, are never seen outside Borland. When one rears its ugly head in operation, it means that something has gone wrong in some routine, probably miles away from the current routine.

Fortunately, if you are developing a routine such as CALENDAR.PRG using the built-in Program Editor, you run by pressing Ctrl+D. This saves first, then compiles and runs. You can recover just by leaving Visual dBASE and starting it again. Except for losing a minute and getting mad, there's no harm done.

You should, however, watch those resources. Use the About choice in the Help pulldown menu in both Visual dBASE and in Windows Program Manager.

The GDI resources (Graphics Device Interface) come from a single, 64K segment. This was a horrible design decision, but as long as you use Windows 3.x you have to live with it. GPFs, and even programs that don't die on GPFs, can cause you to lose resources. (Free resources, as reported by Windows, are the lowest percentage free of the GDI and two other fixed-length segments.)

Visual dBASE, and most other Windows programs, likes to have a lot of available resources. When you start to get below 50% free, you ought to think about closing down some of your open programs. After a GPF, check resources to be sure that some weren't orphaned by the crash.

Since the three resource pools are taken from fixed, 64k segments, you won't solve this problem by adding more RAM to your system.

How to Handle Keystrokes

Now let's see how to do it right. As I said before, it's simple.

You need a way for the keystroke handler to reference the right object when it runs. I do this through a PUBLIC variable, which I call focus_object. Focus_object is a reference to the object that currently has focus. Each object that gets focus assigns itself to focus_object through the OnGotFocus handler.

With that technique, the keystroke handlers can just refer to focus_object and they will be referring to whatever has focus at the moment the key is pressed.

If there are three calendars launched, for example, each one will assign a reference to itself to focus_object each time each calendar object gets focus. When you press PgUp (or any other key with a handler) it will refer to the focus_object. That will always work. If the current object that has focus doesn't use keystroke handlers, it might not have followed this convention. That means that the keystrokes will be processed by the last object that was able to handle them — which probably isn't a bad way to go.

Listing 9-1 shows the new additions to handle four keystrokes.

Code Listing 9-1

```
* CALENDAR.PRG -- The calendar class                                1
* copyright 1995, Martin L. Rinehart                                2
                                                                    3
#define HIGH_COLOR    '+W/N'                                        4
#define PLAIN_COLOR   'N/W'                                         5
                                                                    6
#define DAY_SPACE     0.4                                           7
#define MONTH_WIDTH   5.5                                           8
                                                                    9
PUBLIC focus_object                                                10
                                                                   11
foo = new calendar( "Test Calendar", date() )                      12
...
                                                                  298
   PROCEDURE set_keys                                             299
                                                                  300
   * This is the calendar, focus_object is a public variable
   focus_object = This                                            302
                                                                  303
   ON KEY && clear all previously set keys                        304
                                                                  305
   ON KEY LABEL PgUp focus_object.next_month(-1)                  306
   ON KEY LABEL PgDn focus_object.next_month(1)                   307
   ON KEY LABEL Home focus_object.go_home(focus_object)           308
```

198

```
    ON KEY LABEL End   focus_object.go_end(focus_object)    309
                                                            310
    * end of calendar::set_keys                             311
                                                            312
                                                            313
ENDCLASS && calendar                                        314
```

The whole key to making this work is in line 302. The This variable is assigned to the PUBLIC variable focus_object. Focus_object will be reassigned by every object that has keystroke handlers, but that is exactly what you want.

Note that the first ON KEY has no following code, which serves to clear all ON KEY assignments. You need to do that, because the last focus_object might have handled Ctrl+PgUp, which you don't handle here. You want to handle only the keystrokes you assign.

With that code added, your PgUp key should do precisely the same as a mouse click on the PgUp button. It's always a good idea to have functionality available from both the mouse and the keyboard in a GUI program.

Other Keys

Unfortunately, we haven't met the goal of having functionality available from mouse and keyboard with what we've done so far. We've got PgUp/Dn and Home/End duplicated, but from the keyboard there's no way to highlight another day in the current month.

For this purpose, using the arrow keys would be logical. Let's add keystroke handlers that slide the highlight up, down, left and right. I'll write the simplest possible routines to achieve the goal.

It might be nicer if your up arrow didn't just stop at the top line. There is, after all, no shortage of dates in earlier months that you could back into. But mine will just respect the boundaries of the current display.

The code that does these keystrokes is in Listing 9-2.

Code Listing 9-2

```
PROCEDURE set_keys                                          299
                                                            300
    * This is the calendar, focus_object is a public variable
    focus_object = This                                     302
                                                            303
```

```
   ON KEY                && clear all previously set keys                 304
                                                                          305
   ON KEY LABEL PgUp focus_object.next_month(-1)                          306
   ON KEY LABEL PgDn focus_object.next_month(1)                           307
   ON KEY LABEL Home focus_object.go_home(focus_object)                   308
   ON KEY LABEL End  focus_object.go_end(focus_object)                    309
                                                                          310
   ON KEY LABEL UpArrow focus_object.go_up()                              311
   ON KEY LABEL DnArrow focus_object.go_down()                            312
   ON KEY LABEL LeftArrow focus_object.go_left()                          313
   ON KEY LABEL RightArrow focus_object.go_right()                        314
                                                                          315
* end of calendar::set_keys                                               316
                                                                          317
                                                                          318
PROCEDURE go_up                                                           319
                                                                          320
* 'This' is the calendar object                                           321
                                                                          322
IF This.selected_date - This.start_date > 6                               323
                                                                          324
   This.lolight_date(This)                                                325
   This.selected_date = This.selected_date - 7                            326
   Form[ Form.selected_date - This.start_date + 1 ;                       327
        ].ColorNormal = HIGH_COLOR                                        328
                                                                          329
ENDIF                                                                     330
                                                                          331
* end of calendar::go_up                                                  332
                                                                          333
                                                                          334
PROCEDURE go_down                                                         335
                                                                          336
* 'This' is the calendar object                                           337
                                                                          338
IF This.selected_date - This.start_date < 35                              339
                                                                          340
   This.lolight_date(This)                                                341
   This.selected_date = This.selected_date + 7                            342
   Form[ Form.selected_date - This.start_date + 1 ;                       343
        ].ColorNormal = HIGH_COLOR                                        344
                                                                          345
```

Chapter 9 — Finishing the Calendar

```
    ENDIF                                                    346
                                                             347
* end of calendar::go_down                                   348
                                                             349
                                                             350
PROCEDURE go_left                                            351
                                                             352
* 'This' is the calendar object                              353
                                                             354
IF This.selected_date > This.start_date                      355
                                                             356
    This.lolight_date(This)                                  357
    This.selected_date = This.selected_date - 1              358
    Form[ Form.selected_date - This.start_date + 1 ;         359
        ].ColorNormal = HIGH_COLOR                           360
                                                             361
ENDIF                                                        362
                                                             363
* end of calendar::go_left                                   364
                                                             365
                                                             366
PROCEDURE go_right                                           367
                                                             368
* 'This' is the calendar object                              369
                                                             370
IF This.selected_date - This.start_date < 41                 371
                                                             372
    This.lolight_date(This)                                  373
    This.selected_date = This.selected_date + 1              374
    Form[ Form.selected_date - This.start_date + 1 ;         375
        ].ColorNormal = HIGH_COLOR                           376
                                                             377
ENDIF                                                        378
                                                             379
* end of calendar::go_right                                  380
                                                             381
                                                             382
ENDCLASS && calendar                                         383
```

Each handler is basically similar. First, you check to see if there is any space available in the indicated direction. If there is, you lolight() the current date, change dates, and then highlight the new one.

201

This does, by the way, give you wrap from one edge to the next on either a left or right arrow. Perhaps you'll want to continue so that you can wrap right on into the next or previous months.

Adjusting the Buttons

For our final job, let's get the pushbuttons neatly arranged and add ones that say OK and Esc. (Actually, making those words Enter and Esc might be more in keeping with the names I've used so far, and OK and Cancel would be more in line with Windows conventions. You'll see when we get there that OK and Esc have the distinct advantage of fitting on very small buttons, however.)

As I look at my calendar, I see that Home is lined up on the left, where it belongs. End is about half a day-width left of where it belongs. And both PgUp and PgDn could be shoved out toward the edges a little.

Moving the Existing Buttons

Let's adjust those buttons first, to make room for the two new ones. The buttons are positioned in the draw() routine. It's the assignment to their Left properties that we'll need to change.

I've been adjusting my buttons' Left properties. While I've been doing that, I've discovered something very annoying that I should have remembered. If an object sets an ON KEY for something like the Up arrow, it stays set until you change it, or turn it off.

It even stays set in the Command window, where it can be really annoying. Any object that sets the arrow keys had better clear its sets. Now, let's do those coordinates. Listing 9-3 shows both changes (turning off the sets and adjusting the position of the buttons).

Code Listing 9-3

```
    This.OnGotFocus = { ;This.set_keys(This) }           82
    This.OnLostFocus= { ;ON KEY }                        83
    This.draw(This)                                      84
    This.OnSize = { ;This.draw(This) }                   85
                                                         86
    * end of constructor                                 87
...
                                                        173
```

Chapter 9 — Finishing the Calendar

```
* PgUp/Dn buttons                                          174
   STORE cal[207].Top + .25 TO ;                           175
      cal.pgup_button.Top, ;                               176
      cal.pgdn_button.Top                                  177
                                                           178
   LOCAL wid; wid = cal[102].Left - cal[101].Left          179
   cal.pgup_button.Left = cal[101].Left + 1.25*wid         180
   cal.pgdn_button.Left = cal[108].Left - 2.5*wid          181
   STORE wid * 1.25 TO ;                                   182
      cal.pgup_button.Width, ;                             183
      cal.pgdn_button.Width                                184
                                                           185
* Home/End buttons                                         186
   STORE cal.pgup_button.Top TO ;                          187
      cal.home_button.Top, ;                               188
      cal.end_button.Top                                   189
                                                           190
   cal.home_button.Left = cal[101].Left                    191
   cal.end_button.Left = cal[108].Left - 1.25*wid          192
   STORE wid * 1.25 TO ;                                   193
      cal.home_button.Width, ;                             194
      cal.end_button.Width                                 195
                                                           196
cal.Visible = .T.                                          197
                                                           198
* end of calendar::draw                                    199
```

With those changes, your buttons should be right up next to each other, as the ones shown in Figure 9-1 are.

Adding the New Buttons

To get an OK and Esc button, we'll need some way of remembering the value that the calendar started out with. When we use the calendar for data entry, we'll let the user select a date by clicking or using the keyboard. As always, though, if the user presses Esc or clicks the Esc button, we don't want the program to get the new value.

The easy way to do this is to assign a value property. (Entryfields, among others, have a built-in Value property. Ours will be similar.) We'll assign the value property in the constructor. When the user presses Enter or clicks OK, we'll assign

Learn Visual dBASE Programming

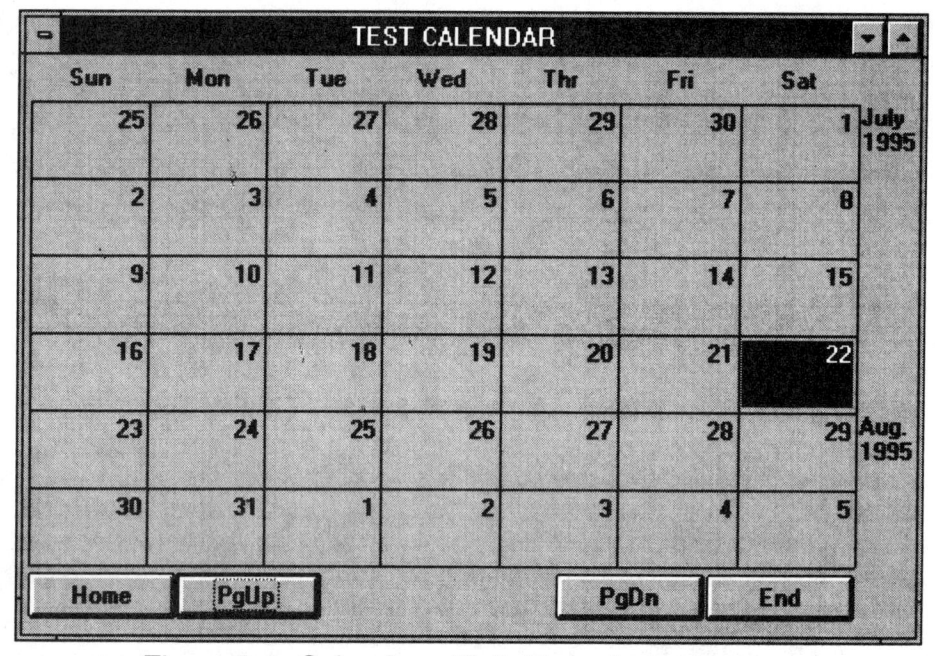

Figure 9-1: Calendar with tightened pushbuttons

the new selected_date property. If the user presses Esc or clicks Esc, we don't need to change a thing.

What we need are two close routines. Both can do any required cleanup (or call a cleanup routine) and the OK one can do the assignment from the selected_date property to the value property.

We'll need to assign these routines to the event handlers of the associated pushbuttons, and we'll want to attach them to ON KEY events for the Enter and Esc keys, as well. As you see in Listing 9-4, most of the code we need to implement this is the code that creates and positions the pushbuttons.

Code Listing 9-4

```
CLASS calendar(title, sdate) OF Form(title)               15
   STATIC day_names = "SunMonTueWedThrFriSat"             16
                                                          17
   This.selected_date = sdate                             18
   This.value = sdate                                     19
                                                          20
```

Chapter 9 — Finishing the Calendar

```
      This.month_label1 = NEW Text(This)                      21
...
                                                              54
   * Add OK/Esc pushbuttons                                   55
     This.OK_button = NEW pushbutton(This)                    56
     This.esc_button = NEW pushbutton(This)                   57
     This.OK_button.Text = "OK"                               58
     This.esc_button.Text = "Esc"                             59
     STORE 1.5 TO ;                                           60
        This.OK_button.Height, ;                              61
        This.esc_button.Height                                62
     This.OK_button.OnClick = { ; class::ok_close() }         63
     This.esc_button.OnClick = { ; class::esc_close() }
                                                              65
   * create the lines                                         66
...
                                                             207
   * OK/Esc buttons                                          208
     STORE cal.pgup_button.Top TO ;                          209
        cal.OK_button.Top, ;                                 210
        cal.esc_button.Top                                   211
                                                             212
     STORE wid-1 TO ;                                        213
        cal.OK_button.Width, ;                               214
        cal.esc_button.Width                                 215
     cal.OK_button.Left = cal.pgup_button.Left + ;           216
                    cal.pgup_button.Width + .75              217
     cal.esc_button.Left = cal.pgdn_button.Left - ;          218
                    cal.esc_button.Width - .75
                                                             220
   cal.Visible = .T.                                         221
                                                             222
   * end of calendar::draw                                   223
                                                             224
                                                             225
   PROCEDURE OK_close                                        226
                                                             227
   Form.value = Form.selected_date                           228
   ON KEY                                                    229
   Form.close()                                              230
                                                             231
   * end of calendar::OK_close                               232
```

```
                                                            233
                                                            234
    PROCEDURE esc_close                                     235
                                                            236
    ON KEY                                                  237
    Form.close()                                            238
                                                            239
    * end of calendar::esc_close                            240
                                                            241
                                                            242
    PROCEDURE go_end                                        243
...
    PROCEDURE set_keys                                      341
                                                            342
    * This is the calendar, focus_object is a public variable
    focus_object = This                                     344
                                                            345
    ON KEY && clear all previously set keys                 346
                                                            347
    ON KEY LABEL PgUp  focus_object.next_month(-1)          348
    ON KEY LABEL PgDn  focus_object.next_month(1)           349
    ON KEY LABEL Home  focus_object.go_home(focus_object)   350
    ON KEY LABEL End   focus_object.go_end(focus_object)    351
                                                            352
    ON KEY LABEL UpArrow    focus_object.go_up()            353
    ON KEY LABEL DnArrow    focus_object.go_down()          354
    ON KEY LABEL LeftArrow  focus_object.go_left()          355
    ON KEY LABEL RightArrow focus_object.go_right()         356
                                                            357
    ON KEY LABEL Enter focus_object.OK_close()              358
    ON KEY LABEL Esc   focus_object.esc_close()             359
                                                            360
    * end of calendar::set_keys                             361
```

With this code added, you can exit from the calendar with an Enter or Esc keypress, or by clicking the OK or Esc pushbuttons. While we don't really have access to the calendar's value property after it's closed, you'll have to assume that this code works. (At any rate, even if it doesn't there are only a handful of lines associated with those properties.)

Chapter 9 Finishing the Calendar

The Full Listing

Again, for those of you who may not have access to the disk, the Listing 9-5 duplicates the one found on disk as L09-04.PRG.

Code Listing 9-5

```
* CALENDAR.PRG -- The calendar class
* copyright 1995, Martin L. Rinehart

#define HIGH_COLOR   '+W/N'
#define PLAIN_COLOR  'N/W'

#define DAY_SPACE    0.4
#define MONTH_WIDTH  5.5

PUBLIC focus_object

foo = new calendar( "Test Calendar", date() )
foo.open()

CLASS calendar(title, sdate) OF Form(title)
   STATIC day_names = "SunMonTueWedThrFriSat"

   This.selected_date = sdate
   This.value = sdate

   This.month_label1 = NEW Text(This)
   This.month_label2 = NEW Text(This)
   STORE MONTH_WIDTH-.5 TO ;
      This.month_label1.Width, ;
      This.month_label2.Width
   STORE 9 TO ;                        && Left wrap
      This.month_label1.Alignment, ;
      This.month_label2.Alignment
   STORE 2 TO ;
      This.month_label1.Height, ;
      This.month_label2.Height

   * Add pgup/pgdn pushbuttons
      This.pgup_button = NEW pushbutton(This)
      This.pgdn_button = NEW pushbutton(This)
```

207

Learn Visual dBASE Programming

```
      This.pgup_button.Text = "PgUp"
      This.pgdn_button.Text = "PgDn"
      STORE 1.5 TO ;
         This.pgup_button.Height, ;
         This.pgdn_button.Height
      This.pgup_button.OnClick = { ; class::next_month(-1) }
      This.pgdn_button.OnClick = { ; class::next_month(1) }

   * Add home/end pushbuttons
      This.home_button = NEW pushbutton(This)
      This.end_button = NEW pushbutton(This)
      This.home_button.Text = "Home"
      This.end_button.Text = "End"
      STORE 1.5 TO ;
         This.home_button.Height, ;
         This.end_button.Height
      This.home_button.OnClick = { ; class::go_home() }
      This.end_button.OnClick = { ; class::go_end() }

   * Add OK/Esc pushbuttons
      This.OK_button = NEW pushbutton(This)
      This.esc_button = NEW pushbutton(This)
      This.OK_button.Text = "OK"
      This.esc_button.Text = "Esc"
      STORE 1.5 TO ;
         This.OK_button.Height, ;
         This.esc_button.Height
      This.OK_button.OnClick = { ; class::ok_close() }
      This.esc_button.OnClick = { ; class::esc_close() }

   * create the lines
      LOCAL i

      FOR i = 101 TO 108
         This[i] = NEW Line(This)
      ENDFOR

      FOR i = 201 TO 207
         This[i] = NEW Line(This)
      ENDFOR

   * create the day labels
```

Chapter 9 *Finishing the Calendar*

```
      FOR i = 301 to 307
         This[i] = NEW Text(This)
         This[i].Text = SUBSTR(day_names, 1+3*(i-301), 3)
         This[i].Alignment = 4 && Centered
         This[i].Top = .25
         This[i].Height = 1
      ENDFOR

   * add the days
      FOR i = 1 TO 42
         This[i] = NEW Text(This)
         This[i].Alignment = 2 && Top, right
         This[i].OnLeftMouseDown = { ;class::day_click() }
      ENDFOR
      This.set_days(This)

   This.OnGotFocus = { ;This.set_keys(This) }
   This.draw(This)
   This.OnSize = { ;This.draw(This) }

   * end of constructor


PROCEDURE day_click
* This is the day (Text object) which was clicked.

* ignore clicks on the currently selected date
   IF This.date = Form.selected_date
      RETURN
   ENDIF

Form.lolight_date(Form)

This.ColorNormal = HIGH_COLOR
Form.selected_date = This.date

RETURN && end of calendar::day_click


PROCEDURE draw(cal)
LOCAL i, lft, rgt, stp, tp, btm
cal.Visible = .F.
```

209

```
lft = .5
rgt = cal.width - MONTH_WIDTH
stp = (rgt - lft) / 7

tp = 1.5
btm = cal.height - 2.25

FOR i = 101 TO 108

   cal[i].Top = tp
   cal[i].Left = lft + (i-101)*stp
   cal[i].Bottom = btm
   cal[i].Right = cal[i].Left

ENDFOR

stp = (btm-tp) / 6

FOR i = 201 TO 207

   cal[i].Top = tp + (i-201)*stp
   cal[i].Left = lft
   cal[i].Bottom = cal[i].Top
   cal[i].Right = rgt

ENDFOR

* Day labels
   LOCAL wdth; wdth = (rgt - lft) / 7
   FOR i = 301 TO 307
      cal[i].Left = cal[i-200].Left
      cal[i].Width = wdth
   ENDFOR

* Days
   LOCAL j, k, ht, wd

   ht = cal[202].Top  - cal[201].Top  - DAY_SPACE
   wd = cal[102].Left - cal[101].Left - DAY_SPACE*2
   k = 1
```

```
      FOR i = 1 TO 6

         FOR j = 1 TO 7
            cal[k].Top    = cal[i+200].Top  + DAY_SPACE/2
            cal[k].Height = ht
            cal[k].Left   = cal[j+100].Left + DAY_SPACE
            cal[k].Width  = wd
            k = k + 1
         ENDFOR

      ENDFOR

* Month labels
   STORE cal[108].Left + .25 TO ;
      cal.month_label1.Left, cal.month_label2.Left
   cal.month_label1.Top = cal[201].Top
   * start_date + 34 is Saturday, row 5
   cal.month_label2.Top = ;
         IIF( DAY(cal.start_date + 34) < 7, ;
             cal[205].Top, ;
             cal[206].Top )

* PgUp/Dn buttons
   STORE cal[207].Top + .25 TO ;
      cal.pgup_button.Top, ;
      cal.pgdn_button.Top

   LOCAL wid; wid = cal[102].Left - cal[101].Left
   cal.pgup_button.Left = cal[101].Left + 1.25*wid
   cal.pgdn_button.Left = cal[108].Left - 2.5*wid
   STORE wid * 1.25 TO ;
      cal.pgup_button.Width, ;
      cal.pgdn_button.Width

* Home/End buttons
   STORE cal.pgup_button.Top TO ;
      cal.home_button.Top, ;
      cal.end_button.Top

   cal.home_button.Left = cal[101].Left
   cal.end_button.Left  = cal[108].Left - 1.25*wid
```

```
      STORE wid * 1.25 TO ;
         cal.home_button.Width, ;
         cal.end_button.Width

   * OK/Esc buttons
      STORE cal.pgup_button.Top TO ;
         cal.OK_button.Top, ;
         cal.esc_button.Top

      STORE wid-1 TO ;
         cal.OK_button.Width, ;
         cal.esc_button.Width
      cal.OK_button.Left = cal.pgup_button.Left + ;
                           cal.pgup_button.Width + .75
      cal.esc_button.Left = cal.pgdn_button.Left - ;
                           cal.esc_button.Width - .75

cal.Visible = .T.

* end of calendar::draw


PROCEDURE OK_close

Form.value = Form.selected_date
ON KEY
Form.close()

* end of calendar::OK_close


PROCEDURE esc_close

ON KEY
Form.close()

* end of calendar::esc_close


PROCEDURE go_end

Form.lolight_date(Form)
```

Chapter 9 — Finishing the Calendar

```
   LOCAL dt;  dt = Form.selected_date

IF (MONTH(dt) < 12) .OR. (DAY(dt) < 31)
   Form.selected_date = make_date( 12, 31, YEAR(dt) )
 ELSE
   Form.selected_date = make_date( 12, 31, YEAR(dt)+1 )
ENDIF

Form.set_days(Form)

* end of calendar::go_end


PROCEDURE go_home

Form.lolight_date(Form)

LOCAL dt;  dt = Form.selected_date

IF (MONTH(dt) > 1) .OR. (DAY(dt) > 1)
   Form.selected_date = make_date( 1, 1, YEAR(dt) )
 ELSE
   Form.selected_date = make_date( 1, 1, YEAR(dt)-1 )
ENDIF

Form.set_days(Form)

* end of calendar::go_home


PROCEDURE lolight_date(cal)

LOCAL dnum
dnum = Form.selected_date - Form.start_date + 1
Form[dnum].ColorNormal = PLAIN_COLOR

* end of lolight_date


PROCEDURE set_days(cal)
STATIC month_names = ;
```

213

```
      'Jan.Feb.Mar.Apr.May JuneJulyAug.Sep.Oct.Nov.Dec.'

   cal.start_date = find_start(cal.selected_date)

   LOCAL dt; dt = cal.start_date

   FOR i = 1 TO 42
      cal[i].date = dt
      cal[i].Text = LTRIM( STR(DAY( dt )) )

      IF dt = cal.selected_date
         cal[i].ColorNormal = HIGH_COLOR
      ENDIF

      dt = dt + 1
   ENDFOR

   * set month labels
      dt = cal.start_date + 6 && Saturday, 1st row
      cal.month_label1.Text = month_id( dt )
      cal.month_label2.Text = month_id( ;
            make_date( MONTH(dt)+1, 1, YEAR(dt) ) )

   * end of calendar::set_days


   PROCEDURE next_month( months_to_add )

   LOCAL dt; dt = Form.selected_date
   LOCAL mo; mo = MONTH(dt) + months_to_add
   LOCAL yr; yr = YEAR(dt)

   IF mo > 12
      mo = mo - 12
      yr = yr + 1
   ELSEIF mo < 1
      mo = mo + 12
      yr = yr - 1
   ENDIF

   Form.lolight_date(Form)
```

Chapter 9 Finishing the Calendar

```
Form.selected_date = make_date( mo, DAY(dt), yr )

DO WHILE MONTH(Form.selected_date) > mo
   Form.selected_date = Form.selected_date - 1
ENDDO

Form.set_days(Form)

* end of calendar::next_month


PROCEDURE set_keys

* This is the calendar, focus_object is a public variable
focus_object = This

ON KEY && clear all previously set keys

ON KEY LABEL PgUp focus_object.next_month(-1)
ON KEY LABEL PgDn focus_object.next_month(1)
ON KEY LABEL Home focus_object.go_home(focus_object)
ON KEY LABEL End  focus_object.go_end(focus_object)

ON KEY LABEL UpArrow focus_object.go_up()
ON KEY LABEL DnArrow focus_object.go_down()
ON KEY LABEL LeftArrow focus_object.go_left()
ON KEY LABEL RightArrow focus_object.go_right()

ON KEY LABEL Enter focus_object.OK_close()
ON KEY LABEL Esc   focus_object.esc_close()

* end of calendar::set_keys


PROCEDURE go_up

* 'This' is the calendar object

IF This.selected_date - This.start_date > 6

   This.lolight_date(This)
   This.selected_date = This.selected_date - 7
```

215

Learn Visual dBASE Programming

```
       Form[ Form.selected_date - This.start_date + 1 ;
           ].ColorNormal = HIGH_COLOR

ENDIF

* end of calendar::go_up


PROCEDURE go_down

* 'This' is the calendar object

IF This.selected_date - This.start_date < 35

   This.lolight_date(This)
   This.selected_date = This.selected_date + 7
   Form[ Form.selected_date - This.start_date + 1 ;
       ].ColorNormal = HIGH_COLOR

ENDIF

* end of calendar::go_down


PROCEDURE go_left

* 'This' is the calendar object

IF This.selected_date > This.start_date

   This.lolight_date(This)
   This.selected_date = This.selected_date - 1
   Form[ Form.selected_date - This.start_date + 1 ;
       ].ColorNormal = HIGH_COLOR

ENDIF

* end of calendar::go_left


PROCEDURE go_right
```

Chapter 9   *Finishing the Calendar*

```
   * 'This' is the calendar object

   IF This.selected_date - This.start_date < 41

      This.lolight_date(This)
      This.selected_date = This.selected_date + 1
      Form[ Form.selected_date - This.start_date + 1 ;
           ].ColorNormal = HIGH_COLOR

   ENDIF

   * end of calendar::go_right


ENDCLASS && calendar


FUNCTION find_start(dt)

* Given any date, this function returns a start date for a
* calendar's page. It assumes that the first of the month
* of the given date should be in the top line of the
* calendar.

LOCAL first

first = make_date( MONTH(dt), 1, YEAR(dt) )

RETURN first - (DOW(first)-1)

* end of find_start()


FUNCTION make_date(mo, da, yr)

* This function returns a date when passed three numbers,
* representing the month, day, and year, respectively.

SET DATE TO MDY

RETURN CTOD( STR(mo,2) + '/' + ;
             STR(da,2) + '/' + ;
```

Learn Visual dBASE Programming

```
            STR(yr,4) )

* end of make_date()


FUNCTION month_id(dt)

* returns 9 character string: "Mmmm YYYY"

STATIC month_names = ;
   'Jan.Feb.Mar.Apr.May JuneJulyAug.Sep.Oct.Nov.Dec.'

LOCAL mo; mo = MONTH(dt)

RETURN SUBSTR(month_names, mo*4 - 3, 4) + ;
       ' ' + LEFT( DTOS(dt), 4 )

* end of month_id()


* end of CALENDAR.PRG
```

Summary

Well, congratulations. You've got a good calendar that can be driven by the mouse or from the keyboard. Its manipulation is either self-evident or has the sort of GUI interface that encourages the user to explore and discover the capabilities.

You've built the underlying event handlers that empower the user. Along the way, you've seen how an object can be launched and given to the user, but still be programmed by you.

Best of all, you haven't built an object. You've built a class. Whenever your systems need a calendar you can launch one with almost no trouble.

In the next chapter we'll stop coding our own programs and let Visual dBASE help us write code.

Chapter 10

Beginning an Application

This chapter is about using the Menu Designer and the Form Designer to help your programming along. I told you that I wasn't going to be teaching you how to use Visual dBASE user interface, since I believe that you have enough experience and enough smarts to figure most of it out for yourself.

As you'll see, the Menu Designer is both thoroughly hidden and completely obtuse. After you finish this chapter, you'll be delighted with the tool, but I sure would have liked some help when I got started. This is that help.

The Form Designer is neither hidden nor obtuse. I'll get you started using it the way I've learned is most efficient after several months of trial and error. I assume that you'll learn most of the ins and outs of this tool on your own, but won't

Learn Visual dBASE Programming

mind a few pointers. We'll use both these tools together to build an old-fashioned application shell.

Warning: There are no listings on the disk for this chapter. Almost all the code is generated by the Menu Designer or the Form Designer. The few exceptions are clearly explained in the text.

In the old days (in software, that's yesterday or earlier) our applications generally started with a main menu, and then sub-menus that eventually got us to some work. We'd have choices like:

- Enter data
- Query data
- Write reports
- File maintenance
- Exit

In a GUI environment, this sort of programming is called modal and it is thought to be a bad thing. In a modeless environment, the user is free to open data entry windows along with query and report windows, all at once. Using the mouse (or pressing Ctrl+Tab) the user picks one and uses it, then goes on to another. These modeless programs *can* be much more flexible, powerful, and friendly.

Of course, menus are still with us. They provide one of several means for controlling your program. (At least, you hope there are several means.) In Visual dBASE, for example, you could drive your work by making menu choices, or ignore the menus and use the Navigator, or just enter commands in the Command window.

In this chapter, we'll use the tools that Visual dBASE provides to build a form with a menu system and create some modal windows that go along with the menus.

Creating a Scratch Form

If you haven't already tried it, Visual dBASE has a helpful fellow called the Form Expert built in. If you have created a table (.DBF, .DB, or SQL database table) when you launch the Form Designer, you'll be given a chance to let the Form Expert go to work for you. Answer a few questions and you will get an instant data entry form.

You will also get a chance to tell the Form Expert that you don't want help, you'll do it yourself, thank you. This is what we'll do here. (If you're going to build a data-entry form for a table, as we'll see later, it's almost always helpful to let the Form Expert go to work for you. When you don't have a table, you'll want to build your own forms from scratch.)

Creating an Empty Form

The Form is the base object for our applications. We'll start by building an empty one and then adding a title. You can access the Form Designer from the Command window or through the Navigator.

Launching the Form Designer from the Command window

The Form Designer can be launched in these ways from the Command window:

- Enter CREATE FORM
- Enter MODIFY FORM
- Enter CREATE FORM <form name>
- Enter MODIFY FORM <form name>

The first two launch the Form Designer on an untitled, new form. The latter two launch the Form Designer on either a new form (if the form you name doesn't exist) or an existing form. The CREATE FORM command will ask you if you want to work with an existing form, if your form name already exists. The MODIFY FORM command will create a new form or go to work on an existing one, in neither case prompting you.

Tip: Always use CREATE FORM. Because it prompts you on an existing form, you'll always know that you have spelled your form's name correctly. MODIFY FORM would be better if it prompted you with a "Do you want to create a new one?" dialog, but it doesn't.

Figure 10-1 shows a Form Designer session launched from the Command window.

221

Learn Visual dBASE Programming

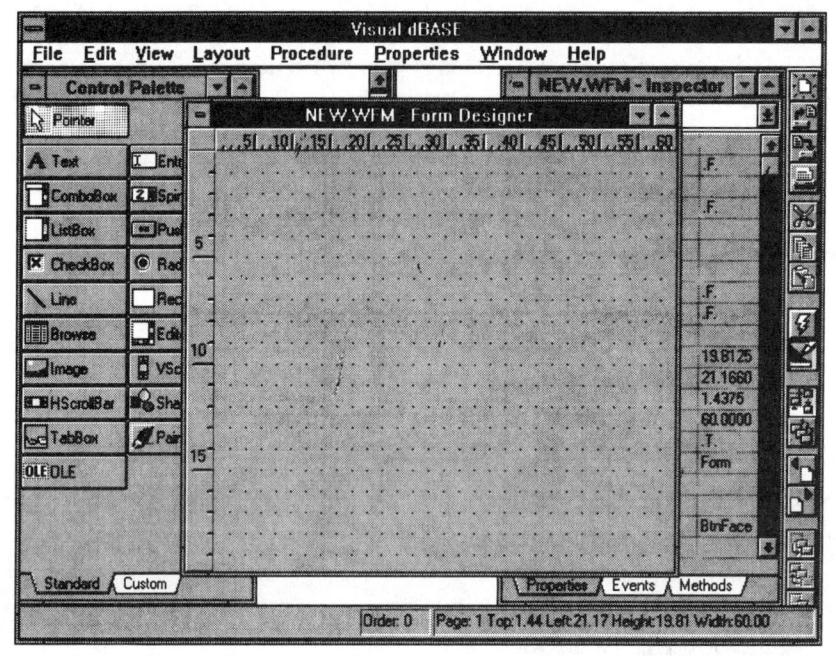

Figure 10-1: Form Designer launched from the Command Window

Note the layout carefully. The Form Designer has four main sub-tools associated with it:

- The Controls palette
- The object properties Inspector
- The Procedures editor
- The Field Palette

These tools are all available on the SpeedMenu (right-click over the Form) and on the View menu.

I've got the Controls palette on the left, beneath the Form Designer window, and the object properties Inspector on the right, also beneath the Form Designer window. You can clearly see the side of each one.

More important than the side, the tabs of both these tools are sticking out under the Form Designer window. When you want to grab a control, you click the

Chapter 10 — Beginning an Application

Standard or Custom tab. When you want to look at or change a property, you click the Properties, Events, or Methods tab.

Figure 10-2 shows the Procedures editor. To bring it to the top, I clicked on the space between the Controls palette and the object properties Inspector, below the Form Designer window.

Launching the Form Designer from the Navigator

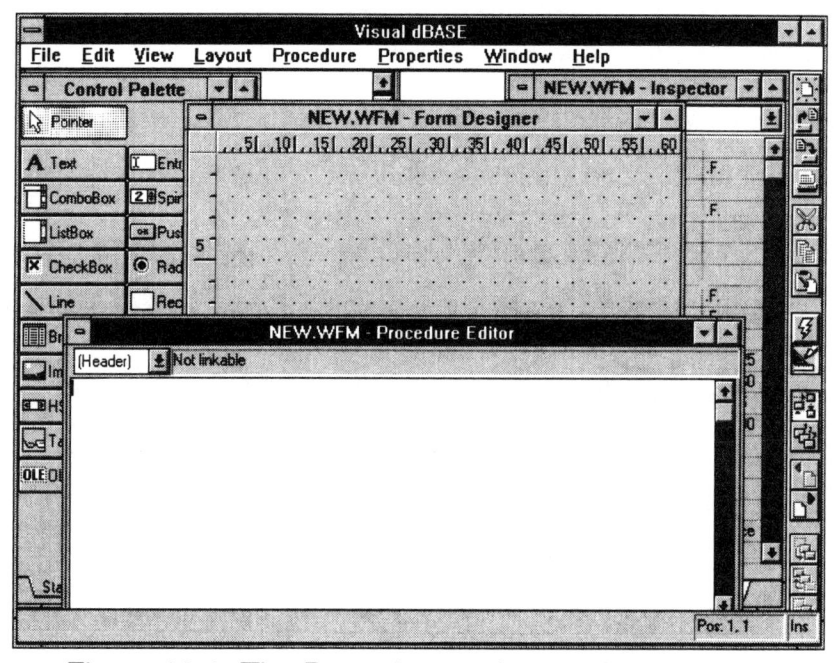

Figure 10-2: The Procedures editor is also available.

You can also launch the Form Designer from the Navigator, if you are working with that tool. Start by selecting Forms (click it, or Tab to the file type list and use the Up and Down arrows, or, from the menu, choose View Forms). Then select either the Untitled form to work on a new form, or choose an existing form (again, click on your choice, or press Tab followed by Up and Down arrows).

After selecting the Untitled form or an existing form, these are some of the ways to launch the Form Designer:

Learn Visual dBASE Programming

- Double right-click it
- Press Shift+F2
- Right click to bring up the SpeedMenu, then choose Design Form
- From the Navigator menu, choose Design Form

Tip: There are lots of ways to navigate around Visual dBASE. This is a virtue that your own systems should try to achieve.

Launching the Form Expert Directly

Unlike launching a form from the Command window, launching a form from the Navigator invokes the Form Expert by default. Its first screen is shown in Figure 10-3.

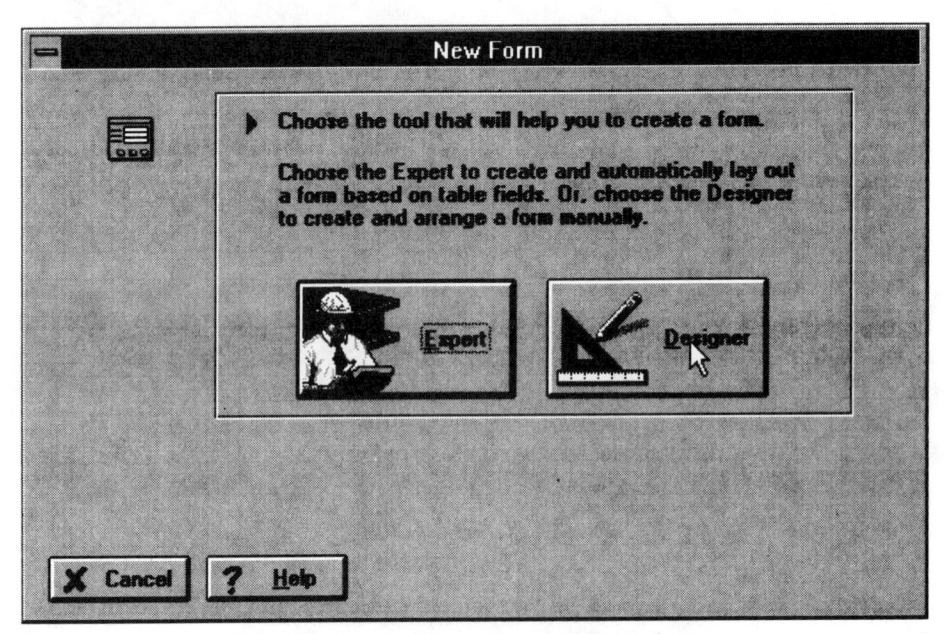

Figure 10-3: Choosing a blank form

224

When you launch a new form with the Form Expert, through either the Navigator or directly, you'll see the command:

```
CREATE FORM EXPERT PROMPT
```

As with most of the work you do, the mouse clicks and menu choices you make are translated into Command window commands and echoed into the Command window. In this case, it teaches you how to invoke the Form Expert from the Command window.

Saving Your Form

Once you make any changes to a form, any method for exiting from the Form Designer will prompt you to save the current form. Figure 10-4 shows the Changes Made - Form Designer dialog box.

There are many ways to leave the Form Designer:

- Double-click its system button
- Press Esc
- Choose Close from its system menu
- Exit with ^W or ^Q

Only the latter choice skips the dialog shown in Figure 10-4. If you choose ^W the Form Designer will save and exit. If your form is Untitled, you will be presented the Save As dialog, where you give it a name. ^Q exits without saving, of course.

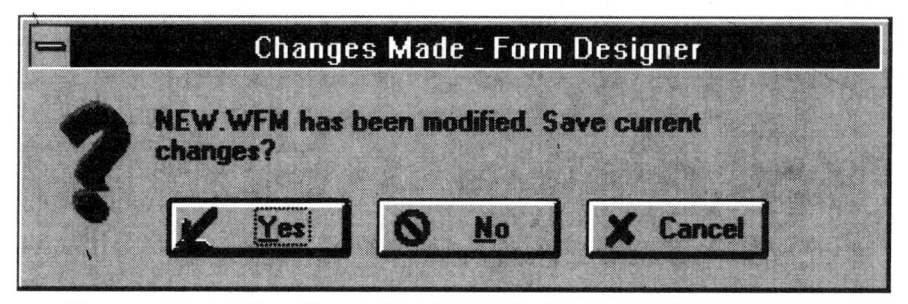

Figure 10-4: The Form Designer helps you when you exit.

If you run the form from the Form Designer you will also get the Changes Made - Form Designer dialog. This lets you alternate between design and run mode and will be a great convenience. The Form Designer is the design mode for a Form, of course. There are several ways to switch directly to run mode from the Form Designer, including:

- Press F2
- Choose Run from the system menu
- Click the lightning icon on the SpeedBar
- Choose View/Form from the menu

Each of these will save the form and then run it. This is the form's equivalent of pressing Ctrl+D in the Program Editor.

The Output of the Form Designer

The Form Designer is a Two-Way Tool (tm). This is Borland's trademarked name for a very slick technology, which you can expect will be copied by all of Borland's competitors. It's one of those ideas that is so obvious, once you see it in action, that you are surprised it wasn't invented 20 years ago.

There is only one storage form for all your Form Designer work: program code. The output of the Form Designer is a program with the extension .WFM. This is dBASE source code.

Output of a Plain Form

Listing 10-1 shows a blank form's saved listing. To create your own, launch the Form Designer, move the form a bit, and then exit. On your way out, save your work as T.WFM. (Moving the blank form is enough to make the Form Designer decide that you have modified the form and should be asked about saving your work.)

You can take a look at T.WFM from the Command window with a MODI COMM command. You can also right-click the Form in the Navigator and select Edit as Program from the SpeedMenu.

Chapter 10 — Beginning an Application

Code Listing 10-1

```
** END HEADER -- do not remove this line*
* Generated on 06/22/95
*
parameter bModal
local f
f = new NEWFORM()
if (bModal)
   f.mdi = .F. && ensure not MDI
   f.ReadModal()
else
   f.Open()
endif
CLASS NEWFORM OF FORM
   this.Top = 0.1875
   this.Left = 22
   this.Text = "Form"
   this.Height = 20
   this.Width = 60

ENDCLASS
```

There are three areas in a .WFM program. Listing 10-1 shows the middle area, which is written by the Form Designer. The three areas are

```
HEADER
MIDDLE
GENERAL
```

The default code, as you can see, does not include either a beginning or an end of file comment, which I consider bad style. Let's add these, since doing this will show you more about how the Form Designer's output is structured.

First, launch the Form Designer with T.WFM as your form. (Make it a point of pride to see how many times you can launch the Form Designer with T, or any other form, without using the same launch method — you'll learn a lot.)

Header and General .WFM Output

Let's use the Procedures editor to create a Header comment at the beginning of our file, and the General area to add an end of file comment. Start by selecting the Procedures editor using one of these methods:

227

Learn Visual dBASE Programming

- Click on it, if it is on screen
- Right-click the form and select it from the SpeedMenu
- Choose View/Procedures from the menu
- Choose Window/Procedures from the menu

When it is first launched, the Procedures editor has a dropdown list of choices (near the upper-left corner) showing the default Header. It also has a General choice. In the default Header, type some opening lines, like those shown in Figure 10-5.

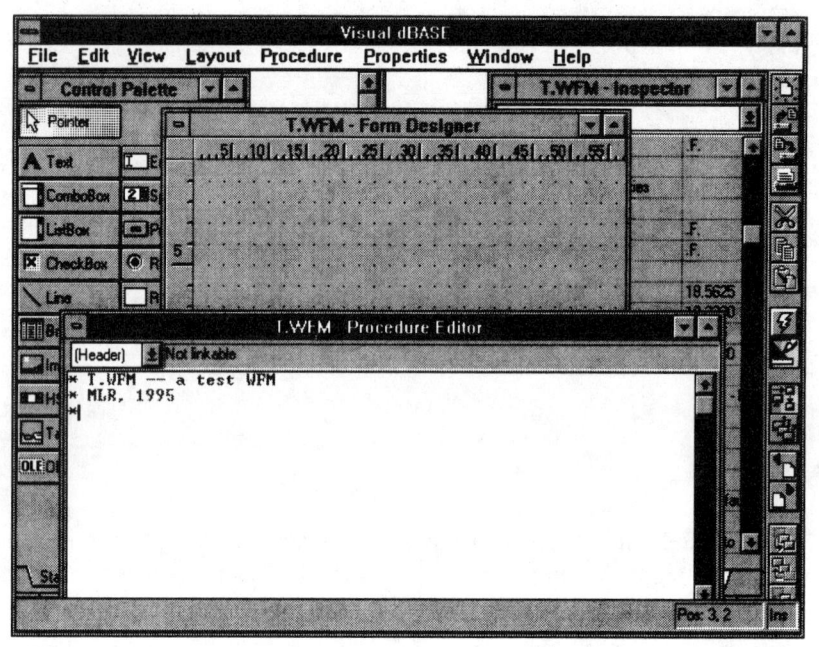

Figure 10-5: A Header program in the Procedures editor

Any code that you place in the Header section will appear in your output file before the code that the Form Designer writes in the Middle section.

Tip: To separate your code from the Middle section, use one or more asterisks trailing below your code. Trailing blank lines in the Header section are not saved by the Form Designer.

228

Chapter 10 Beginning an Application

Add your Header lines and press Ctrl+S to save the addition. My result is shown in Listing 10-2.

Code Listing 10-2

```
* T.WFM -- a test WFM
* MLR, 1995
*
** END HEADER -- do not remove this line*

* Generated on 06/23/95
*
parameter bModal
local f
f = new TFORM()
if (bModal)
   f.mdi = .F. && ensure not MDI
   f.ReadModal()
else
   f.Open()
endif
CLASS TFORM OF FORM
   this.ScrollBar = 2
   this.Left = 19.333
   this.Text = "Form"
   this.Top = 1.8125
   this.ColorNormal = "w"
   this.Height = 18.5625
   this.Width = 57.333

ENDCLASS
```

Listing 10-2 shows the Header code that I added appearing before the Middle code that the Form Designer wrote. As you have probably guessed, Visual dBASE depends on this line:

```
** END HEADER -- do not remove this line*
```

As it reads the .WFM, everything above that line is stored as Header code. From that line through the ENDCLASS statement, it reads its own Middle code.

229

Learn Visual dBASE Programming

You can edit the Header code (as well as the other code) with the Procedures editor, or in any other text editor. When you launch a form in the Form Designer, your Header code will be appropriately separated and available for editing in the Procedures editor as its Header.

Let's continue to add that end of file comment in the General section. Figure 10-6 shows my simple comment.

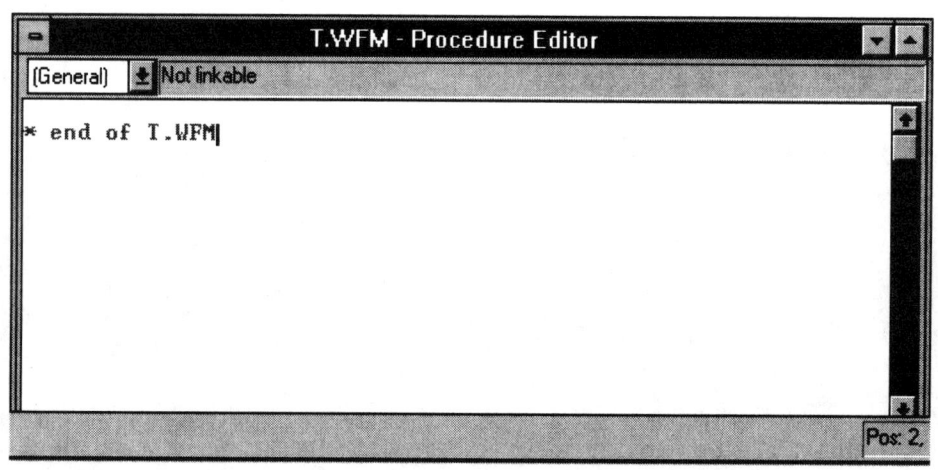

Figure 10-6: An end-of-file comment in the General section

As you would assume, the leading blank lines here are meaningful, but trailing blank lines are discarded, which is probably just what you want. Listing 10-3 shows the full program written by the Form Designer when I pressed Ctrl+S in the Procedures editor.

Code Listing 10-3

```
* T.WFM -- a test WFM
* MLR, 1995
*
** END HEADER -- do not remove this line*
* Generated on 06/23/95
*
parameter bModal
local f
f = new TFORM()
if (bModal)
   f.mdi = .F. && ensure not MDI
```

230

```
      f.ReadModal()
else
      f.Open()
endif
CLASS TFORM OF FORM
   this.ScrollBar = 2
   this.Left = 19.333
   this.Text = "Form"
   this.Top = 1.25
   this.ColorNormal = "w"
   this.Height = 18.25
   this.Width = 57.333

ENDCLASS
```

* end of T.WFM

This listing is beginning to resemble the sort of code I'd write myself. The Header and General sections are completely under your control. You can edit them in the Procedures editor and save them to T.WFM. You can edit T.WFM in any text editor and your changes to the Header and General sections will be available the next time you launch the Form Designer.

You can also edit the Middle section with MODI COMM or your favorite text editor. The Form Designer will recognize many, but not all, changes to this section. As an example, if you were to edit the location and size values (change this.Left from 14 to another number) your changes would be correctly read and preserved.

On the other hand, if you changed the 14 in this.Left to a formula, the Form Designer would evaluate that formula to set the Left property. Unfortunately, when it writes the code again, it will write the value, not your formula.

Tip: Experiment with a sample program when you edit the Middle of a .WFM. The Two-Way Tools right now are really closer to 1.7- or 1.8-Way Tools.

Let's get on to using the Menu Designer to create a menu for our form.

Creating a Menu System

Everything else you do with a form is attached to the form, but not menus. Menus exist in a separate .MNU file, which you can attach to a form. You can attach one .MNU to many forms, if you like, through the MenuFile property of the form.

This means, among other things, that we can attach a menu to T.WFM. As the name T suggests, this is not a permanent form; it's one that we'll delete later on. If we build a nice menu, it doesn't matter. Our menu is in a separate file where we can use it with other forms. In this section we'll create a skeleton menu that we can quickly attach to any form that needs a menu.

To do this, you'll have to find the Menu Designer. I'm tempted to make this a contest. First one to find it gets a big prize. Anyone finding it in less than 15 minutes gets second prize.

Finding the Menu Designer

The Menu Designer is a superb tool, but it has two glaring defects. The first is that you can't find it. If you'll pass up the prizes, I'll also let you pass up the time it takes to remedy that problem. Start by launching T in the Form Designer.

With T launched, click the Properties tab of the object properties Inspector. If you haven't used this tool before, double-click on any property that has a plus sign on the left. It will expand to show all its component properties, and the plus will turn into a minus. Double-click on any property that has a minus sign on the left. It will contract, showing none of its components and the minus sign is replaced by the plus sign.

Some properties, including the property of most interest to us, stand outside any group. We're most interested in the MenuFile property. Click on this property and the entryfield to its right is highlighted. Additionally, a tool icon shows up on a pushbutton to the far right. Figure 10-7 shows my MenuFile's tool icon about to be clicked.

If you have no menu file listed for the MenuFile property, clicking the MenuFile's tool icon will immediately launch the Menufile Property Builder dialog box, shown in Figure 10-8.

I've chosen the name SKELETON. As we proceed through this section, we'll create a skeleton menu file that can be the starting point for any Windows program's menu.

Chapter 10   *Beginning an Application*

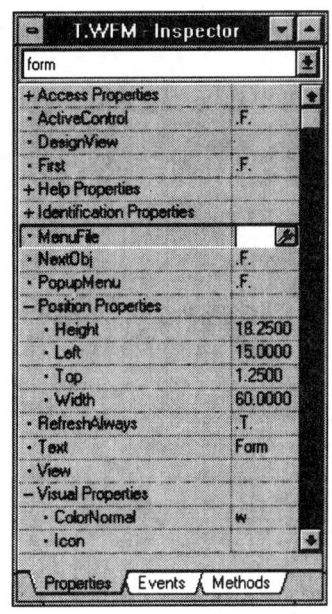

Figure 10-7: Clicking the MenuFile's tool icon

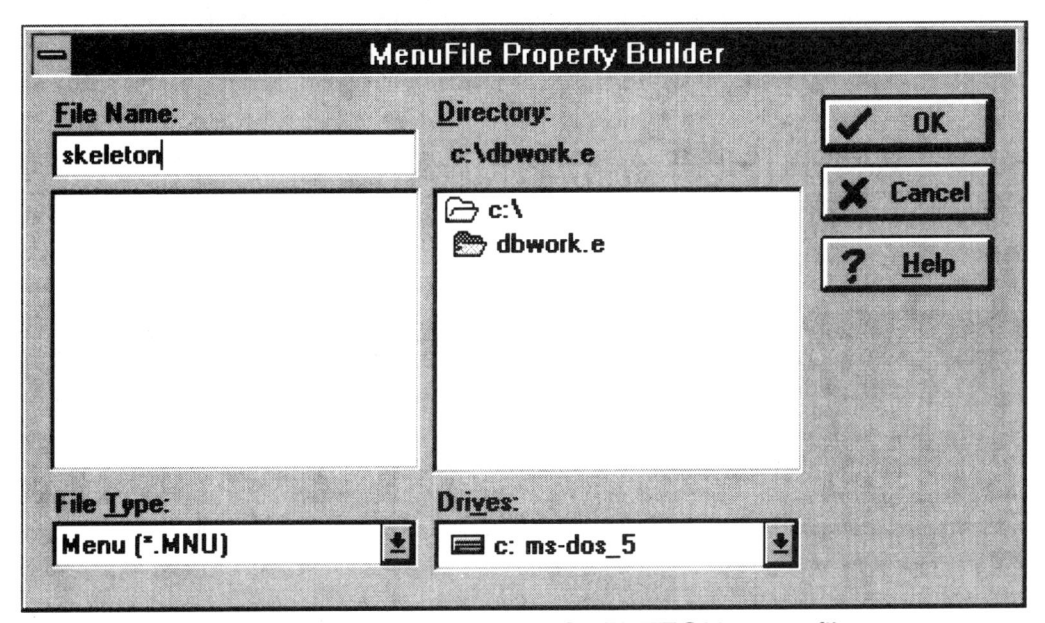

Figure 10-8: Choosing the SKELETON menu file

233

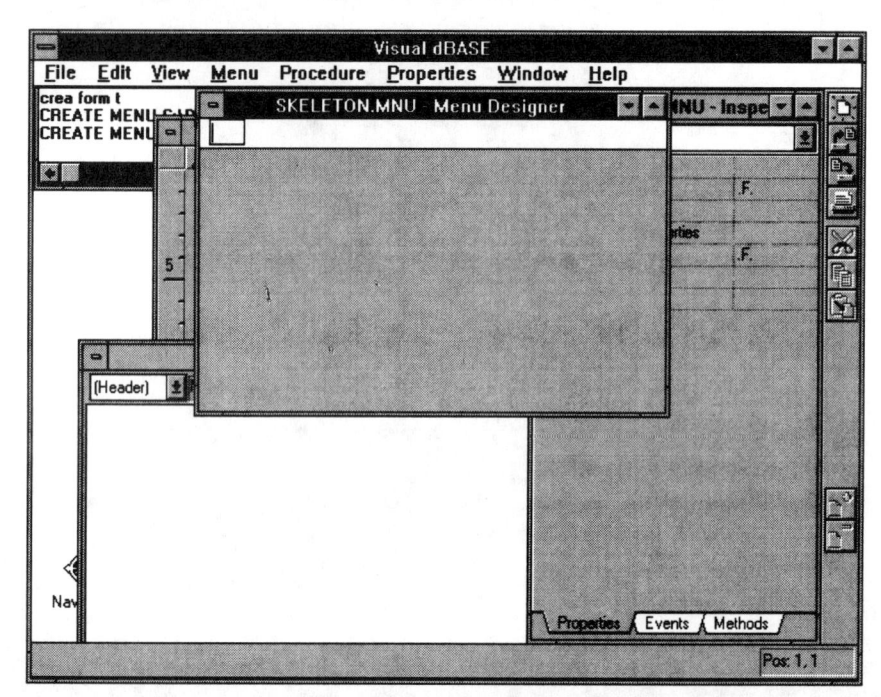

You've now found the Menu Designer. It's shown in Figure 10-9.

Figure 10-9: The Menu Designer is launched.

This brings us to the second major problem with this tool.

Using the Menu Designer

This tool is very simple to use and has all the power you need to do complete, Windows-style menus. But it starts you off with no help whatsoever. It sits there blinking an insertion point inside a rectangle.

I guess that the designer of this tool had programmers like us in mind. You'll find that the dumb stare here conceals a tool that makes the best possible use of every one of your keystrokes. This is an amazingly agile environment. You'll be in and out of the Menu Designer in no time, once you understand it.

Chapter 10   *Beginning an Application*

Getting Started with the Menu Designer

Of course, that may be comforting, but right now, if you're new to the Menu Designer, it's hard to know how to begin. Follow these instructions and you'll be an expert in no time. Let's begin by creating a menu with some standard Windows' menu prompts, in the standard order:

- File
- Edit
- Window
- Help

Each prompt is an object of the Menu class. To create one, just type a word. Start by typing "File" in the rectangle the Menu Designer starts with. Figure 10-10 shows this step.

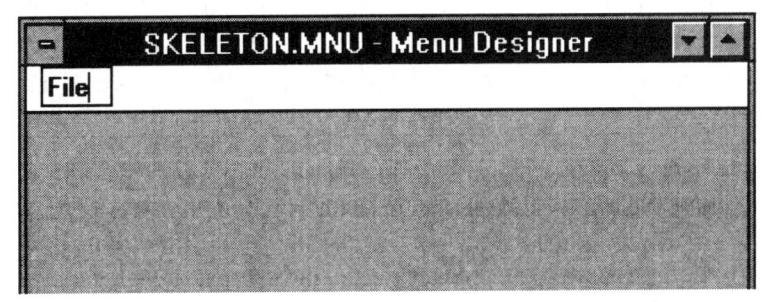

Figure 10-10: The File prompt was typed.

Do this on your own machine. Notice that the object properties Inspector is now showing you the properties of a menu object. For example, the Text property (the last one) shows the word File which you just typed. (As you type, the object properties Inspector is updated, which is what makes the apparent response so slow. You can type at full speed; it will catch up.)

To create the next menu object in the main menu, press the Tab key. This will move to the right into a new rectangle. Add the four standard prompts in our skeleton menu, tabbing after each one is entered. Figure 10-11 shows this step.

235

Learn Visual dBASE Programming

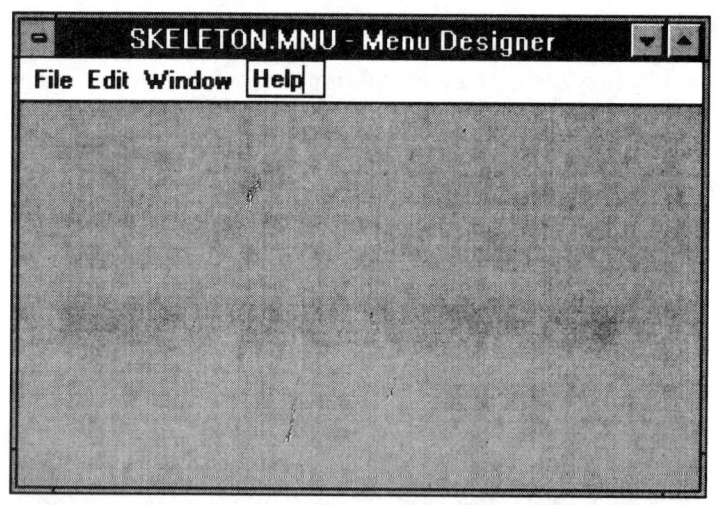

Figure 10-11: The four standard prompts added

After you have added all four, use the Tab and Shift+Tab keystrokes to move back and forth from one to the other. This is very efficient, isn't it?

Now let's add a pulldown menu under the File menu object. At a minimum, our pulldown will have two options:

- Print

- Exit

(Why are these options under the File menu? Why should our skeleton file have the ultimate stupidity, a File menu with no file-related options? Ask the wise designers at IBM and Microsoft. I don't know. I do know that since every Windows program is built that way, we'll do our users a disservice if we don't go along.)

To add these, use Shift+Tab to get back to the File option. (You can click on it, if you like, but this tool works marvelously from the keyboard.) When you are at the File option, press the Down arrow. An empty option will appear below the File options, as you see in Figure 10-12.

Chapter 10 *Beginning an Application*

Figure 10-12: A dropdown from the File option

In this new menu object, type Print. Then press the Down arrow again and type Exit in the second menu object. You'll now have a dropdown menu, as shown in Figure 10-13.

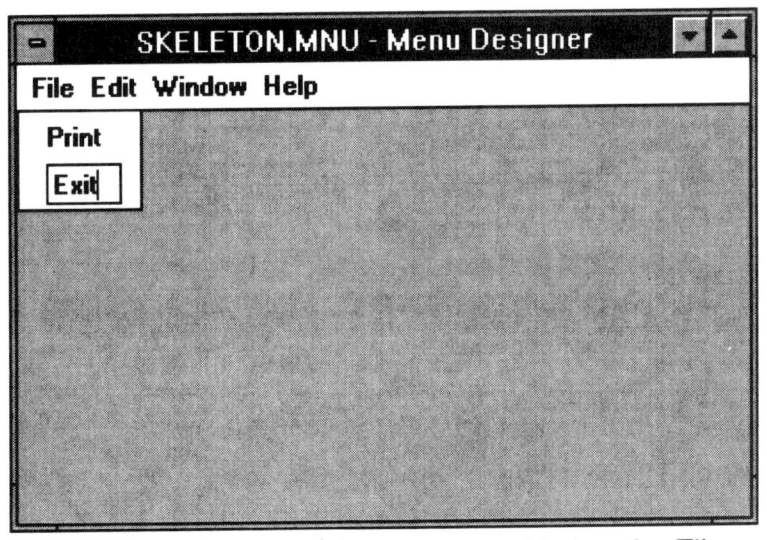

Figure 10-13: A dropdown menu added under File

237

Learn Visual dBASE Programming

Now you know how to create menu objects, how to add main menu objects, and how to create and add to dropdown menus. You can save your work with Ctrl_W. Now let's take a look at the work the Menu Designer is doing.

The Output of the Menu Designer

The Menu Designer is a Two-Way Tool, like the Form Designer. It stores its data as a program file, with the extension .MNU. The menu you have created so far generates a short file, shown in Listing 10-4.

Code Listing 10-4

```
** END HEADER -- do not remove this line*
* Generated on 06/23/95
*
Parameter FormObj
NEW SKELETONMENU(FormObj,"Root")
CLASS SKELETONMENU(FormObj,Name) OF MENUBAR(FormObj,Name)

   DEFINE MENU FILE OF THIS;
      PROPERTY;
         Text "File"

         DEFINE MENU PRINT OF THIS.FILE;
            PROPERTY;
               Text "Print"

         DEFINE MENU EXIT OF THIS.FILE;
            PROPERTY;
               Text "Exit"

   DEFINE MENU EDIT OF THIS;
      PROPERTY;
         Text "Edit"

   DEFINE MENU WINDOW OF THIS;
      PROPERTY;
         Text "Window"

   DEFINE MENU HELP OF THIS;
```

Chapter 10 — Beginning an Application

```
        PROPERTY;
    Text "Help"
ENDCLASS
```

The first line (** END HEADER) should remind you of the Form Designer output. Like a .WFM, the .MNU has three sections:

- Header
- Middle
- General

Anything you care to add before the ** END HEADER line is the Header portion of your .MNU. You can add header code with the Procedures editor. (In the Menu designer you launch the Procedures editor with View/Procedures from the menu or by right clicking and choosing Procedures from the SpeedMenu. If it is already launched, just click on it or choose Window from the menu and pick Procedures from the Window menu.)

If you press Ctrl+W in the Menu Designer, your work will be saved and you'll return to the Form Designer, which is what I'd like you to try now.

Back in the Form Designer, use Alt+W to access the Window menu and choose window 2, the Command window. In the Command window, type "MODIFY COMMAND SKELETON.MNU".

The .MNU extension is mandatory, if you don't want to edit a .PRG. The uppercase and the fully spelled commands are not mandatory. In practice, I'd actually type "modi comm skeleton.mnu".

Whichever you choose, your .MNU file will be launched in the Program Editor, where you can add a header and general section. The ones I've added are in Listing 10-5.

Code Listing 10-5

```
* SKELETON.MNU -- skeleton menu file
* Copyright 1995, Martin L. Rinehart
*
** END HEADER -- do not remove this line*
```

239

Learn Visual dBASE Programming

```
* Generated on 6/23/95
...

ENDCLASS

* end of SKELETON.MNU
```

Use Ctrl+W to save those, or similar additions, to your own .MNU file. Then click on the object properties Inspector's Properties tab to return to it. Again, click on the MenuFile property and then on the tool icon to the right of the entryfield. You will get the Modify Menu File Property dialog box and can choose the Design Current Menu choice.

When you return to your Menu Designer, use the Procedures editor to look at the code. You should see your additions when you check both Header and General sections. Bear in mind that the file the Procedures editor looks at in the Menu Designer is not the same as the one it examines in the Form Designer.

Getting Fancy with the Menu Designer

Now that you've got the basics down, let's get to some of the fancier features of good Windows menus. First, one letter should be underscored in each menu choice and pressing that letter should immediately activate that option. The *F* in File is always underscored, for example, as is the *x* in Exit. This lets you press Alt+F to get the File menu and then x to exit from the program.

To underscore a letter in the Menu Designer, just put an ampersand (&) in front of it. Figure 10-14 shows the menu choices with underscores. The ampersand that you type (in this case, in the E&xit menu object) is converted to an underscore letter as soon as you leave the menu object, and is turned back into an ampersand when you return to the menu object, so you can easily change it.

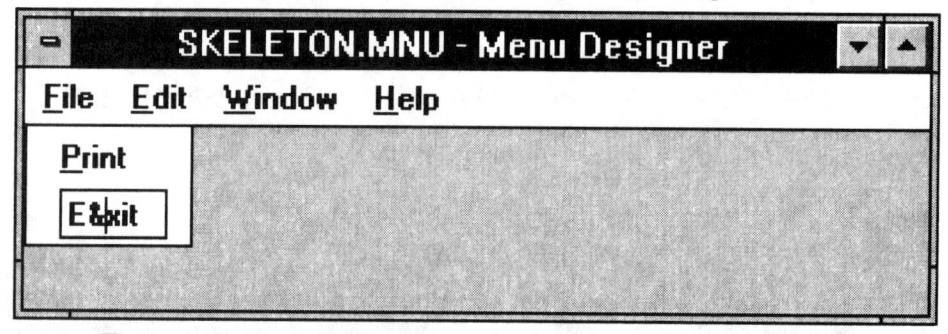

Figure 10-14: Adding ampersands to underscore letters

You haven't just underscored the letters. You've turned those letters into *mnemonic keys* which respond in all the ways you'd expect. Outside the menu, pressing Alt+a mnemonic key triggers that menu option (usually a pulldown menu). When a menu is active, pressing the mnemonic key alone hops immediately to that action. You've completed your work in this regard. (You do remember that I told you that this was a fast, powerful tool, don't you? I bet you're beginning to agree.)

In addition to mnemonic keys, a menu can have accelerator keys. Those are the ones you can press that bypass the menus to simply execute a command. On a well-designed menu, they're shown to the right of the menu choices for which they substitute.

Let's add an About choice to the Help menu and assign Ctrl+A as an accelerator key to go straight to our Help/About dialog. Start by using Shift+Tab and Tab to get to the Help menu object, or, with the mouse, clicking on Help.

Press the Down arrow to add a pulldown and type "&About...". The ellipses following a menu choice tell you that a dialog box is launched from that choice. You have to type them if that is what will happen. This is shown in Figure 10-15.

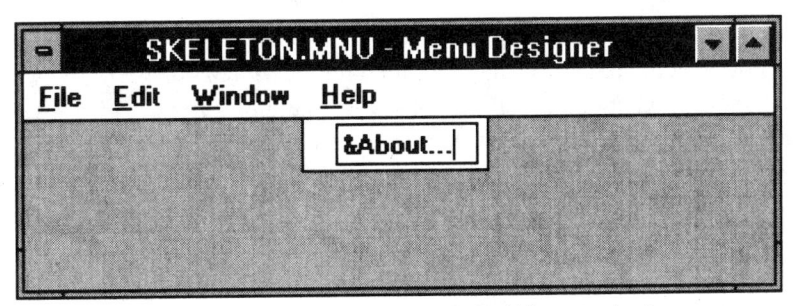

Figure 10-15: Adding a Help/About choice

Once you've added this choice, you want to add an accelerator key. (Borland's documentation calls accelerators *shortcut* keys.) To do this, select the Properties tab of the object properties Inspector, then click on the Shortcut property. In the entryfield of this property, type "Ctrl+A".

You will see the entryfield turn yellow (warning, or caution) as you type. This is true of all fields where you type things like expressions, color specifications or key specifiers. The yellow means that Visual dBASE hasn't checked your work. Press Enter and your field will return to the normal colors, indicating that your entry is acceptable.

Learn Visual dBASE Programming

That's all you have to do. As you can see, your accelerator key is now shown in the menu prompt and will be effective when you run the menu.

With an accelerator installed, let's add a menu separator between the Print and Exit options of the File menu. Return to the File menu and press the Down arrow twice to get to the Exit option.

From the Menu pulldown, choose Insert Separator. A separator-type Menu object will hop into place above the current option, as you see in Figure 10-16.

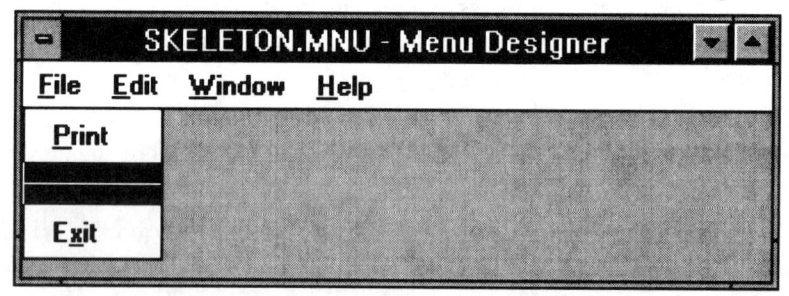

Figure 10-16: A menu separator added

You may have noticed that the Menu pulldown contained four key tools for editing menus. Each one has a control key accelerator, or shortcut, which you can use after the Menu pulldown starts to become one keystroke more than you like. These are:

- Ctrl+N — inserts a menu object before the current one
- Ctrl+M — inserts a new menu (pulldown or cascading)
- Ctrl+T — inserts a separator above the current option
- Ctrl+U — deletes the currently selected Menu object

Tip: Always check the main menu option that has a name matching the current tool. An option such as Menu is bound to have interesting actions when you are in the Menu Designer.

We haven't asked any of our terminal menu nodes to do any work yet. Without our doing any additional work, the File menu option knows that when it is selected it should drop the pulldown menu we attached to it, and so does the Help option. But the other options don't have jobs, yet.

Chapter 10   *Beginning an Application*

Let's attach an exit action to the Exit menu object in the File pulldown. For the simplest possible use, you'll just have it quit Visual dBASE. When your applications get smarter, they'll probably want this option to first do any necessary cleanup work, and then return to Visual dBASE, but it will be easy enough to change this for individual applications, as you'll see later.

For now, select Exit and then click on the object properties Inspector's Events tab. You'll see two events: OnClick and OnHelp. These do just what you'd think. Type the following statement-type codeblock into the OnClick property:

```
{ ; QUIT }
```

Actually, this works fine, but it can be annoying to test. If you don't have a machine that loads Windows programs like greased lightning (and who does?) you might want to try:

```
{ ; ? "File/Exit Selected"}
```

That won't leave dBASE when you test it. You'll have to remember to change it after you test it, however.

Now you've gone through all of the key points to building menus. You might want to try some of your own menus, until you are fully comfortable with this tool. Once you have a SKELETON.MNU that you like, run it by pressing Ctrl+W to return to the Form Designer and press F2 or click the lightning icon to run your form. You'll see that your menu replaces Visual dBASE menu while your form is active.

If you don't like what you see, press Shift+F2 to return to the Form Designer. Get back to the Menu Designer by clicking the tool icon to the right of your Form's MenuFile property in the object properties Inspector. Continue this cycle until you have a SKELETON.MNU that you think will be a useful starting point for your systems.

Then exit to the Command window. From now on you can start work on an individual menu like this:

```
COPY FILE skeleton.mnu TO new_one.mnu
MODI MENU new_one
```

That will launch you straight into the Menu Designer without going through the Form Designer.

243

Help About Menu Objects

Of course, there's no reason to use the Menu Designer. You can write code the old-fashioned way, by hand. Let's take another look at the code we've generated, now that we've added some more bells and whistles. Listing 10-6 shows the new .MNU file.

Code Listing 10-6

```
* SKELETON.MNU -- skeleton menu file
* Copyright 1995, Martin L. Rinehart
*
** END HEADER -- do not remove this line*
* Generated on 06/23/95
*
Parameter FormObj
NEW SKELETONMENU(FormObj,"Root")
CLASS SKELETONMENU(FormObj,Name) OF MENUBAR(FormObj,Name)

   DEFINE MENU FILE OF THIS;
      PROPERTY;
         Text "&File"

         DEFINE MENU PRINT OF THIS.FILE;
            PROPERTY;
               Text "&Print"

         DEFINE MENU EXIT OF THIS.FILE;
            PROPERTY;
               Text "E&xit",;
               OnClick {; ? "File/Exit selected"}

   DEFINE MENU EDIT OF THIS;
      PROPERTY;
         Text "&Edit"

   DEFINE MENU WINDOW OF THIS;
      PROPERTY;
         Text "&Window"

   DEFINE MENU HELP OF THIS;
```

```
      PROPERTY;
         Text "&Help"

ENDCLASS

* end of SKELETON.MNU
```

The DEFINE syntax shown here is an alternate for the syntax we have been using. These two code pieces do the same thing:

```
parent_menu.option_1 = NEW Menu(parent_menu, "Option_1")
parent_menu.option_1.Text = "Option 1"

* same as:

DEFINE MENU option_1 OF parent_menu ;
  PROPERTY ;
     TEXT "Option 1"
```

In the New syntax, you write:

```
obj.prop1 = value1
obj.prop2 = . . .
```

In the DEFINE syntax, you write:

```
DEFINE . . . ;
  PROPERTY ;
     prop1 value1, ;
     prop2 value2, . . .
  CUSTOM ;
     cust_prop1 cust_val1, . . .
```

There is an advantage to using the DEFINE syntax. The properties that follow the PROPERTY keyword must be built-in object properties and those that follow the CUSTOM keyword must *not* be built-in properties. If you don't get this right, you've got a syntax error.

In the NEW syntax, you can assign built-in or custom properties when and where you wish. This means that when you use the NEW syntax, the compiler can't catch your typing mistakes, which it will do for you using the DEFINE syntax.

245

Learn Visual dBASE Programming

The downside to the DEFINE syntax is that it won't work at all for numbered properties, so you can't do something like:

```
* This isn't correct

FOR i = 101 TO 108
   DEFINE LINE i OF calendar . . .
NEXT i
```

With that syntax explained, here are some of the features SKELETON uses:

- Text is assigned to the Text property

- Ampersands (&) precede mnemonic keys in the Text property

- Accelerator keys are assigned to the Shortcut property

- Actions are assigned to the OnClick event property

- Nested menus are assigned to their parent menus

Of these five points, the first four are straightforward. The last can use a word of explanation.

The top level menu is a Menubar object. Each dropdown is attached to the Menubar. Additional nested menus may be attached to these Menu objects, in turn. (The Menubar object is new with Visual dBASE. In dBASE 5, the top level was a hidden Menu object called "Root", which was not shown anywhere.) In the class constructor, the Menubar is the object called This.

Studying the code generated by the Menu Designer will help you get a better understanding of another way that Visual dBASE object-oriented code can be written. On the other hand, totally ignoring the output code, except to add some intelligent comments in the Header and General sections, will still give you well-behaved, Windows-compatible menus.

Warning: Do not copy the style of the Two-Way Tools code when it comes to matters such as capitalization. The coding style does not follow any consistent conventions, unfortunately.

Creating Modal Windows

Now that you know how to build a menu system, let's create a complete application by hooking up a couple of modal windows to a parent window with an attached menu. A modal window refuses to let you proceed with anything else until you have responded to it.

I don't really like modal windows, and I hope you use them sparingly. They prevent you from changing your mind or doing something else that might be useful.

One of my favorites is the modal window (in a product I will not name) that tells me I can't write the file I've specified when I include a non-existent subdirectory in my path specification. If it weren't modal, I could use the File Manager or another tool to create the directory I need to write the file. But it's modal, so I can't fix the problem.

On the other hand, modal windows are so widely used for information and other messages that we'll not be doing our users a favor if we don't go along with the convention. So let's begin with a window that simply informs us that a feature is not yet available. Begin by launching the Form Designer with a new, blank form.

The Not_Yet Window

Make a habit of beginning your forms by setting the Form.Text property in the object properties Inspector. This text will appear in the title bar of your form. It's not visible when you work on your form, so it's pretty easy to forget if you don't get in the habit of starting here.

Tip: Set Form.Text first, or you'll end up with a lot of forms titled *Form*.

Adding the Text Object

After setting the title, we want a Text object to state something like:

```
The feature you just chose has not been implemented
in this release.
```

To do that, click on the Text object in the Controls palette and then drag a big outline on your form, as shown in Figure 10-17.

Once you've added a Text object, you are ready to put text into the object. By default, the text of the first Text object you add is *Text1*, which is probably not

247

Learn Visual dBASE Programming

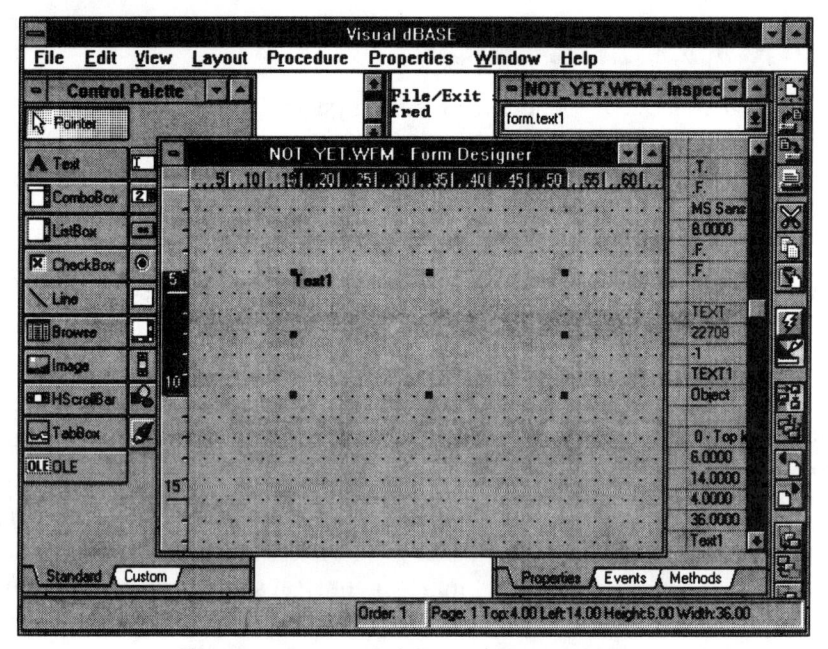

Figure 10-17: Adding a Text object

exactly what you want your form to say. (It's a good default choice, since it reminds you that you have something to do.)

Immediately after you add any control, it is selected, as you see by its outline on the form. With your new Text object selected (click on it, if it isn't selected) go back to the object properties Inspector's Properties tab and select the Text property. Type in a sentence, such as the one above, explaining that the feature isn't ready. As you type in the entryfield, your words will be copied onto the Form as shown in Figure 10-18.

With the text entered, return to the object properties Inspector and click the tool icon to the right of the Alignment property (it's one of the Position properties). Alignment defaults to top, left. We want Wrap Left (word-wrapped, left-justified). Click on Wrap Left and your Alignment will be set to 9.

With Wrap Left specified, go on to the FontSize property (it's one of the Font properties, of course). This has a tiny spinbutton to its right. Click the up arrow to grow your text. As you click the FontSize higher, your text size is adjusted accordingly and your text is rewrapped in the Text object. In Figure 10-19 you can see the size I chose.

248

Chapter 10   ***Beginning an Application***

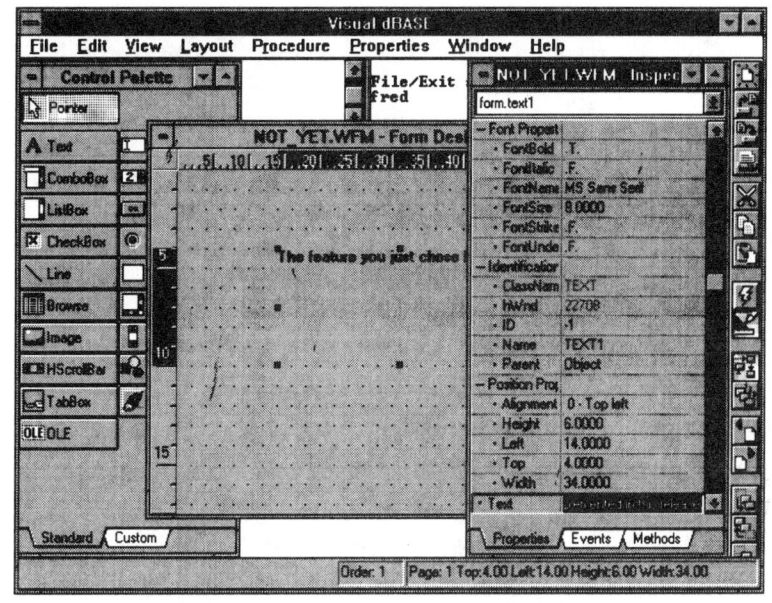

Figure 10-18: Entering the text

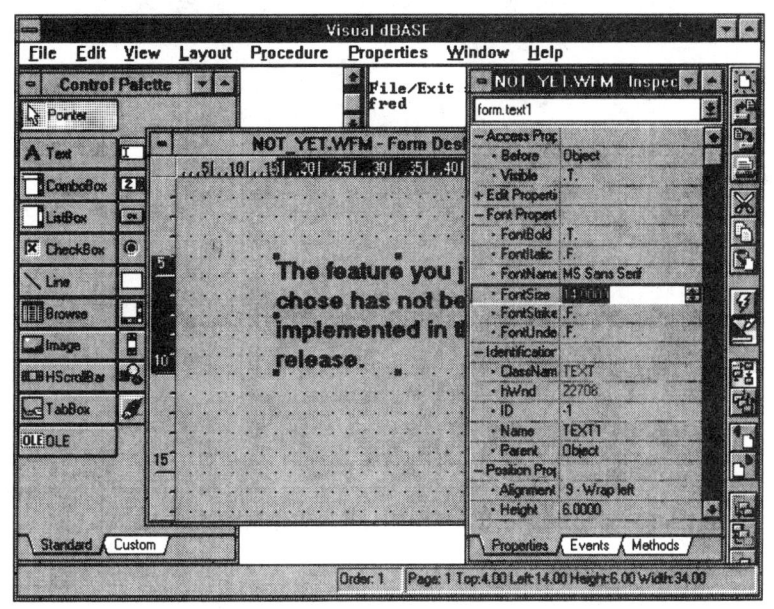

Figure 10-19: Growing bigger text

Learn Visual dBASE Programming

Go ahead and test the other Font properties, or anything else that interests you. I'm happy with the results so far, so I'm going on to add an OK pushbutton.

Adding an OK Pushbutton

All the NOT_YET Form needs now is an OK pushbutton, so the user can click it after seeing the message. Personally, I find these tremendously annoying. ("I just asked for the Framis option! I don't want a message telling me there's no Framis option. It's definitely *not* OK.") On the other hand, when every application behaves like every other application, I at least know what to expect.

Tip: If we improved everything we saw that could use a little improving, our programs would stop being Windows programs, which is definitely worse than an occasional annoyance. Go with the flow.

To add a pushbutton, click the pushbutton object on the Controls palette and drag its outline into place on your Form. Then, leaving the pushbutton selected, go back to the object properties Inspector and click on the Text property in the Properties tab. Enter "OK" as you see me doing in Figure 10-20.

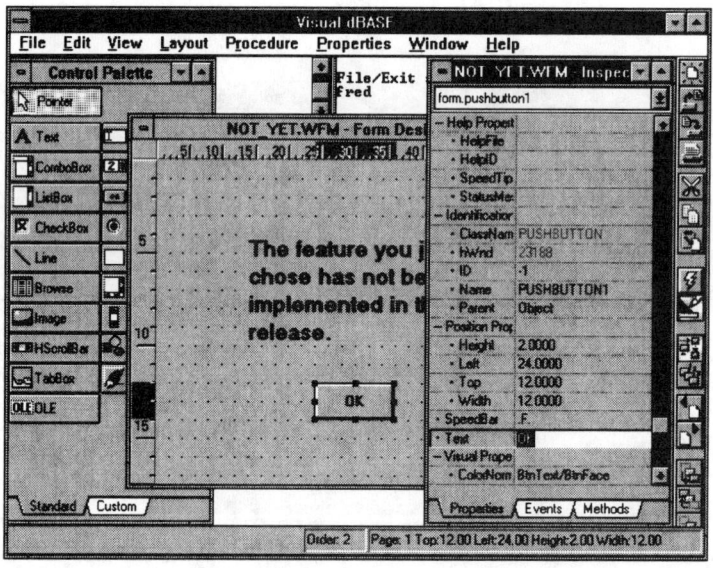

Figure 10-20: Entering OK for the Pushbutton's Text property

250

With that done, it's time to test the Form. Click the lightning icon or press F2 to run it. You should detect several bugs on your first try. Let's get after them one at a time.

For starters, the pushbutton is completely ineffective. It doesn't do anything. We want it to close the form. If you haven't done so, return to the Form Designer (press Shift+F2) and we'll fix that.

Enter this codeblock in the pushbutton's OnClick event property:

```
{ ;Form.Close() }
```

Warning: If you press F2 with the cursor still in the event or other property, your last change will be undone. Complete your entry with and Enter keypress and use the Up or Down arrow to move to the next property before you test your changes.

When you test this version (press F2) you'll see that the pushbutton promptly closes the form. Launch NOT_YET in the Form Designer again and we'll correct some bugs.

Did you notice that the form was not, in fact, modal? You could easily switch to another window. To change that, you have to set the MDI property (Multiple Document Interface, more specifically, an MDI child window) to False. MDI is one of the Window properties.

While you're at it, set all these False:

```
Maximize    .F.
MDI         .F.
Minimize    .F.
Sizeable    .F.
```

A proper modal form should not be able to be maximized, left open, turned into an icon or resized, which is what these properties do, respectively. When next you test your window, you'll see that you have a proper modal window that insists on an answer. You'll even see that the border has lost the double-line look that means you can resize it. My NOT_YET is shown in Figure 10-21.

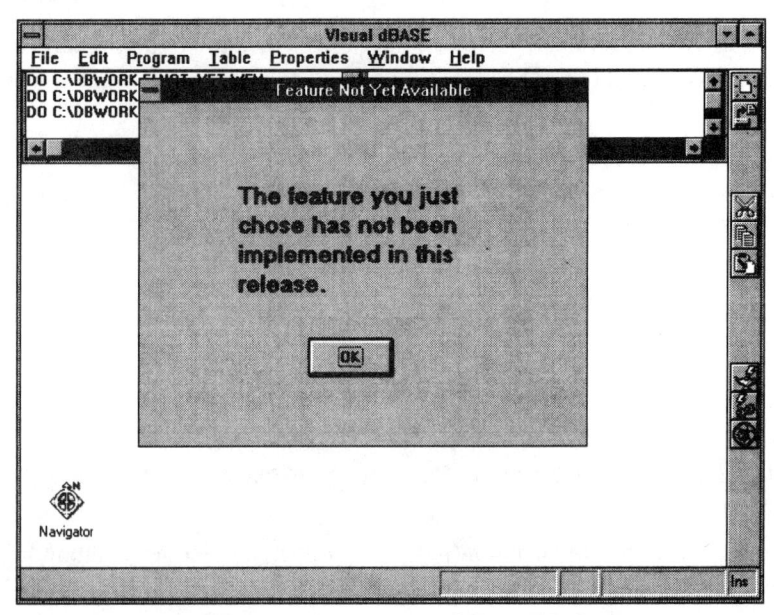

Figure 10-21: The completed NOT_YET form in action

It's time to call this a serviceable window. Listing 10-7 shows the program that the Form Designer wrote for me.

Code Listing 10-7

```
* NOT_YET.WFM -- Not Yet Implemented message form
* copyright 1995, Martin L. Rinehart
*
** END HEADER -- do not remove this line*
* Generated on 06/23/95
*
parameter bModal
local f
f = new NOT_YETFORM()
if (bModal)
   f.mdi = .F. && ensure not MDI
   f.ReadModal()
else
   f.Open()
endif
```

252

```
CLASS NOT_YETFORM OF FORM
   this.Left = 17.833
   this.Text = "Feature Not Yet Available"
   this.Top = 3.125
   this.Maximize = .F.
   this.Minimize = .F.
   this.Sizeable = .F.
   this.Height = 17.5
   this.Width = 63
   this.MDI = .F.

   DEFINE TEXT TEXT1 OF THIS;
      PROPERTY;
         Left 14,;
         Text "The feature you just chose has" + ;
            " not been implemented in this release.",;
         Top 4,;
         Alignment 9,;
         FontSize 14,;
         Border .F.,;
         Height 6,;
         Width 34

   DEFINE PUSHBUTTON PUSHBUTTON1 OF THIS;
      PROPERTY;
         Left 24,;
         Text "OK",;
         Top 12,;
         Default .T.,;
         OnClick {; form.close();},;
         Height 2,;
         Group .T.,;
         Width 12
ENDCLASS

* end of NOT_YET.WFM
```

(Actually, the Text1.Text property was written on a single line by the Form Designer. I wrapped it by hand to make it fit into this book.)

Learn Visual dBASE Programming

A Help/About Window

Now let's get on to building a Help/About message window. For this one, you'll be mostly on your own. First, launch a new form, SKEL_ABT.WFM, in the Form Designer.

Next, make it look like my SKEL_ABT, which you see in Figure 10-22. Try it yourself, and then check the following hints.

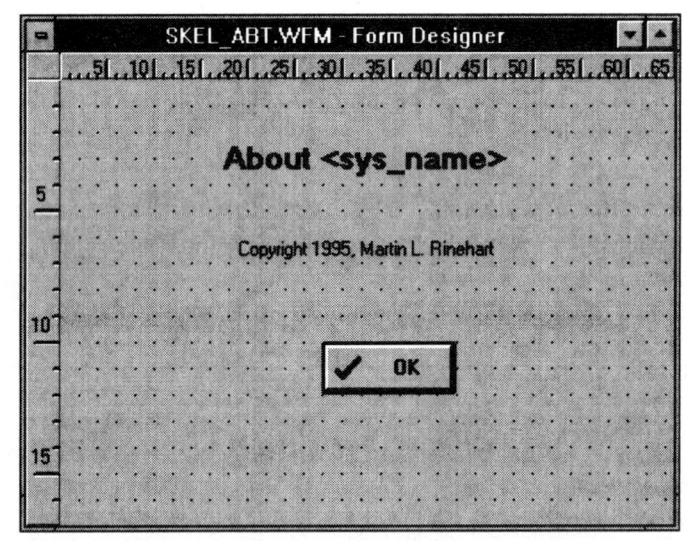

Figure 10-22: A skeleton About Form

Don't forget to set the Form's Text property, to get the title.

I've only used one font. The difference between the two text objects is the font's size and the FontBold property.

You can add that Borland-style check mark to your OK button through the Bitmap properties in the object properties Inspector, but it's a lot easier to just use the Custom tab of the Controls palette and choose the OK button.

Remember to make the Form none of the following: minimizable, maximizable, MDI and sizable. (Borland's name for the latter property is spelled Sizeable. Their spell-checker must have been in the shop for repairs that day.)

Add a Header and General section to comment your code.

For your reference (and so you can use your object properties Inspector to fix things up) Listing 10-8 is my complete program.

254

Code Listing 10-8

```
* SKEL_ABT.WFM -- a skeleton About modal dialog
* copyright 1995, Martin L. Rinehart
*
** END HEADER -- do not remove this line*
* Generated on 06/23/95
*
parameter bModal
local f
f = new SKEL_ABTFORM()
if (bModal)
   f.mdi = .F. && ensure not MDI
   f.ReadModal()
else
   f.Open()
endif
CLASS SKEL_ABTFORM OF FORM
   Set Procedure To C:\VISUALDB\SAMPLES\BUTTONS.CC additive
   this.Left = 12
   this.Text = "Skeleton About Dialog"
   this.Top = 3
   this.Maximize = .F.
   this.Minimize = .F.
   this.Sizeable = .F.
   this.Height = 17
   this.Width = 65
   this.MDI = .F.

   DEFINE TEXT TEXT1 OF THIS;
       PROPERTY;
         Left 15,;
         Text "About ys_name",;
         Top 2,;
         Alignment 4,;
         FontSize 14,;
         ColorNormal "N/W",;
         Border .F.,;
         Height 2,;
         Width 35

   DEFINE TEXT TEXT2 OF THIS;
       PROPERTY;
```

Learn Visual dBASE Programming

```
            Left 10,;
            Text "Copyright 1995, Martin L. Rinehart",;
            Top 6,;
            Alignment 4,;
            ColorNormal "N/W",;
            FontBold .F.,;
            Border .F.,;
            Height 1,;
            Width 45

    DEFINE OKBUTTON OKBUTTON1 OF THIS;
        PROPERTY;
            Left 28,;
            Top 10,;
            OnClick {; Form.Close()},;
            Height 2,;
            Group .T.,;
            Width 14

ENDCLASS

* end of SKEL_ABT.WFM
```

Tying It All Together

What we want now is to tie the SKELETON menu we built earlier to the NOT_YET and SKEL_ABT dialog boxes, so we'll have a complete application. (At least it will be complete in the sense that it responds to everything by telling you that it can't do anything.)

For this, launch SKELETON.WFM, a new Form, in the Form Designer. Start by setting the Text property to *Skeleton Application* or whatever you choose. Then go to the MenuFile property and click the tool icon that lets you select a menu. This time, you can select your SKELETON menu.

Modifying the Menu

Through the SKELETON menu, you'll access your NOT_YET and SKEL_ABT forms. Once SKELETON.MNU is inserted as the MenuFile property of your SKELETON Form, clicking the tool icon next to MenuFile will give you the opportunity to Design Current Menu, which you want to do.

Chapter 10 **Beginning an Application**

You want to attach codeblocks to the OnClick property of your Print, Edit and Window Menu objects that call the NOT_YET routine. They each have this form:

`{ ;DO not_yet.wfm }`

> **Tip:** The keyword DO isn't needed to run .PRG code anymore. It *is* still needed, however, to run code in files with other extensions, such as .MNUs.

After you attach those three codeblocks, attach one more to the About menu object that calls SKEL_ABT.WFM. When you are done, use Ctrl+W to save your work and return to the Form Designer. Your SKELETON.MNU should look like the one in Listing 10-9.

Code Listing 10-9

```
* SKELETON.MNU -- skeleton menu file
* Copyright 1995, Martin L. Rinehart
*
** END HEADER -- do not remove this line*
* Generated on 06/23/95
*
Parameter FormObj
NEW SKELETONMENU(FormObj,"Root")
CLASS SKELETONMENU(FormObj,Name) OF MENUBAR(FormObj,Name)


   DEFINE MENU FILE OF THIS;
      PROPERTY;
         Text "&File"

         DEFINE MENU PRINT OF THIS.FILE;
            PROPERTY;
               Text "&Print",,;
               OnClick {;do not_yet.wfm}

         DEFINE MENU EXIT OF THIS.FILE;
            PROPERTY;
               Text "E&xit",;
               OnClick {; ? "File/Exit selected"}

   DEFINE MENU EDIT OF THIS;
      PROPERTY;
         Text "&Edit",;
```

257

Learn Visual dBASE Programming

```
        OnClick {; do not_yet.wfm}

DEFINE MENU WINDOW OF THIS;
    PROPERTY;
       Text "&Window",;
       OnClick {;do not_yet.wfm}

DEFINE MENU HELP OF THIS;
    PROPERTY;
       Text "&Help"

       DEFINE MENU ABOUT OF THIS.HELP;
           PROPERTY;
              Text "&About",;
              OnClick {; do skel_abt.wfm}

ENDCLASS

* end of SKELETON.MNU
```

When you run an MDI window with a .MNU attached, that menu replaces the Visual dBASE menu. If you could run the child window maximized, you'd get a very nice approximation of a main program. (For the real thing, you can use the SHELL() function. Try HELP SHELL() in the Command window when you want to experiment.)

For a simple approximation of a maximized window, you can simply make your window big. It's not the same, but it's not much trouble, either. Use the Position properties. Set your Top and Left to 0, set Height to 25 and set Width to 100 or so. (You'll have to experiment to get it exact.)

Tip: Big Form objects are a nuisance in the Form Designer. You can't click on the object properties Inspector or the Controls palette. If you need to go large, do this last.

Now when you run your form, it will grow to nearly full-size and its menu will replace the Visual dBASE menu. As you click on the menu choices, you'll be politely informed that nothing has been implemented.

Don't forget to press Ctrl+A to test that accelerator we put in as the Shortcut for the Help/About choice. It should get you to the SKEL_ABT dialog box you built.

If you are having trouble, compare your SKELETON.WFM to the one in Listing 10-10.

Code Listing 10-10

```
* SKELETON.WFM -- a skeleton window application
* Copyright 1995, Martin L. Rinehart
*
** END HEADER -- do not remove this line*
* Generated on 06/23/95
*
parameter bModal
local f
f = new SKELETONFORM()
if (bModal)
   f.mdi = .F. && ensure not MDI
   f.ReadModal()
else
   f.Open()
endif
CLASS SKELETONFORM OF FORM
   this.MenuFile = "SKELETON.MNU"
   this.Left = 0
   this.Text = "Skeleton Application"
   this.Top = 0
   this.Sizeable = .F.
   this.Height = 24
   this.Width = 99

ENDCLASS

* end of SKELETON.WFM
```

In SKELETON, everything works just like a Windows application, except that it's totally useless. If your job is learning Visual dBASE programming (which I presume it is, at the moment) you're making excellent progress.

Summary

In this chapter we used the built-in tools, the Form Designer, and the Menu Designer.

You found out that the Menu Designer was well hidden, but we dug it out at last. You also discovered that its blank face didn't really tell you where to begin, but we overcame this hurdle, too.

Before we were done with the Menu Designer, you had learned to build a main menu, pulldown and cascading menus, add mnemonic and shortcut keys, and use menu separators. You built a real Windows menu system as a skeleton for future use.

Back in the Form Designer, you saw that this is a much less obtuse tool, and did some simple things. You created forms, added text and pushbutton objects, and turned your MDI child forms into non-MDI modal forms.

Finally, we tied two forms together with our SKELETON menu into a SKELETON application, that at least looks like a true Windows application.

In the next chapter, we'll leave the tools behind again and pick up where we left off with more object-oriented programming. This time we'll begin building a speed_bar class that can add a polished look to our Windows applications.

Chapter 11

Building a Speed_bar Class

In this chapter we're going to add a class that emulates one that Visual dBASE uses. This is a useful class that dBASE doesn't provide as a built-in.

When I first began programming Visual dBASE's predecessor, dBASE for Windows, I thought that the lack of classes such as a built-in Speedbar class was an oversight. Now I'm not so sure. After all, if there's no built-in Speedbar class, that's our opportunity to write a speed_bar class of our own and tailor it to our liking.

For example, I don't think that Borland's SpeedBar has big enough buttons. My speed_bar buttons are going to be a lot bigger than the ones in Borland's (and everybody else's) Windows applications.

In this chapter we'll start by building a small test program to develop a good-looking speed_bar button. This will lead us into programming in pixel-width increments, not just Visual dBASE Turpins.

When we finish our experiments, we'll go on to build the speed_bar class and a speed_bar_button class. The latter will involve an object that needs to inherit characteristics from two of the built-in classes, which is impossible in Visual dBASE — impossible, that is, unless you can simulate multiple inheritance, which we will do.

As you'll find in lots of Visual dBASE programming, the techniques may take a lot of explanation, but actually doing the program takes very few lines of code. Let's get to work on our speed_bar's buttons.

The Speed_bar's Button Object

For a very fast speed_bar, you can put a row of Pushbuttons across the top of your Form. The Pushbutton has a Speedbar property, which you can set to True. If True, the Pushbutton is removed from the tabbing order, so it behaves like a speedbar button.

I tried that for my very first speed_bar, but I wasn't happy with it. Among other problems, the image size is restricted to the size you used when you made the bitmap. I had become used to the Alignment features of the Image object for my bitmaps.

An Image can center a bitmap or locate the bitmap at the top-left corner. Either way, the image stays in its original size, and the Image shows as much as fits. Alternatively, you can use stretch alignment, which adjust the bitmaps size to fit the image area. This means that you have a lot of choices.

Importantly for me, you can paint a big picture. I find about 1 inch (2.5 centimeters) square is easier to work with than the finished button size. I use Microsoft Paint, which is about as good a program as you have a right to expect for free. MS Paint has trouble writing a bitmap file if you use any size much smaller than an inch square.

I experimented with various objects until I came up with a combination of the Image and the Rectangle.

Bouncing Rectangles

Let's start with a simple test program. I'll go right to the experiments I ran that worked. When I built my first speed_bar, of course, I tried lots of things that didn't work. As you go along, I hope that you'll try some experiments of your own, in addition to the ones that I talk about.

Begin by writing a simple T.PRG to launch a Form, like the one in Listing 11-1.

Code Listing 11-1

```
foo = new form()

foo.open()
```

This is in my all-lowercase, throwaway style. Next, add a Rectangle object somewhere in the Form. Mine is shown in Listing 11-2.

Code Listing 11-2

```
foo = new form()

rec = new rectangle(foo)

rec.top = 5; rec.left = 10
rec.height = 2; rec.width = 5

foo.open()
```

That will launch a form, like the one you see in Figure 11-1.

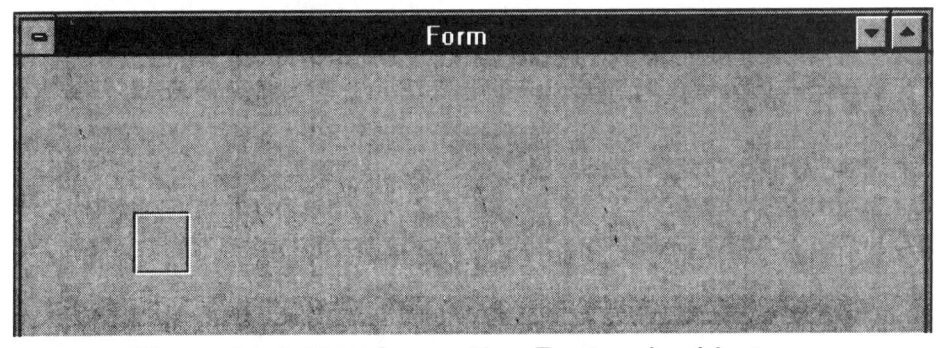

Figure 11-1: Test form with a Rectangle object

This Rectangle shows the default border. It uses BorderStyle 0, since we haven't changed that property. Next, change the border to raised, as you see in Listing 11-3.

Code Listing 11-3
```
foo = new form()

rec = new rectangle(foo)

rec.top = 5; rec.left = 10
rec.height = 2; rec.width = 5

rec.borderstyle = 1 && raised border

foo.open()
```

Figure 11-2 shows each of the three border styles: 0 is the default; 1 is raised and 2 is lowered.

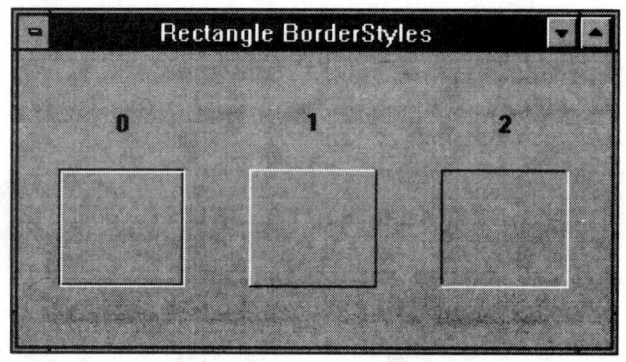

Figure 11-2: The three Rectangle border styles

Now let's make our rectangle pop up and down. We can use the OnLeftMouseDown and OnLeftMouseUp event properties to switch the BorderStyle property. Listing 11-4 shows my version.

Code Listing 11-4
```
foo = new form()
```

Chapter 11   *Building a Speed_bar Class*

```
rec = new rectangle(foo)

rec.top = 5; rec.left = 10
rec.height = 2; rec.width = 5

rec.borderstyle = 1 && raised border

rec.onleftmousedown = { ;this.borderstyle = 2 }
rec.onleftmouseup   = { ;this.borderstyle = 1 }

foo.open()
```

With those two codeblocks attached, your rectangle should look like it is popping up and down when you click on it. I really like this object-oriented code, don't you? Look at how little code you wrote to get this effect.

Adding the Image

What we need now is an Image object. You can use a paint program or the MS Paint utility to create bitmap images. For now, let's start with the collection of images that comes in the Visual dBASE resource file.

Launch your Form Designer on an empty form and then drag in the OK button from the Custom tab of the Controls palette. You'll see that this has Borland's check icon.

Grab an Image object from the Controls palette's Standard tab and you can get another copy of this check mark. The Image object is fourth from the bottom on the left. With the Image selected, click on the DataSource property in the object properties Inspector. When you click the tool icon to the right of the DataSource entryfield, you'll get the DataSource Property Builder dialog box, shown in Figure 11-3.

Figure 11-3: The DataSource Property Builder dialog box

265

The dropdown list on the left lets you choose one of the following:

- Resource
- Filename
- Binary

The Resource choice accesses the bitmaps in RESOURCE.DLL, a dynamic link library that is used by Visual dBASE for its own bitmaps. The Filename choice lets you use your own image files, such as .BMPs. The Binary choice lets you pick images from binary fields in your tables.

If you leave the Resource choice selected, clicking the tool icon in the Bitmap field launches the Visual dBASE Bitmaps dialog. This lets you scroll through the bitmaps in RESOURCE.DLL. The very first one, #20, is the check mark used in the OK button.

When you select Resource #20 as the DataSource for an Image object, you'll see that the default alignment is stretch: the image expands and contracts as you change the size of your Image object. If you stretch your OK button, you'll see that the check mark does not change size — it stays a little check mark even on a very big button.

For an Image, Alignment is one of the Position properties in the object properties Inspector. Try TopLeft and Center and you'll see the check mark revert to its original size. With KeepAspectStretch the image's aspect ratio (vertical to horizontal) is maintained as you stretch. (Only the first three options were available in dBASE 5.0 for Windows.)

Let's add this check mark on top of our test button.

Pixel-Sized Coordinates

To add the Image on top of the Rectangle, we'll need pixel-sized coordinates, which Visual dBASE does not appear to provide. Let me explain why.

I'm going to get ahead of myself here. Bear with me. In Visual dBASE, click on a speedbar button and watch the image very carefully. You may need to place the tip of a sharp pencil on the corner of the image to convince yourself that this is true.

What you see is that the image shifts down and to the left as you push the button. This is a subtle little shift, but without it the *clicky* feel of that button is really diminished. We're going to want the same sort of wiggle in our button's walk, or we'll have a distinctly inferior speed_bar.

As it turns out, when we wiggle our image, it will work better with the rectangle border to shift it a pixel or two toward the top-left corner as it's pressed. But as you'll see when we get there, this little shift makes a big difference in the feel of the button.

Of course, our pixel-sized coordinates will come in very handy whenever we need to do detailed drawing work on any object, so let's bite the bullet and figure out where the pixel coordinates are hidden.

This is going to take a bit of what we used to proudly call *hacking*. Try entering the program in Listing 11-5 as T2.PRG. (Save T.PRG for later. We'll get back to it when we finish this little hack.)

Code Listing 11-5

```
#define VPIX_SIZE   (1/5)
#define HPIX_SIZE   (1/2)

#define HORIZONTAL 100
#define VERTICAL   200

foo = new form()

for i = 1 to 20 step 2

  fh = new line(foo)
  fv = new line(foo)

  fh.top =  2 + i*VPIX_SIZE
  fv.top =  2 + i*VPIX_SIZE

  fh.left =  5 + i*HPIX_SIZE
  fv.left =  5 + i*HPIX_SIZE

  fh.bottom = fh.top
  fv.bottom = fv.top + 10

  fh.right = fh.left + 25
  fv.right = fv.left

endfor
```

Learn Visual dBASE Programming

```
foo.open()
```

That program won't do very much that's useful. Here's a trick. Change all these:

```
fh
```

change to:

```
foo[i+HORIZONTAL]
```

And then change these:

```
fv
```

change to:

```
foo[i+VERTICAL]
```

This will expand your program to the working one shown in Listing 11-6.

Code Listing 11-6

```
#define VPIX_SIZE   (1/5)
#define HPIX_SIZE   (1/2)

#define HORIZONTAL 100
#define VERTICAL   200

foo = new form()

for i = 1 to 20 step 2

   foo[i+HORIZONTAL] = new line(foo)
   foo[i+VERTICAL  ] = new line(foo)

   foo[i+HORIZONTAL].top =  2 + i*VPIX_SIZE
   foo[i+VERTICAL  ].top =  2 + i*VPIX_SIZE

   foo[i+HORIZONTAL].left =  5 + i*HPIX_SIZE
   foo[i+VERTICAL  ].left =  5 + i*HPIX_SIZE

   foo[i+HORIZONTAL].bottom = foo[i+HORIZONTAL].top
```

```
    foo[i+VERTICAL  ].bottom = foo[i+VERTICAL  ].top + 10

    foo[i+HORIZONTAL].right = foo[i+HORIZONTAL].left + 25
    foo[i+VERTICAL  ].right = foo[i+VERTICAL  ].left

endfor

foo.open()
```

This program draws a pattern of horizontal and vertical lines, meeting at their corners. Figure 11-4 shows my result.

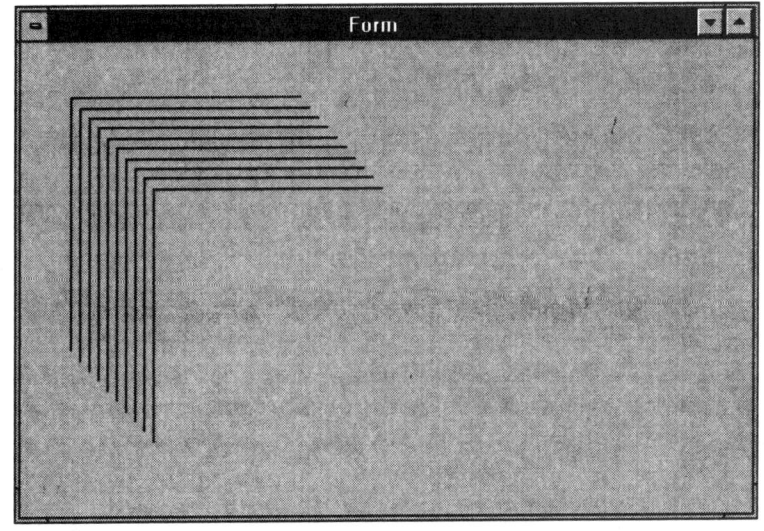

Figure 11-4: HPIX_SIZE = 1/2; VPIX_SIZE = 1/5

Since the program steps from 2 to 20 by 2's, what we need to do now is adjust the #define_ sizes until our lines appear separated by exactly one pixel. (The default line width is 1 pixel.)

It's time for you to take a break from this text and experiment with the VPIX_SIZE and HPIX_SIZE values on your own. You want your display to look like Figure 11-5.

Did you get it on your own? The answer is that each character is 16 pixels tall and 6 pixels wide. You can change these dimensions by changing your Form's

Learn Visual dBASE Programming

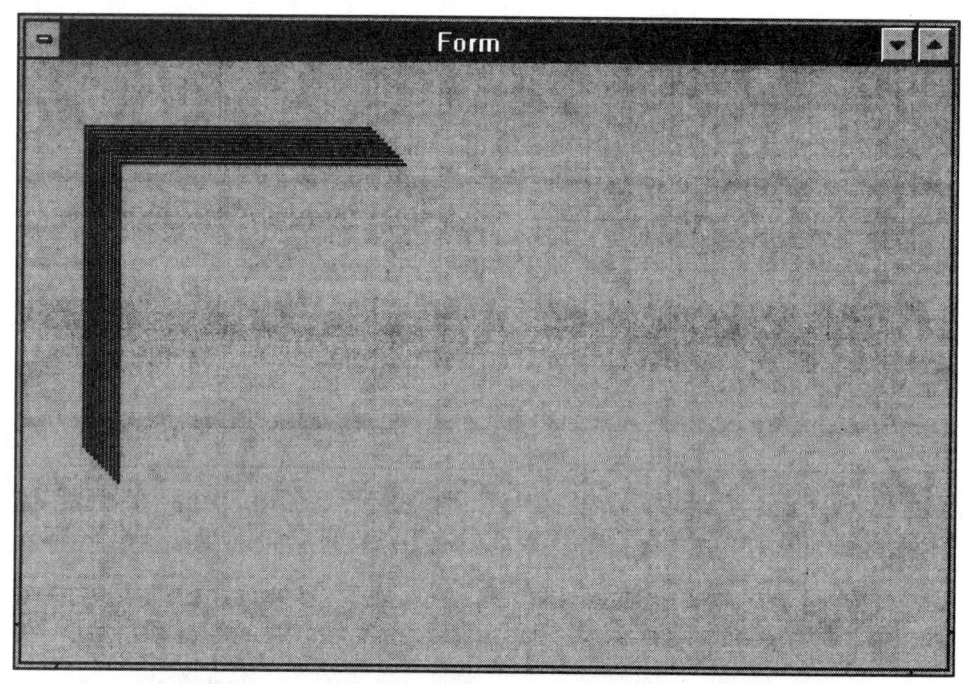

Figure 11-5: Correctly hacked pixel sizes

ScaleFont property. These dimensions are based on the default 8 point bold MS Sans Serif.

Tip: Never change the ScaleFont properties. The only effect changing these has is to change the pixel-size equivalent values, so you'll have to go back to hacking to figure these out, and very probably not come up with a scale font where these values are integral multiples of a pixel-width size.

Now that we know how to convert character (or Turpin) coordinates into pixels, we can get back to placing our Image objects on Rectangles.

Drawing the Image

Let's grab resource #20, the check mark, since it's handy. We'll lay this carefully on top of our Rectangle. I'm going to shrink it so that there's an even border of Rectangle object showing around the Image. So we can play with it, I'll *#define* a constant called SHRINKAGE, which we can adjust.

We need to make the Image's Top and Left SHRINKAGE pixels greater than the Rectangle's Top and Left. The Height and Width will be twice SHRINKAGE

270

Chapter 11 Building a Speed_bar Class

pixels less than the Rectangle's, to allow for borders on both sides and at top and bottom.

Listing 11-7 shows the new T.PRG.

Code Listing 11-7

```
#define VPIX_SIZE (1/16)
#define HPIX_SIZE (1/6)

#define SHRINKAGE (3)

foo = new form()

rec = new rectangle(foo)

rec.top = 5; rec.left = 10
rec.height = 2; rec.width = 5

rec.borderstyle = 1 && raised border

rec.onleftmousedown = { ;this.borderstyle = 2 }
rec.onleftmouseup   = { ;this.borderstyle = 1 }

img = new image(foo)
img.top    = rec.top    + SHRINKAGE*VPIX_SIZE
img.left   = rec.left   + SHRINKAGE*HPIX_SIZE
img.height = rec.height - 2*SHRINKAGE*VPIX_SIZE
img.width  = rec.width  - 2*SHRINKAGE*HPIX_SIZE

img.DataSource = "RESOURCE #20"

foo.open()
```

With these additions, when you press Ctrl+D you'll get an Image neatly placed on your Rectangle. If you click on the Image, nothing will happen. Place your mouse pointer very carefully in the Rectangle but outside the Image — when you click there you'll see the Rectangle flip its border as it did before.

This shows that the object that responds to the mouse events is the one on top, when you stack up more than one object. We'll have to switch our click handling from the Rectangle to the Image.

Learn Visual dBASE Programming

Warning: A bug in version 0.638 (use "? version(0)" in the Command window to get your version number) causes the Rectangle not to be reliably redrawn when you change the BorderStyle property. If your Rectangle is not "clicking" set its Visible property to False, then change the BorderStyle and then set its Visible back to True.

Putting a Wiggle in the Image

When you clicked your Rectangle, you probably were a bit disappointed in the overall effect. It just didn't look as good as it did before you added the Image. The fix is to make the Image wiggle.

First, we'll need to get the Image to respond to the mouse events. While we're at it, we'll need to switch to calling subroutines instead of just using codeblocks, since we'll be adding more code to them.

Listing 11-8 shows the new program.

Code Listing 11-8

```
#define VPIX_SIZE (1/16)
#define HPIX_SIZE (1/6)

#define SHRINKAGE (3)

foo = new form()

rec = new rectangle(foo, 'rec')

rec.top = 5; rec.left = 10
rec.height = 2; rec.width = 5

rec.borderstyle = 1 && raised border

* rec.onleftmousedown = { ;this.borderstyle = 2 }
* rec.onleftmouseup   = { ;this.borderstyle = 1 }

img = new image(foo)
img.top    = rec.top    + SHRINKAGE*VPIX_SIZE
img.left   = rec.left   + SHRINKAGE*HPIX_SIZE
img.height = rec.height - 2*SHRINKAGE*VPIX_SIZE
img.width  = rec.width  - 2*SHRINKAGE*HPIX_SIZE

img.DataSource = "RESOURCE #20"
```

Chapter 11 — Building a Speed_bar Class

```
img.onleftmousedown = pusher
img.onleftmouseup   = popper

foo.open()

proc pusher

form.rec.borderstyle = 2

proc popper

form.rec.borderstyle = 1
```

Go through these changes carefully, so you don't miss any. The first is critical: I've added the name rec as the second parameter to the NEW Rectangle() constructor. The second parameter is the name of the property that is used to attach it to the parent form.

Then remember to comment out (or delete) the assignments to the Rectangle's OnLeftMouseDown and Up event handlers. They are replaced by assignments to the same properties in the Image object. These events get assigned subroutine references (Borland calls them function pointers) to the two new methods.

In both pusher() and popper(), the This handler is the Image that is responding to the event. Where This is available, the Form automatic variable is also available. It is, of course, the form to which This is attached. The Form.rec property is the rectangle.

You see the reason for adding the name rec to the constructor call — it lets us refer to the rectangle here as a named property. (If you don't assign a name, the first rectangle attached to a form is named "Rectangle1." We could have used this name just as we're using rec but that isn't a very general technique.

With that background, we're ready to wiggle the rectangle. Let's start by emulating the Borland wiggle, and going down and to the right. Add a #define so you can change this easily, as you see in Listing 11-9.

Code Listing 11-9

```
#define VPIX_SIZE (1/16)
#define HPIX_SIZE (1/6)
```

273

Learn Visual dBASE Programming

```
#define SHRINKAGE (3)

#define WIGGLE    (1)

foo = new form()

...

foo.open()

proc pusher

form.rec.borderstyle = 2
This.Top  = This.Top  + WIGGLE*VPIX_SIZE
This.Left = This.Left + WIGGLE*HPIX_SIZE


proc popper

form.rec.borderstyle = 1
This.Top  = This.Top  - WIGGLE*VPIX_SIZE
This.Left = This.Left - WIGGLE*HPIX_SIZE
```

Tip: When you add these lines, make sure that you are always thinking about horizontal and vertical directions. You have to keep reminding yourself that all vertical adjustments are in VPIX_SIZE units and horizontal adjustments are based on HPIX_SIZE units.

When you run this program, you'll see lots of movement. Unfortunately, it's terribly uncoordinated. It looks like the rectangle's going north and the image is going south.

To sort this out, adjust WIGGLE to -1. You'll see the image and the rectangle start to work together as a team.

Beginning to like it? Let's try some fine-tuning adjustments and talk about a bug. Click your button down and hold the mouse button depressed. Slide the mousepointer off the button and then release. You've left the Form's button depressed and the Image moved.

Click on the Image again and you will see the up/down motion return, but the Image will be moved one pixel up and left. Get it back by reversing the strategy:

move the mousepointer off the button, click and hold the mouse button, and then release it over the Form's button.

You've just lifted the Form's button and slid the Image one pixel down and right. Try it again. I think that this button looks best if you start the Image 3 pixels from the top and left, but only one pixel from the bottom right.

Another experiment you'll want to try is changing the WIGGLE constant to -2, which also looks good. Today I'm more impressed with the more subtle 1-pixel movement, but I change my mind on that almost as often as I try it. Whichever you decide, modify the code in the next section appropriately.

The Speed_bar

We've dug into Visual dBASE and discovered how to make a very good speed_bar button. Now we need to put together the speed_bar itself. As always, start with design.

Designing the Speed_bar

The speed_bar almost designs itself. First, there's the bar. This is a rectangular area, a Rectangle object should do the trick, which contains a row of speed_bar buttons.

The speed_bar button is another object that we can derive from a custom class. The obvious design choice is whether the speed_bar_button class should be derived from the Rectangle or the Image class. I'm going to derive it from the Rectangle, since the coordinates of the Rectangle are the coordinates of the speed_bar_button object. You could make it work the other way, too.

The next question is how we attach speed_bar_button objects to the speed_bar object. There are lots of ways to do this. I do it by creating an array of speed_bar_button objects and passing that array to the speed_bar's constructor. As you'll see, this leads to a mainline program that is reasonably direct about its work.

The last design problem is devising a way to build the class that makes testing an integral part of programming. My strategy is to build the visible components first, starting with the speed_bar and then the speed_bar_buttons. After they're staring at us from a Form, we can work on bringing them to life.

Building the Visual Components

To start, we'll need a .PRG file with a Form object. Listing 11-10 shows my first version of SPEEDBAR.PRG, which started as a copy of SKELETON.PRG and then had some additions that I already knew we'd need.

Code Listing 11-10

```
* SPEEDBAR.PRG -- A speed_bar class with speed_bar_buttons
* copyright 1995, Martin L. Rinehart

foo = NEW Form('Test Speed_bar')
sb = NEW speed_bar(??)

CLASS speed_bar(??) OF Rectangle(??)

ENDCLASS


CLASS speed_bar_button(??) OF Rectangle(??)

ENDCLASS

* end of SPEEDBAR.PRG
```

Obviously, Visual dBASE won't handle ?? as a valid argument or parameter. In fact, it will fail to compile, which is exactly what I want — it's a personal reminder that there's more work to do to get this started. Let's go ahead and do this work.

Launching the Speed_bar

I'm not sure about all the parameters that I'll want to use, but I know that the Form will be needed. Let's start there and that will give us a Form object that we can actually launch. Also, I'll add the height of the speed_bar as a parameter. Listing 11-11 shows these additions.

Code Listing 11-11

```
* SPEEDBAR.PRG -- A speed_bar class with speed_bar_buttons
* copyright 1995, Martin L. Rinehart

foo = NEW Form('Test Speed_bar')
```

Chapter 11   Building a Speed_bar Class

```
sb = NEW speed_bar(foo, 3)

foo.Open()

CLASS speed_bar(frm, hgt) OF Rectangle(frm, 'speed_bar')
   This.Height = hgt
   This.Width  = frm.Width

ENDCLASS


CLASS speed_bar_button(frm) OF Rectangle(frm)

ENDCLASS

* end of SPEEDBAR.PRG
```

    That works when you press Ctrl+D, but it doesn't look perfect. What I think it needs is to have the speed_bar carefully offset within the Form, by just 1 or 2 pixels. So let's add pixel coordinates, and add a surround-width constant. Listing 11-12 shows these improvements.

Code Listing 11-12

```
* SPEEDBAR.PRG -- A speed_bar class with speed_bar_buttons
* copyright 1995, Martin L. Rinehart

#define VPIX_SIZE (1/16)
#define HPIX_SIZE (1/6)

#define SB_SRRND_WIDTH (2)

foo = NEW Form('Test Speed_bar')
sb  = NEW speed_bar(foo, 3)

foo.Open()

CLASS speed_bar(frm, hgt) OF Rectangle(frm, 'speed_bar')
   This.Top    = SB_SRRND_WIDTH*VPIX_SIZE
   This.Left   = SB_SRRND_WIDTH*HPIX_SIZE
   This.Height = hgt
   This.Width  = frm.Width - 2*SB_SRRND_WIDTH*HPIX_SIZE
```

Learn Visual dBASE Programming

```
ENDCLASS

CLASS speed_bar_button(frm) OF Rectangle(frm)

ENDCLASS

* end of SPEEDBAR.PRG
```

This version draws the rectangle you see in Figure 11-6.

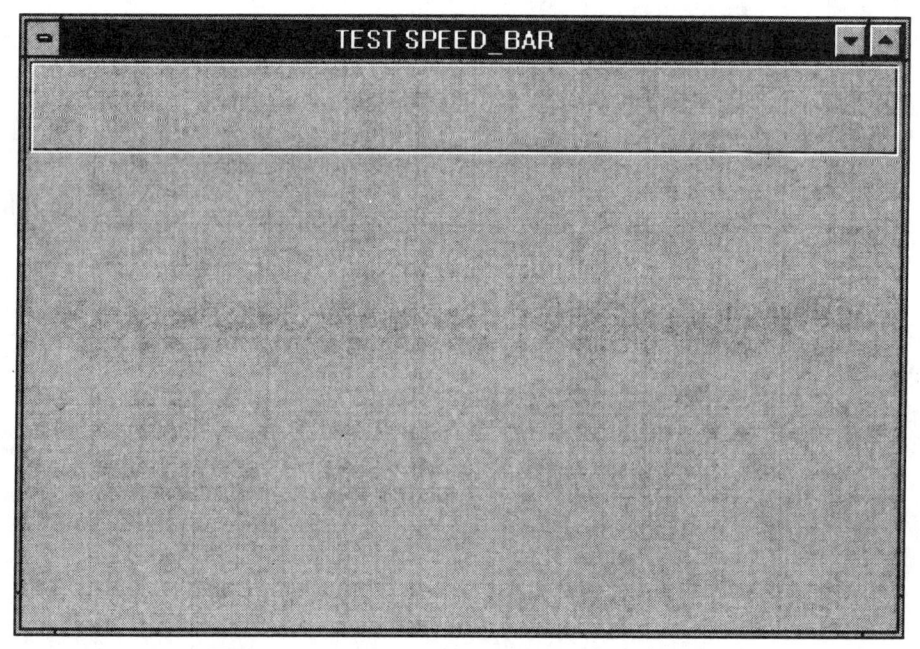

Figure 11-6: A well-drawn speed_bar

Isn't it nice to see your very precise spacing specifications handsomely drawn on the screen? Try different SB_SRRND_WIDTH values to see what you like best.

Tip: You will never get perfect pixel-width placement of every element on your Forms. The fractions 1/6 and 1/16 are only approximately represented as binary fractions. Don't worry about it. No one will ever notice, except you and me.

Have you wondered why all my #define constants are placed in parentheses? It's a habit that you should copy. In most cases, it won't matter, but sometimes it's vital. Consider these:

```
#define RIGHT  (2/10)
#define WRONG  2/10

? RIGHT^2    && returns 0.04
? WRONG^2    && returns 0.02
```

That constant WRONG looks a lot like 0.2, doesn't it? When you square it, you expect to get 0.04, don't you? Well, that's not what happens. The #define mechanism is a text substitution system that is called before the line is compiled. Here's what happens:

```
#define WRONG  2/10
? WRONG^2

   && preprocessor converts this to:

? 2/10^2
```

The effects of this bug source can get very subtle and devilishly difficult to trace when you start using #define to create inline functions.

Tip: The compiler strips extra parentheses so they are essentially free. Always parenthesize #define constants and you will never be wrong.

With the speedbar itself drawn, let's get on to drawing the buttons.

Drawing the Buttons

Visual dBASE provides two models for ways we could implement our speed_bar. We could place the buttons in fixed locations, as the Visual dBASE SpeedBar does, or we could let the speed_bar object decide the spacing, based on its size.

The problem with the first approach is that the button placement doesn't change when you change Visual dBASE SpeedBar. For example, if you follow my advice about the vertical SpeedBar position, you've chopped off some of the SpeedBar buttons. With most Visual dBASE tools active, there is space for the buttons that you chop off.

279

Learn Visual dBASE Programming

I think the menus are a better model to follow. When you add Menu objects through the Menu Designer, you don't specify their position. That happens automatically based on their number. I'd like our speed_bar to do the same things for our speed_bar_button objects.

I don't implement it here, but if you like, you could have a speed_bar_button separator property which, if true, said that this isn't a real button — you just want some spacing (to divide the buttons into logical groups). This would serve the same purpose as the menu separators you add to pulldown menus.

Using the menu convention means that we don't need to worry about the size or position of the buttons — we'll have the speed_bar class take care of that. We do have to figure out where to go for each button's bitmap, and we have to have an action for each button to perform.

In addition to properly initializing each button, we'll have to add some constants and logic to the speed_bar class to position the buttons. Listing 11-13 shows these additions to SPEEDBAR.PRG.

Code Listing 11-13

```
* SPEEDBAR.PRG -- A speed_bar class with speed_bar_buttons
* copyright 1995, Martin L. Rinehart                              2
                                                                  3
#define VPIX_SIZE (1/16)                                          4
#define HPIX_SIZE (1/6)                                           5
                                                                  6
#define SB_SRRND_WIDTH (2)                                        7
#define BTN_SRRND_WIDTH (2)                                       8
                                                                  9
foo = NEW Form('Test Speed_bar')                                 10
sb = NEW speed_bar(foo, 3)                                       11
                                                                 12
* Build an array of speed_bar_button objects                     13
   btns = NEW Object()                                           14
                                                                 15
   btns[1] = NEW speed_bar_button( ;                             16
      foo, "RESOURCE #20", { ;? 'OK'} )                          17
   btns[2] = NEW speed_bar_button( ;                             18
      foo, "RESOURCE #24", { ;? 'Not allowed!'} )                19
   btns[3] = NEW speed_bar_button( ;                             20
      foo, "RESOURCE #28", { ;? 'Wrong'} )                       21
   btns[4] = NEW speed_bar_button( ;                             22
      foo, "RESOURCE #32", { ;? 'Help!'} )                       23
```

```
          btns.number = 4                                          24
                                                                   25
                                                                   26
sb.attach(btns)                                                    27
                                                                   28
foo.Open()                                                         29
                                                                   30
CLASS speed_bar(frm, hgt) OF Rectangle(frm, 'speed_bar')           31
   This.Top    = SB_SRRND_WIDTH*VPIX_SIZE                          32
   This.Left   = SB_SRRND_WIDTH*HPIX_SIZE                          33
   This.Height = hgt                                               34
   This.Width  = frm.Width - 2*SB_SRRND_WIDTH*HPIX_SIZE            35
                                                                   36
   PROCEDURE attach(b_list)                                        37
   LOCAL i                                                         38
                                                                   39
   This.button_array = b_list                                      40
                                                                   41
   FOR i = 1 TO b_list.number                                      42
      b_list[i].Left = i*8                                         43
      b_list[i].picture.Left = i*8 + .5                            44
   ENDFOR                                                          45
                                                                   46
ENDCLASS                                                           47
                                                                   48
                                                                   49
CLASS speed_bar_button(frm, img, act) OF Rectangle(frm)            50
   This.picture = NEW Image(frm)                                   51
   This.picture.DataSource = img                                   52
   This.picture.button = This                                      53
   This.action = act                                               54
                                                                   55
ENDCLASS                                                           56
                                                                   57
* end of SPEEDBAR.PRG                                              58
```

    I've made far more changes here than I like to make at one pass, and I've still left a lot of work to do. At line 8 I added a new constant that will be the space between the speed_bar rectangle and the outside edges of the buttons.

    At lines 13 through 27 I've created an array of speed_bar_button objects. The array itself is a plain Object object (line 14), since these are very handy for quick arrays. Lines 16 through 23 assign new speed_bar_button objects to the elements of this array.

I've chosen four convenient bitmap resources. They are the check mark, the international don't sign (slash in a circle), Borland's *X* from their Cancel button, and the question mark. For the moment, the actions are codeblocks that will appropriately comment in the Command window's results pane.

Line 25 assigns another property, number, to the array Object. This is used by the attach() method that is called at line 27. Attach() is defined as a speed_bar class method at lines 37 through 45. For the moment, it assigns the speed_bar_button array to the new button_array property of the speed_bar object and then assigns Left properties to each button's Rectangle and Image objects.

The assignments to Left are just enough to get the result, shown in Figure 11-7. It shows that we've added rectangles with images, but have more work to do to get them properly positioned.

Figure 11-7 shows that we've got all the right pieces coming together, which is one good thing to say about it. Now let's go after the exact positioning of the Rectangles and Images that make a speed_bar_button look good.

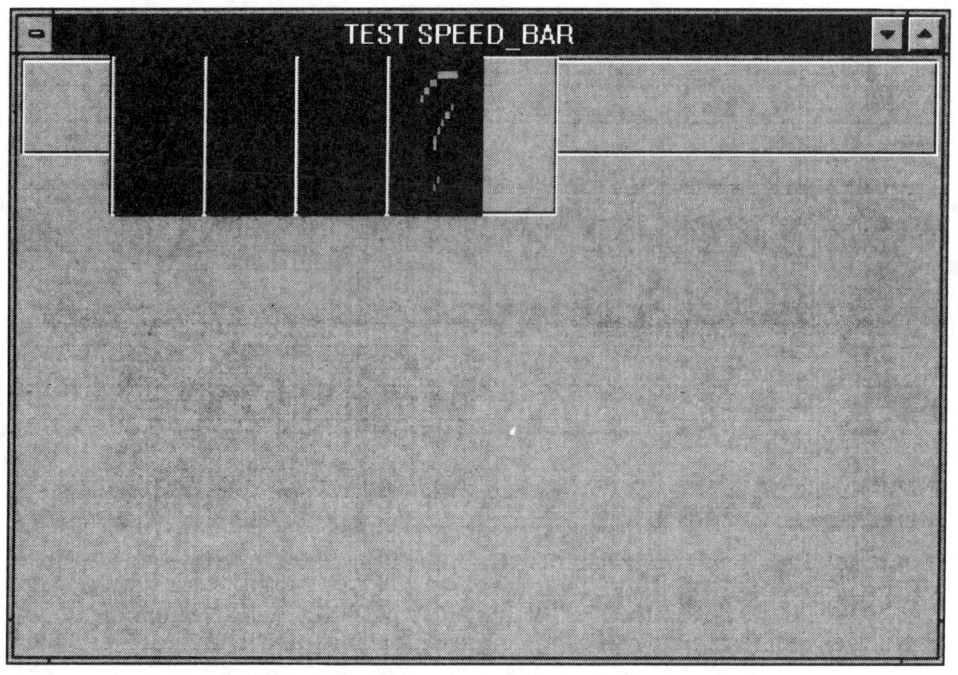

Figure 11-7: The parts are there, but out of place

Chapter 11   Building a Speed_bar Class

The positioning code all goes in the attach() method. My improved attach() is shown in Listing 11-14.

Code Listing 11-14

```
PROCEDURE attach(b_list)                                    37
LOCAL i                                                     38
                                                            39
This.button_array = b_list                                  40
                                                            41
LOCAL tp, lft, ht, wd                                       42
                                                            43
tp  = This.Top + BTN_SRRND_WIDTH*VPIX_SIZE                  44
lft = This.Left + BTN_SRRND_WIDTH*HPIX_SIZE                 45
ht  = This.Height - 2*BTN_SRRND_WIDTH*VPIX_SIZE             46
wd  = This.Height * (HPIX_SIZE/VPIX_SIZE)                   47
                                                            48
FOR i = 1 TO b_list.number                                  49
   b_list[i].Top    = tp                                    50
   b_list[i].Left   = lft                                   51
   b_list[i].Height = ht                                    52
   b_list[i].Width  = wd                                    53
                                                            54
   b_list[i].picture.Top  = b_list[i].Top  + 3*VPIX_SIZE
   b_list[i].picture.Left = b_list[i].Left + 3*HPIX_SIZE
                                                            57
   b_list[i].picture.Height = b_list[i].Height - ;          58
                              4*VPIX_SIZE                   59
   b_list[i].picture.Width  = b_list[i].Width - ;           60
                              4*HPIX_SIZE                   61
                                                            62
   lft = lft + wd + BTN_SRRND_WIDTH*HPIX_SIZE               63
                                                            64
ENDFOR                                                      65
                                                            66
ENDCLASS                                                    67
```

I added four new locals to hold top, left, height and width values. The top and left are calculated by adding the button surround width to the top and left of the speed_bar Rectangle. The height is calculated by subtracting twice the surround size from the speed_bar Rectangle's Height.

283

Learn Visual dBASE Programming

The non-obvious calculation is the width. I want a square button, so I want to set the width equal to the height. Since we're giving Visual dBASE dimensions in Turpins, you have to adjust for the ratio of horizontal to vertical Turpin size.

The actual assignments to the speed_bar_button Rectangle objects (lines 50 through 53) and to the speed_bar_button Image objects (lines 55 through 61) are straightforward. I'm offsetting the Images 3 pixels from the top and left, inside a Rectangle that's 4 pixels bigger than the Image. (This was what I liked best from the experimenting we did with buttons in the previous section.)

Finally (line 63), I increment the left-side variable by the width of the button plus the surround width, in pixels. All this gives the much better-looking appearance shown in Figure 11-8.

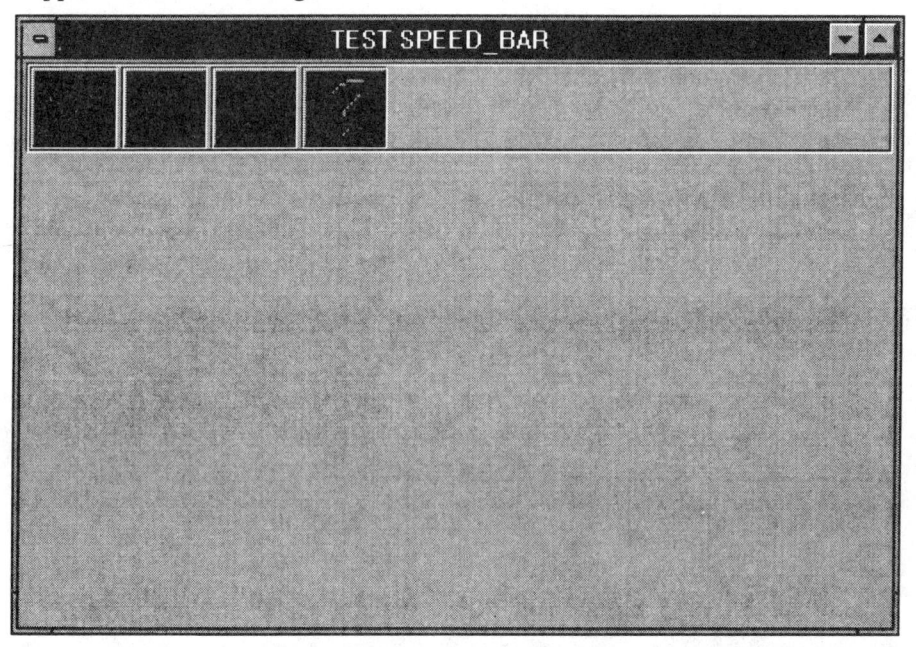

Figure 11-8: Rectangles and Images organized correctly

At this point, I think it looks pretty good, but I'm wondering how many of those pixel-width adjustments will have to be adjusted some more. There's no way of telling, until we get this speed_bar to come to life, with real buttons that we can actually click. That's the next job.

Bringing the Speed_bar to Life

Our speed_bar_buttons need to learn how to click and to respond to the clicks. Let's begin by getting the buttons to pop in and out as our test button did.

Clicking the Buttons

As we did with our test button, we want to flip the Rectangle's border and wiggle the Image. Let's start with the border. First, we'll have to add to the attach() method. It has to tell every speed_bar_button's underlying Rectangle that its Border-Style should be raised (1). It also needs to attach function pointers to push down and pop up routines to each Image's appropriate mouse event handlers.

Listing 11-15 shows these changes, along with the two event handlers.

Code Listing 11-15

```
  PROCEDURE attach(b_list)                                37
  ...
    lft = lft + wd + BTN_SRRND_WIDTH*HPIX_SIZE            63
                                                          64
    b_list[i].BorderStyle = 1 && raised                   65
                                                          66
    b_list[i].picture.OnLeftMouseDown = class::pusher     67
    b_list[i].picture.OnLeftMouseUp   = class::popper     68
                                                          69
  ENDFOR                                                  70
                                                          71
  * end of speed_bar::attach                              72
                                                          73
                                                          74
  PROCEDURE pusher                                        75
  This.button.BorderStyle = 2 && lowered                  76
                                                          77
  * end of speed_bar::pusher                              78
                                                          79
                                                          80
  PROCEDURE popper                                        81
  This.button.BorderStyle = 1 && raised                   82
                                                          83
```

```
    * end of speed_bar::popper                                      84
                                                                    85
                                                                    86
ENDCLASS                                                            87
```

In the constructor function for the speed_bar_button class there's one somewhat strange line:

```
This.picture.button = This
```

As in any constructor, This is a reference to the object being built. That's a speed_bar_button object, which inherits from the Rectangle class. Its picture property is a reference to the Image object that you use for the image on the button. The button property is a custom property that we are attaching. It is assigned a reference to This, which is the underlying speed_bar_button object.

That all seems pretty circular when you do it in the speed_bar_button's constructor. Sort of like handing yourself your own business card so you'll know how to get in touch with yourself.

It's in the handlers for the OnLeftMouseDown and OnLeftMouseUp events that it makes sense. The object that receives those events is the Image (the picture property of the speed_bar_button object). The Image doesn't know that there is a rectangle lying underneath it.

Visual dBASE doesn't understand what we are doing, either. We could refer to This or Form in the event handler. This would be the Image and Form would be the underlying form, of course. What we need to do is manipulate the correct speed_bar_button's border.

The speed_bar_button inherited all the characteristics of the Rectangle class, so it has a BorderStyle property. In the pusher() and popper() routines, you manipulate that property. What really happened in the speed_bar_button constructor was that the Rectangle handed the Image its business card. The Image filed that card (attached it as the button property) so that it knows how to contact the Rectangle.

Some object-oriented languages permit what is called multiple inheritance — an object that inherits from two or more classes at once. Visual dBASE supports single inheritance only. You can't do this:

```
* This isn't supported:

CLASS sb_button OF Rectangle AND Image
```

The technique I've used here gets around this seeming limitation. You inherit from one class (call it the senior class) and attach an object of the other class (call it the junior class). The only problem is that the senior class knows about the attached junior object, but the junior object doesn't know about the senior object. You have to tell the junior object who its senior object is.

After this explanation, this line shouldn't look quite as strange — it's just the senior object handing the junior object its business card:

```
This.picture.button = This
```

In general terms, the senior constructor has to hand junior its card:

```
* code in Senior's constructor

This.junior.senior = This
```

Only if junior has senior's card can junior correctly identify senior. If junior responds to an event in the event handler, This is junior. So you refer to senior by the attached business card:

```
* code in an event Junior traps

This.senior.??? && whatever senior needs to do
```

Tip: Remember that attachments are one-way references. Attaching one object reference to another lets the attacher know about the attachee, but not the other way around. You have to tell the attachee about the attacher explicitly.

If you understand all this, you're well on your way to being a complete, object-oriented programmer. If it's still fuzzy, rest assured that we'll be using it often throughout the rest of this chapter and the remainder of this book.

Let's get on to the other part of clicking the button, wiggling the Image. A little trick makes this dead simple. I attach an extra pair of properties, home_top and home_left, when I first position the Images. These just save the originally calculated positions. With that done, wiggling by a pixel is dead simple. Listing 11-16 shows the additions.

287

Code Listing 11-16

```
      b_list[i].picture.Top  = b_list[i].Top  + 3*VPIX_SIZE
      b_list[i].picture.Left = b_list[i].Left + 3*HPIX_SIZE
                                                                57
      b_list[i].picture.home_top  = b_list[i].picture.Top
      b_list[i].picture.home_left = b_list[i].picture.Left
                                                                60
      b_list[i].picture.Height = b_list[i].Height - ;           61
                   4*VPIX_SIZE                                  62
...
                                                                74
* end of speed_bar::attach                                      75
                                                                76
                                                                77
PROCEDURE pusher                                                78
This.button.BorderStyle = 2 && lowered                          79
                                                                80
This.Top  = This.home_top  - VPIX_SIZE                          81
This.Left = This.home_left - HPIX_SIZE                          82
                                                                83
* end of speed_bar::pusher                                      84
                                                                85
                                                                86
PROCEDURE popper                                                87
This.button.BorderStyle = 1 && raised                           88
                                                                89
This.Top  = This.home_top                                       90
This.Left = This.home_left                                      91
                                                                92
* end of speed_bar::popper                                      93
                                                                94
                                                                95
ENDCLASS                                                        96
```

Lines 58 and 59 simply copy the top and left coordinates into the home_top and home_left properties, for safe keeping. Then lines 81 and 82 move the Image, and lines 90 and 91 put it back where it was. You'll see that doing it this way is helpful when we get on to bug-fixing.

Chapter 11   *Building a Speed_bar Class*

Acting on the Clicks

Ready to respond to the button clicks? You'll be happy to see that exactly one line of code will do the trick. Listing 11-17 shows how.

Code Listing 11-17

```
PROCEDURE pusher                                              78
This.button.BorderStyle = 2 && lowered                        79
                                                              80
This.Top  = This.home_top  - VPIX_SIZE                        81
This.Left = This.home_left - HPIX_SIZE                        82
                                                              83
This.button.action()                                          84
                                                              85
* end of speed_bar::pusher                                    86
```

Again, in an event handled by the Image, This is the Image object. This.button is the senior speed_bar_button object. The action method property of the speed_bar_button is the codeblock or subroutine reference (function pointer) that we passed as an argument to the speed_bar_button's constructor.

Got it? Mine's now clicking along quite happily. Don't worry that the actions this speedbar is performing are trivial comments in the Command window's results pane. Since the actions are parameters passed to the constructor, they could just as easily be launching an ever-to-date simulation of the entire universe.

If you're not perfectly happy with the spacing, don't worry about it. We'll clean this up in Chapter 12.

The Full Listing

If you have the disk, the full listing is L11-17.PRG. For those who do not, it is given here.

Code Listing 11-18

```
* SPEEDBAR.PRG -- A speed_bar class with speed_bar_buttons
* copyright 1995, Martin L. Rinehart

#define VPIX_SIZE (1/16)
#define HPIX_SIZE (1/6)

#define SB_SRRND_WIDTH (2)
```

289

```
#define BTN_SRRND_WIDTH (2)

foo = NEW Form('Test Speed_bar')
sb  = NEW speed_bar(foo, 3)

* Build an array of speed_bar_button objects
   btns = NEW Object()

   btns[1] = NEW speed_bar_button( ;
      foo, "RESOURCE #20", { ;? 'OK'} )
   btns[2] = NEW speed_bar_button( ;
      foo, "RESOURCE #24", { ;? 'Not allowed!'} )
   btns[3] = NEW speed_bar_button( ;
      foo, "RESOURCE #28", { ;? 'Wrong'} )
   btns[4] = NEW speed_bar_button( ;
      foo, "RESOURCE #32", { ;? 'Help!'} )

   btns.number = 4

sb.attach(btns)

foo.Open()

CLASS speed_bar(frm, hgt) OF Rectangle(frm, 'speed_bar')
   This.Top    = SB_SRRND_WIDTH*VPIX_SIZE
   This.Left   = SB_SRRND_WIDTH*HPIX_SIZE
   This.Height = hgt
   This.Width  = frm.Width - 2*SB_SRRND_WIDTH*HPIX_SIZE

   PROCEDURE attach(b_list)
   LOCAL i

   This.button_array = b_list

   LOCAL tp, lft, ht, wd

   tp  = This.Top + BTN_SRRND_WIDTH*VPIX_SIZE
   lft = This.Left + BTN_SRRND_WIDTH*HPIX_SIZE
   ht  = This.Height - 2*BTN_SRRND_WIDTH*VPIX_SIZE
   wd  = This.Height * (HPIX_SIZE/VPIX_SIZE)

   FOR i = 1 TO b_list.number
```

```
    b_list[i].Top    = tp
    b_list[i].Left   = lft
    b_list[i].Height = ht
    b_list[i].Width  = wd

    b_list[i].picture.Top  = b_list[i].Top  + 3*VPIX_SIZE
    b_list[i].picture.Left = b_list[i].Left + 3*HPIX_SIZE

    b_list[i].picture.home_top  = b_list[i].picture.Top
    b_list[i].picture.home_left = b_list[i].picture.Left

    b_list[i].picture.Height = b_list[i].Height - ;
                               4*VPIX_SIZE
    b_list[i].picture.Width  = b_list[i].Width - ;
                               4*HPIX_SIZE

    lft = lft + wd + BTN_SRRND_WIDTH*HPIX_SIZE

    b_list[i].BorderStyle = 1 && raised

    b_list[i].picture.OnLeftMouseDown = class::pusher
    b_list[i].picture.OnLeftMouseUp   = class::popper

ENDFOR

* end of speed_bar::attach


PROCEDURE pusher
This.button.BorderStyle = 2 && lowered

This.Top  = This.home_top  - VPIX_SIZE
This.Left = This.home_left - HPIX_SIZE

This.button.action()

* end of speed_bar::pusher


PROCEDURE popper
This.button.BorderStyle = 1 && raised
```

```
      This.Top  = This.home_top
      This.Left = This.home_left

   * end of speed_bar::popper

ENDCLASS


CLASS speed_bar_button(frm, img, act) OF Rectangle(frm)
   This.picture = NEW Image(frm)
   This.picture.DataSource = img
   This.picture.button = This
   This.action = act

ENDCLASS

* end of SPEEDBAR.PRG
```

Summary

In this chapter, you've done some typical programming. We started with a test program to develop our techniques. The techniques we worked out in our testing included coding in pixel-width increments and combining the Rectangle object with an Image object to make an effective speedbar button.

After we developed the techniques, we went on to build the speed_bar class. This was more interesting since it used a supporting speed_bar_button class. The speed_bar class is built from an array of speed_bar_button objects. We used an Object class object to hold the array of speed_bar_buttons.

The speed_bar_button object itself used simulated multiple inheritance, since it needed to be partly a Rectangle object and partly an Image object. We had the Rectangle object attach an Image object as one of its properties.

Attaching one object to another provides a one-way link between the objects. We add an explicit reference from one object to the other to get the link in the second direction, which we needed to use to handle mouse events.

In Chapter 12, we'll polish our speed_bar class.

Chapter 12

Polishing the Speed_bar

In this chapter we're going to add the finishing touches to our speed_bar class.

There are a number of places where we'll look at the precise spacing of items on the speed_bar and make pixel-sized adjustments. Presumably, all your systems (or all the more important ones) will use speed_bars, so it makes sense to spend a little time being more than normally fussy about this.

After we get it looking just right, we'll go on to the status messages. If all our buttons were self-explanatory, we wouldn't need status messages. Have you ever seen a Windows program where all the buttons were self-explanatory? I haven't. The status messages provide a helpful second place to look.

Finally, we'll make it impossible for the user to leave our buttons punched in, or otherwise destroy our good work. As you'll see, we'll be assigning cleanup responsibilities in key places, to make sure we never have these problems.

There are three items that you have to handle before you can claim that your speed_bar class is fully professional. First, there are those spacings. Once those are done we've got to look at the status bar — a good speedbar tells you what a button click will do before you click the button. Finally, there's the subtle problem of the user not completing the button click over the button.

The Speed_bar's Spacing

In a lot of GUI programming work, you'll be using programmer's tools but your work is really more art than engineering. In this section, you'll see a very good example of that.

Except for the problems of not always being released by the user, our buttons work correctly. They go in when pressed and they pop back out on release. But experience tells me that if we spent a few minutes looking at their appearance, we could come up with a significant improvement.

The Surround Width

I think my buttons are too big, relative to their enclosing speedbar rectangle. Let's try to shrink them, to let the three-dimensional look of those underlying rectangle borders stand out a little more.

Luckily for us, we've used a #define constant to set this surround width. All we have to do is change the constant, recompile, and run the code. In Visual dBASE that just means changing the constant and pressing Ctrl+D.

Try 4 pixels instead of 2, as shown in Listing 12-1.

Code Listing 12-1

```
* SPEEDBAR.PRG -- A speed_bar class with speed_bar_buttons
* copyright 1995, Martin L. Rinehart

#define VPIX_SIZE (1/16)
#define HPIX_SIZE (1/6)
```

Chapter 12   *Polishing the Speed_bar*

```
#define SB_SRRND_WIDTH (2)
#define BTN_SRRND_WIDTH (4)

foo = NEW Form('Test Speed_bar')
```

Run the version with the 4-pixel surround and what do you think? For me, it looks like we've gone too far. I backed off and tried 3 pixels, as shown in Listing 12-2.

Code Listing 12-2

```
* SPEEDBAR.PRG -- A speed_bar class with speed_bar_buttons
* copyright 1995, Martin L. Rinehart

#define VPIX_SIZE (1/16)
#define HPIX_SIZE (1/6)

#define SB_SRRND_WIDTH (2)
#define BTN_SRRND_WIDTH (3)

foo = NEW Form('Test Speed_bar')
```

I like the 3-pixel surround best. I wouldn't be surprised if some of you chose different sizes, due to differences in equipment and maybe just to tastes. Go ahead and do it your way; I'm not Rembrandt.

By the way, there was a reason for my jumping from two pixels to four, even though I rather guessed that three would be best. If we had gone to three first, we would have seen an improvement. We wouldn't have stopped, though. We would have gone on to check four to see if that was better still, or was too much.

Tip: By going toward what you guess is the opposite extreme (in this case, from two to four) you can actually save time. You tune these things toward the middle. You only know if you're in the middle by looking at both sides.

With the surround looking better, let's consider the image within the button. As you recall, I used an uneven offset based on my experimental results. I offset the images three pixels left and down leaving only one pixel on the right and bottom. To my eye, the images we've got are a little big.

Listing 12-3 isn't really a code listing. I've substituted question marks for the constants in the code. Experiment by substituting values of your own for these

295

Learn Visual dBASE Programming

question marks. Return to this text when you've tested both too much and too little and think you have the best solution.

Code Listing 12-3

```
FOR i = 1 TO b_list.number
   b_list[i].Top    = tp
   b_list[i].Left   = lft
   b_list[i].Height = ht
   b_list[i].Width  = wd

   b_list[i].picture.Top  = b_list[i].Top  + ?*VPIX_SIZE
   b_list[i].picture.Left = b_list[i].Left + ?*HPIX_SIZE

   b_list[i].picture.home_top  = b_list[i].picture.Top
   b_list[i].picture.home_left = b_list[i].picture.Left

   b_list[i].picture.Height = b_list[i].Height - ;
                              ?*VPIX_SIZE
   b_list[i].picture.Width  = b_list[i].Width - ;
                              ?*HPIX_SIZE

   lft = lft + wd + BTN_SRRND_WIDTH*HPIX_SIZE
```

Tip: While you're studying your buttons' appearance, don't forget that you can press one down and leave it down, by sliding the mousepointer off the **speed_bar** button before you release your mouse button.

When I finished experimenting with mine, I decided on a 3-pixel offset in a 5-pixel frame. If you decided on something else your answer is right, too, as long as it looks good to you.

The code for my final version is in Listing 12-4.

Code Listing 12-4

```
FOR i = 1 TO b_list.number
   b_list[i].Top    = tp
   b_list[i].Left   = lft
   b_list[i].Height = ht
   b_list[i].Width  = wd

   b_list[i].picture.Top  = b_list[i].Top  + 3*VPIX_SIZE
   b_list[i].picture.Left = b_list[i].Left + 3*HPIX_SIZE
```

Chapter 12   **Polishing the Speed_bar**

```
b_list[i].picture.home_top  = b_list[i].picture.Top
b_list[i].picture.home_left = b_list[i].picture.Left

b_list[i].picture.Height = b_list[i].Height -';
                           5*VPIX_SIZE
b_list[i].picture.Width  = b_list[i].Width - ;
                           5*HPIX_SIZE

lft = lft + wd + BTN_SRRND_WIDTH*HPIX_SIZE
```

    My speedbar now looks like the one in Figure 12-1. Yours should be as attractive as you can make it. Remember, you'll create lots of speedbars from this class.

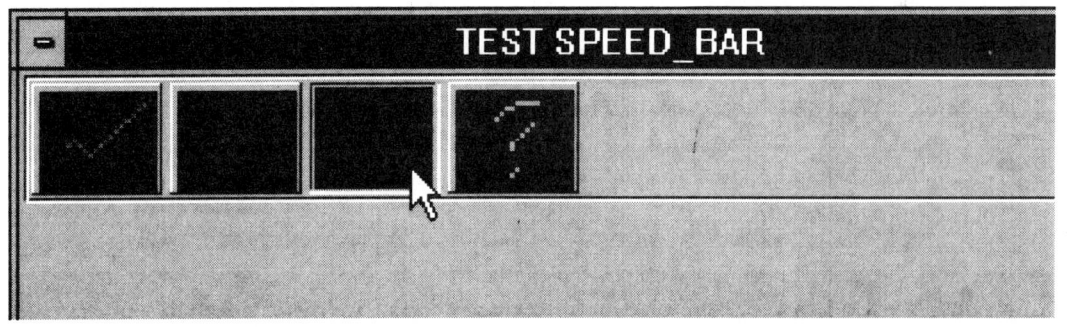

Figure 12-1: The speed_bar button spacing adjusted

Status Messages for Speed_bar Buttons

    Some products, such as Visual dBASE, show you explanatory status messages as you move your mousepointer over the speedbar buttons. This is a good design — it tells you what will happen before you press the button.

    Other products, such as Word for Windows, display a status message only when you click the button — which may or may not be soon enough. Still others don't even have the decency to display any message at all. You just guess, click, and hope that nothing too bad happens.

    Our speed_bar class is now in the latter, ill-mannered category. I want to switch it into the first, best category. Fortunately, that's almost trivially simple to achieve.

297

You set the status bar message with a SET MESSAGE TO command. Try this in the Command window:

```
SET MESSAGE TO "Hello, from the status bar!"
```

When you try that, you'll see that you have set the status bar message. The only trick is to be sure that the status bar message is blanked out after the mousepointer leaves the speedbar button.

Setting the Status Message

To set messages when the mousepointer moves over the buttons, we'll need messages, of course. So the first order of business is to add another parameter, stat_msg, to the speed_bar_button constructor, and to add another argument to each of the four calls, providing appropriate messages for the buttons.

The next bit of coding needed is to save those parameters as properties of the Image objects. Then you can add an OnMouseMove event handler to the Image which will set the status message. The added code to do all this is probably shorter than this explanation. It's shown in Listing 12-5.

Code Listing 12-5

```
* SPEEDBAR.PRG -- A speed_bar class with speed_bar_buttons
...
* Build an array of speed_bar_button objects
  btns = NEW Object()

  btns[1] = NEW speed_bar_button( ;
     foo, "RESOURCE #20", { ;? 'OK'}, ;
     "Click here if it's all OK" )
  btns[2] = NEW speed_bar_button( ;
     foo, "RESOURCE #24", { ;? 'Not allowed!'}, ;
     "Clicks here are not allowed" )
  btns[3] = NEW speed_bar_button( ;
     foo, "RESOURCE #28", { ;? 'Wrong'}, ;
     "Click here if your choice was wrong" )
  btns[4] = NEW speed_bar_button( ;
     foo, "RESOURCE #32", { ;? 'Help!'}, ;
     "Click here to get help" )
```

```
   btns.number = 4
...

CLASS speed_bar_button(frm, img, act, stat_msg) ;
   OF Rectangle(frm)

   This.picture = NEW Image(frm)
   This.picture.DataSource = img
   This.picture.button = This
   This.action = act
   This.picture.message = stat_msg
   This.picture.OnMouseMove = ;
      { ; SET MESSAGE TO This.message }

ENDCLASS

* end of SPEEDBAR.PRG
```

Listing 12-5 shows that you add a fourth argument to each call for a NEW speed_bar_button, the status message to display for that button.

In the constructor you add one assignment statement to attach that parameter to the new property, message. A second assignment builds a code block that displays the message and attaches it to the OnMouseMove event.

When you run this code, your new status messages are displayed as your mousepointer moves over the buttons.

Unsetting the Status Message

As simple as setting the status messages was, you know there's got to be a catch. There is. You've not provided for unsetting the status messages when the cursor leaves the object. Worse, there's no event property like OnMouseOuttaHere that you could use to make this job simple.

Some objects, like Forms and Entryfields have an OnGotFocus property and they have OnLostFocus properties which you could use to reset the status message when the user goes elsewhere. You could clear the status message with:

```
SET STATUS TO
```

You could also have saved the old message and restored it, with code like this:

299

```
PROCEDURE OnGotFocus
This.save_message = SET('message')
...

PROCEDURE OnLostFocus
SET MESSAGE TO This.save_message
...
```

The latter approach is more thorough, but not needed here. We can blank out the speedbar since any other control (or speedbar button or whatever) that wants to display a message will do so when the mousepointer moves over it.

Now we just need a routine that fires whenever the mousepointer is not over a speedbar button, and lets us do our clean up. Fortunately, that routine is precisely what we need to write for the next problem, making sure that buttons aren't left down.

For this one problem, we'll just wait patiently for the solution to appear when we solve the next problem.

Goof-Proofing the Speed_bar

As I've already pointed out, you press the speed_bar_button down by pressing the left mouse button. It pops up when you release the left mouse button, which the user just might not do. You can press the mouse button, depressing the speed_bar_button, and then slide the mousepointer off the speed_bar_button, holding the mouse button down. This leaves the speed_bar_button pressed, which is not what we want.

We want the speed_bar_button to pop up on the first to occur of:

- The mouse button being released

- The mousepointer leaving the speed_bar_button

What we'll need is a clean_up() method. We can call this method whenever the mousepointer moves over either the Form or the speed_bar. The clean_up() method will have two jobs:

- Clearing the status message

- Raising any lowered button

Calling a Clean_up() Method

The clean_up() method would be simpler if it were not for one problem it shares with many others: you want different objects to call it. Since we want to call it when the mousepointer moves over either the speed_bar or the Form, that implies that we want to attach it to the OnMouseMove() event properties of both the speed_bar and the Form. As with any event handler, the This variable will be the calling object.

If the clean_up() method is called from the Form, This.speed_bar will be the speed_bar object. Alternatively, if the call is made from the speed_bar itself, This is the speed_bar. We'll use the identification property ClassName to find out who is who and a local variable to refer to the speed_bar object in the clean_up() method.

Listing 12-6 shows the speed_bar class with an added clean_up() method attached to the OnMouseMove() properties of the Form and the speed_bar. The actual method doesn't do any cleaning up — it reports on who is calling from the Command window.

Code Listing 12-6

```
CLASS speed_bar(frm, hgt) OF Rectangle(frm, 'speed_bar')    
  This.Top    = SB_SRRND_WIDTH*VPIX_SIZE                    36
  This.Left   = SB_SRRND_WIDTH*HPIX_SIZE                    37
  This.Height = hgt                                         38
  This.Width  = frm.Width - 2*SB_SRRND_WIDTH*HPIX_SIZE      39
                                                            40
  This.OnMouseMove = Class::clean_up                        41
  Form.OnMouseMove = Class::clean_up                        42
                                                            43
                                                            44
  PROCEDURE clean_up                                        45
  ? 'Called from a '+This.ClassName                         46
                                                            47
  * end of speed_bar::clean_up                              48
                                                            49
                                                            50
  PROCEDURE attach(b_list)                                  51
```

Learn Visual dBASE Programming

Enter these changes and press Ctrl+D in your own SPEEDBAR.PRG. Be aware that when the form is launched, you'll get hundreds of reported calls from the clean_up() method. Wiggle your mouse very minutely around the border between the speed_bar and the Form and you'll see exactly what's happening.

When you get this working, it's time to get the clean_up() routine to actually do its job. Once it gets a proper object reference to the speed_bar, its job is fairly simple. Listing 12-7 shows my code.

Code Listing 12-7

```
PROCEDURE clean_up                                          45
                                                            46
SET MESSAGE TO                                              47
                                                            48
* Can be called from speed_bar or parent form               49
  LOCAL spd_bar                                             50
  IF This.Classname = "SPEED_BAR"                           51
     spd_bar = This                                         52
  ELSE                                                      53
     spd_bar = This.speed_bar                               54
  ENDIF                                                     55
                                                            56
LOCAL btn, i                                                57
FOR i = 1 TO spd_bar.button_array.number                    58
   btn = spd_bar.button_array[i]                            59
   IF btn.picture.Top <> btn.picture.home_top               60
      btn.picture.Top = btn.picture.home_top                61
      btn.picture.Left = btn.picture.home_left              62
      btn.BorderStyle = 1 && raised                         63
      EXIT                                                  64
   ENDIF                                                    65
ENDFOR                                                      66
                                                            67
* end of speed_bar::clean_up                                68
```

The first line turns off any status bar message. The next block creates a LOCAL variable, spd_bar, and assigns either This or This.speed_bar to it, depending on whether the calling routine is the speed_bar or the Form.

The loop code, lines 57 through 66, looks at each button in turn, checking to see that the home_top is the same as the top. If it finds one where this is not true it resets the Top and Left properties of the Image and the BorderStyle of the Rectangle.

When you enter and run this code, your speed_bar should be polite about turning off the status messages, and it should be almost impossible for you to leave a button pressed.

Yes, I said "almost" impossible. If you really want to leave a button pressed, press the mouse button down when the mousepointer is over one of your speed_bar buttons. Without releasing the mouse button, flick your wrist so that your mousepointer goes across the Form's title bar very quickly.

With a little practice, and perhaps by dragging your form lower down to give your wrist more flicking room, you should be able to get the buttons left down. The reason this happens is that the Microsoft mouse drivers poll the hardware 50 times a second. If your mouse movement is very fast, chances are pretty good that you won't trigger an OnMouseMove event before your mousepointer leaves the form.

Warning: Don't count on all events that you or your user make happen being reflected in calls to your event handlers. Mouse actions can beat the computer.

To be more thorough about trapping every event that happens, you could also call the clean_up() method from other places, such as in your Form's OnGotFocus() and OnLostFocus() event properties. But I'm not going to do this with my class, for a couple of reasons.

First, when the mousepointer returns to the form, it will probably trigger a clean_up() call with the first mouse movement. So your buttons will get lifted anyway.

More importantly, we're doing something very bad, here. We've let one of our classes attach its own idea of what needs to be done to our Form. Specifically, the speed_bar object attaches its own code to the OnMouseMove() property of the form. What would happen if another class or the Form itself wanted to use this property?

Of course, that's a rhetorical question. If more than one class attached its own handlers to a Form property, whichever one did this last would get its way. Obviously, this would result in bugs unless our system was small enough so we could be sure this wouldn't ever happen.

Tip: Don't ever assume that your class is the only one that needs access to a property in an object of another class.

There are two solutions to this problem. The more thorough one is this: save the former handler (if any) in another property and Make sure your new handler runs the saving property. The code should look like this:

```
* Constructor code:
  Form.new_class_save_OnEvent = Form.OnEvent
  Form.OnEvent = new_class_handler

...
* Runtime code:
  PROCEDURE new_class_handler

  * Do new_class work here
  ...
  * Then call the old handler:
  Form.new_class_save_OnEvent()
```

I'm going to implement the simpler, less robust method here. That's this one:

```
* PUT BIG, SCREAMING!!! COMMENTS IN YOUR
* CLASS LISTING!

* WARNING:  THIS DESTROYS THE ... HANDLER!!!
```

Obviously, this is not as good a method, but for personal work it's adequate. The full listing, in the next section, shows the comments I've added near the top.

The Full Listing

For those of you who have the disk, Listing 12-8 adds the warning comments mentioned in the previous section. Otherwise, it's identical to Listing 12-7.

Code Listing 12-8

```
* SPEEDBAR.PRG -- A speed_bar class with speed_bar_buttons
* copyright 1995, Martin L. Rinehart

***********************************************************
* WARNING: speed_bar destroys OnMouseMove in the parent
* Form object.
***********************************************************
```

```
#define VPIX_SIZE (1/16)
#define HPIX_SIZE (1/6)

#define SB_SRRND_WIDTH (2)
#define BTN_SRRND_WIDTH (3)

foo = NEW Form('Test Speed_bar')
sb = NEW speed_bar(foo, 3)

* Build an array of speed_bar_button objects
  btns = NEW Object()

  btns[1] = NEW speed_bar_button( ;
     foo, "RESOURCE #20", { ;? 'OK'}, ;
     "Click here if it's all OK" )
  btns[2] = NEW speed_bar_button( ;
     foo, "RESOURCE #24", { ;? 'Not allowed!'}, ;
     "Clicks here are not allowed" )
  btns[3] = NEW speed_bar_button( ;
     foo, "RESOURCE #28", { ;? 'Wrong'}, ;
     "Click here if your choice was wrong" )
  btns[4] = NEW speed_bar_button( ;
     foo, "RESOURCE #32", { ;? 'Help!'}, ;
     "Click here to get help" )

  btns.number = 4

sb.attach(btns)

foo.Open()

CLASS speed_bar(frm, hgt) OF Rectangle(frm, 'speed_bar')
   This.Top    = SB_SRRND_WIDTH*VPIX_SIZE
   This.Left   = SB_SRRND_WIDTH*HPIX_SIZE
   This.Height = hgt
   This.Width  = frm.Width - 2*SB_SRRND_WIDTH*HPIX_SIZE

   This.OnMouseMove = Class::clean_up
   Form.OnMouseMove = Class::clean_up
```

```
PROCEDURE clean_up

SET MESSAGE TO

* Can be called from speed_bar or parent form
  LOCAL spd_bar
  IF This.Classname = "SPEED_BAR"
     spd_bar = This
  ELSE
     spd_bar = This.speed_bar
  ENDIF

LOCAL btn, i
FOR i = 1 TO spd_bar.button_array.number
   btn = spd_bar.button_array[i]
   IF btn.picture.Top <> btn.picture.home_top
      btn.picture.Top = btn.picture.home_top
      btn.picture.Left = btn.picture.home_left
      btn.BorderStyle = 1 && raised
      EXIT
   ENDIF
ENDFOR

* end of speed_bar::clean_up


PROCEDURE attach(b_list)
LOCAL i

This.button_array = b_list

LOCAL tp, lft, ht, wd

tp  = This.Top + BTN_SRRND_WIDTH*VPIX_SIZE
lft = This.Left + BTN_SRRND_WIDTH*HPIX_SIZE
ht  = This.Height - 2*BTN_SRRND_WIDTH*VPIX_SIZE
wd  = This.Height * (HPIX_SIZE/VPIX_SIZE)

FOR i = 1 TO b_list.number
   b_list[i].Top    = tp
   b_list[i].Left   = lft
   b_list[i].Height = ht
```

```
        b_list[i].Width    = wd

        b_list[i].picture.Top  = b_list[i].Top  + 3*VPIX_SIZE
        b_list[i].picture.Left = b_list[i].Left + 3*HPIX_SIZE

        b_list[i].picture.home_top  = b_list[i].picture.Top
        b_list[i].picture.home_left = b_list[i].picture.Left

        b_list[i].picture.Height = b_list[i].Height - ;
                                   5*VPIX_SIZE
        b_list[i].picture.Width  = b_list[i].Width - ;
                                   5*HPIX_SIZE

        lft = lft + wd + BTN_SRRND_WIDTH*HPIX_SIZE

        b_list[i].BorderStyle = 1 && raised

        b_list[i].picture.OnLeftMouseDown = class::pusher
        b_list[i].picture.OnLeftMouseUp   = class::popper

ENDFOR

* end of speed_bar::attach


PROCEDURE pusher
This.button.BorderStyle = 2 && lowered

This.Top  = This.home_top  - VPIX_SIZE
This.Left = This.home_left - HPIX_SIZE

This.button.action()

* end of speed_bar::pusher



PROCEDURE popper
This.button.BorderStyle = 1 && raised

This.Top  = This.home_top
This.Left = This.home_left
```

Learn Visual dBASE Programming

```
   * end of speed_bar::popper

ENDCLASS


CLASS speed_bar_button(frm, img, act, stat_msg) ;
   OF Rectangle(frm)

   This.picture = NEW Image(frm)
   This.picture.DataSource = img
   This.picture.button = This
   This.action = act
   This.picture.message = stat_msg
   This.picture.OnMouseMove = ;
       { ; SET MESSAGE TO This.message }

ENDCLASS

* end of SPEEDBAR.PRG
```

Summary

In this chapter, we've finished our speed_bar class.

We adjusted the spacing of our speed_bar, getting everything positioned at exactly the pixel where we thought it looked best.

We added status bar messages, just in case we ever used a button that wasn't self-explanatory.

Finally, we eliminated the possibility for some types of user-induced mistakes, such as punching but not releasing a button.

Are you getting the feeling that you can handle this new programming paradigm? I hope so. I think you can.

Chapter 13

Building Tree Classes

In this chapter we're going to do some very interesting work. We'll put together a tree class. We'll build our tree objects from tree node objects.

As we build the tree, we'll use recursive programming techniques, which are a sophisticated way of doing a lot of work with very few lines of code.

I'll spend some time discussing the tree, the design, and the ways you can traverse a tree. You'll see that a tree is an alternative way to show an outline, and that a depth-first traversal of a tree is the same as reading an outline from the top to the bottom.

While we discuss this, we'll get into the subject of recursive programming. You'll see that recursive programs are a good match to recursive data structures, such as trees.

After the preliminary work, we'll build the tree and node classes. Then we'll build an outline-type display class that will show trees as outlines that you can expand or contract.

The classes you create here are powerful ones that you can apply to many systems.

Designing the Tree

I've read a number of books that try to take the mystery out of object-oriented design. I'm trying to figure out why the objects I create don't seem to have any mystery at all about their design. The tree classes we'll build are typical — the overall design seems almost self-evident.

Overall Object Design

We'll want a tree object. Since trees are collections of nodes, we'll build our tree objects out of a collection of node objects. Since we'll be using trees to hold outline-type data, we'll also want a display capability. The Visual dBASE object properties Inspector is a pretty good model.

We'll want a display object to which we can hand a tree and have it take care of displaying the nodes. Nodes can be contracted (not showing children) and we'll show them with a "+" sign to the left of the name. A double click will expand the node, and we'll change the "+" to a "-" sign.

Since Forms can scroll vertically and horizontally, we'll take the easy way out and just write as many lines of Form as our tree requires. We'll let Visual dBASE take care of the messy details of scrolling and handling automatic vertical elevators.

Tree Detailed Design

How should we represent a tree? Using an Object object seems obvious since we don't really have anything to inherit. We'll attach node objects as tree[1], tree[2], and so on.

Each node can have children. These will be node[1], node[2], and so on. Each node will look like a tree, so any function we write that will handle a tree will handle a branch of that tree that starts with a node.

Recursion

We're going to write recursive subroutines to handle our trees. For those of you who haven't worked with recursive routines, they are like a great deal of Visual dBASE because they handle rather sophisticated concepts they seem to work with remarkably few lines of code. We're going to have a very high ratio of thinking to typing!

Let's start the thinking by considering two ways to write an outline. Here's the traditional way:

```
I.
  A.
  B.
II.
  A.
    1.
    2.
  B.
```

That outline is a tree structure. This is the same outline, set out as a tree:

```
      (root)
      /    \
    I.      II.
   / \     / \
  A.  B.  A.  B.
         / \
        1.  2.
```

Depth-First Traversals

There are two ways to *traverse* a tree (go from node to node, reaching all nodes). In a *depth-first* traversal, you visit the nodes in the order you see them written as an outline. You start at point I. Then you go to I. A. If I. A. had more details (child

311

nodes) you would continue on down until you had looked at every detail under I. A. before you got to I. B.

The terminology of tree traversal, such as depth-first traversal, comes from looking at trees in the second way I've shown the outline — as a classic computer science tree structure. You can see that reading top to bottom in the outline view is the same as reading down the leftmost side of the tree view.

Breadth-First Traversal

The complement of the depth-first traversal is the breadth-first traversal. It makes a lot of sense when you look at the tree view. Starting at the top, you read each row left to right before going down to the next row.

When you draw the tree in outline form, the breadth-first traversal doesn't make much sense. You'd read down the main items, I., II., and so on, before getting to the first level of detail (I. A., I. B., and so on).

Recursive Routines

One of the most interesting things about a tree is that you can grab any node of the tree and what you have is a smaller tree. We can use this property to describe a depth-first traversal this way:

```
pseudo_procedure depth_first_traversal(start_node)

start_node is first node in traversal

IF start_node has children

   FOR each child of start_node && left-to-right
      Do depth_first_traversal( child_node )
   ENDFOR

ENDIF

RETURN && done!
```

This pseudo-code calls itself once for each child node. Looked at from the point of view of our outline, a depth-first traversal of the whole outline is a depth-first traversal of point I., followed by a depth-first traversal of point II., and so on.

A depth-first traversal of point I. is a depth-first traversal of point I. A., followed by a depth-first traversal of point I. B., and so on.

If you need more explanation, sketch a more complicated outline than the one I gave you. Redraw it as a tree. Then apply the above algorithm, noting each node in the traversal. Every time the algorithm calls itself, write down the current node. Every time the algorithm returns, cross out the last current node you wrote down. You'll see that you're actually processing a stack.

Non-Recursive Routines

For non-recursive data structures, non-recursive routines work beautifully. For recursive data structures such as trees, non-recursive routines work, but they are absurdly messy compared to the equivalent recursive routine.

The beauties of the algorithm I just gave for depth-first traversals are its brevity and its ability to handle arbitrarily complex trees. It will work fine on a tree of one level or a hundred levels. Let's try this with non-recursive code:

```
pseudo_procedure d_f_traversal2(start_node)

create a stack
push start_node onto stack

DO WHILE stack is not empty

   this node = pop top node from stack

   this node is next node in traversal

   working from right to left,
      push each child of this node onto stack

ENDDO

RETURN && done!
```

Is it obvious to you that this routine does a depth-first traversal of a tree? I don't think it's the least bit obvious. You have to get a pencil out and work an example by hand to convince yourself that this works.

Convince yourself that this routine handles the depth-first traversal as well as the recursive one by reworking your examples by hand. Although it works, you have to create and maintain your own stack to get it to work. In the recursive example, each line of pseudo-code corresponds to a single line of dBASE code, which is not true in the second case.

The reason that the recursive routine is simpler is that the compiler handles building the stack for you. When a subroutine calls another, it pushes all the information it needs onto a stack. It saves everything it needs to begin precisely where it left off, before actually making the call. When it returns, it pops all the information it pushed and resumes operation. The recursive subroutine takes advantage of this fact to let the compiler maintain needed stacks.

Let me summarize before we get into the code.

1. A tree is a recursive structure. You can pick any node and look at it as a tree (although it will be a smaller tree).

2. An outline is a tree structure. The main points, I., II., and so on, are children of an anonymous root node. The next level of detail, A., B., and so on, are the children of point I., or II., or whichever.

3. A depth-first traversal of a tree is the same as writing the tree in outline style and reading it from the top down. It's called depth-first because if you wrote the outline as a tree, with point II. to the right of point I., you'd completely traverse everything under I. before going on to II.; you'd completely traverse everything under I. A. before going on to I. B., and so on.

4. The depth-first traversal can be easily handled by a recursive subroutine.

Now let's start programming. You'll see that we end up with a lot less code than explanation.

Programming the Tree Classes

We'll begin TREE.PRG with the basics from SKELETON.PRG and add the three classes that our design calls for. Listing 13-1 shows my starting point.

Code Listing 13-1

```
* TREE.PRG -- tree and related classes
* copyright 1995, Martin L. Rinehart


CLASS tree(tname) OF Object

ENDCLASS && tree
```

Chapter 13   Building Tree Classes

```
CLASS node(prnt_node, num) OF Object

ENDCLASS && node

CLASS tree_display_form(title, tp, lft, hght, wdth, tree);
   OF Form(title)

ENDCLASS && tree_display_form

* end of TREE.PRG
```

The tree and node classes inherit from the plain Object class. The tree_display_form inherits from Form and, as all classes that I start with a Form, it is called with a title and the four position/size properties' values. The unique item that is in the parameter list is a tree object. We'll attempt to write the tree_display_form class so that we can use it on any tree that we create.

Now we're up to the chicken and egg problem: which do we write first? Obviously, a tree without nodes is impossible. Actually, a tree is really just another node, the root node. We could dispense with the class altogether, but it makes for a more natural expression when, for example, you pass a tree to the tree_display_form() constructor.

Nodes, of course, need to be attached to a tree if we don't want them just floating off into space. We'll have to write a little of both, for starters. We can use the inspect() function to check our work. Listing 13-2 shows constructors for both the tree and the node classes.

Code Listing 13-2

```
CLASS tree(tname) OF Object

   This.name        = tname
   This.tree        = This
   This.depth       = 0
   This.root        = NEW node(This, 1)
   This.root.name   = tname
   This.size        = 1
   This.stop        = .T.
```

315

```
ENDCLASS && tree


CLASS node(prnt_node, num) OF Object

    This.parent           = prnt_node
    This.tree             = prnt_node.tree
    This.num_in_parent    = num
    This.num_kids         = 0

    This.depth = prnt_node.depth + 1

    This.expanded = .T.
    This.name     = ''
    This.stop     = .F.

    * kids are this[1]...this[num_kids]

ENDCLASS && node
```

I'll comment on each of these assignments. The tree constructor is called with the name of the tree, which is assigned to the name property. Then the tree class assigns a reference to itself to its tree property. You'll see that this simplifies the subsequent coding.

The depth property shows the distance from the root of each node. The tree, or root, is at depth zero.

The root property of the tree is a node. In the NEW operation, you assign each node to a parent at a number. The first child of the parent is number 1, and so on. The name of the root node is the same as the name of the tree.

The size property of the tree indicates the total number of nodes. The stop property is used in the traversal routines to keep the traversal from going past the root. It is true in the root, and false for all other nodes. Routines that want to process a sub-tree can temporarily set the stop property true for any node, ensuring that they only process the correct portion of the tree.

The node's constructor assigns the parent property the node object in the first parameter. The tree property is a direct reference to the root, which can be used at any level.

Chapter 13 — Building Tree Classes

The num_in_parent property is used for looping through the child nodes of a parent, much as an ID property can be used for looping through multiple objects. For example, num_in_parent might be 2 and the total number of kids of the parent might be 3, indicating that you were in the middle.

The number of children, the num_kids property, is the number of direct children, not including grandchildren or grandchildren's children, and so on. Again, it can be used to loop through the list of child nodes.

The depth property is, of course, one greater than the parent's depth. The expanded property is used by the display class to show an expanded or contracted node. If expanded is False, the display will be shown as if there were no child nodes.

The name property is not assigned in the constructor, although it could be. In this class I add the name after running the NEW operation.

Finally, the stop property is used as discussed above. Initially, the root's stop is True and the rest are False. By setting a node's stop property to True, a tree traversal routine can limit itself to working on a selected branch of the tree.

With that code, it's time to build a tree.

To build the tree, we'll need to add the first method to the node class, make_child(). Then we can add some mainline code to create a tree and some children. Listing 13-3 shows the new mainline and node class method.

Code Listing 13-3

```
* TREE.PRG -- tree and related classes          1
* copyright 1995, Martin L. Rinehart            2
                                                3
* test data and mainline code:                  4
  test_tree = NEW tree('Family')                5
  r = test_tree.root                            6
                                                7
    t = r.make_child('Tom')                     8
        t.make_child('Tomasina')                9
        t.make_child('Tommy')                  10
                                               11
    d = r.make_child('Dick')                   12
        d.make_child('Richard')                13
        d.make_child('Rich')                   14
        d.make_child('Ricki')                  15
                                               16
    h = r.make_child('Harry')                  17
```

```
            h.make_child('Jane')                        18
            j = h.make_child('June')                    19
                j.make_child('Jillian')                 20
                j.make_child('Jonathan')                21
                                                        22
            h.make_child('Jill')                        23
            j2 = h.make_child('Jack')                   24
            j2.make_child('John')                       25
            j2.make_child('Jeanne')                     26
                                                        27
inspect(test_tree)                                      28
                                                        29
CLASS tree(tname) OF Object                             30
...
    * kids are this[1]...this[num_kids]                 56
                                                        57
    FUNCTION make_child(name)                           58
        LOCAL kid                                       59
                                                        60
        This.num_kids = This.num_kids + 1               61
        kid = NEW node(This, This.num_kids)             62
        This[This.num_kids] = kid                       63
        This[This.num_kids].name = name                 64
        This.tree.size = This.tree.size + 1             65
                                                        66
    RETURN kid                                          67
                                                        68
    * end of node::make_child                           69
                                                        70
                                                        71
ENDCLASS && node                                        72
```

The mainline creates a tree named Family and assigns its root to a variable, r. Beginning with calls to r.make_child(), it creates a family tree. The make_child() method returns an object reference to the node that it creates. Sometimes I've used this, and sometimes the mainline ignores it.

The make_child() routine's basic job is to create a new node, correctly attached as a child of the calling node. The first child of This is This[1]; the second is This[2], and so on. It maintains the bookkeeping detail properties, num_kids and size, as well as assigning the new child a name.

Chapter 13　　　　　　　　　　　　　　　　　　　　　Building Tree Classes

When you run this routine, it calls the inspect() function to launch the object properties Inspector. From any point in the tree you can use this tool to inspect every node. You'll see the number of nodes in the Size property.

Click on the root property and a tool icon will appear. Click on the tool icon to change focus to node 1, the top node of the tree. The object properties Inspector says this node has 3 kids (num_kids) among other things.

The 3 kids are [1], [2], and [3]. Click on one of them and you get another tool icon. Click on the tool and you are looking at the kid node. Click on PARENT and its tool to move the focus back up.

All the properties that have an object as their value (tree.root, for example) will show a tool icon on the right of the properties value. When you click on that icon, you switch to inspecting the object that was the value of the property. When you click the icon next to tree.root, for instance, your object properties Inspector changes to inspecting the root node object.

The property of This that your code references as This[2], for example, is named [2] in the object properties Inspector. Clicking on the [2] property of the root node gets you to the second child of the root.

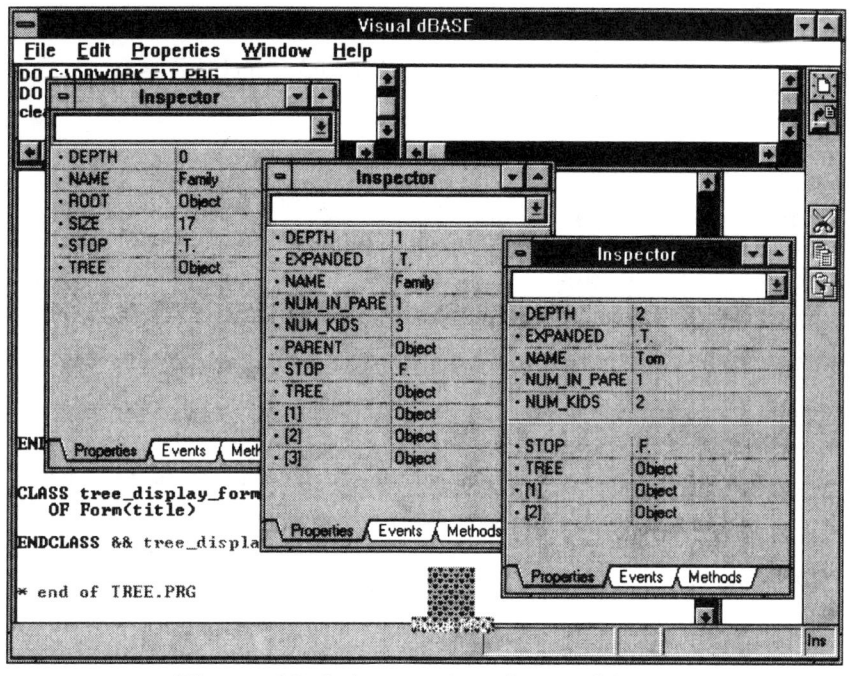

Figure 13-1: Inspecting three objects

In Figure 13-1, I've run TREE.PRG three times, so that I launched three object properties Inspectors. From top left, I started looking at the tree named Family. Then I looked at the root object, which is also named Family. Finally, I looked at the [1] property of the root node, which is the Tom node.

With the object properties Inspector, you can look through your entire tree. This is an invaluable debugging tool. Go ahead and run your TREE.PRG multiple times to launch multiple inspectors, as I've done. It's easier than trusting to memory.

The next method to add to the node class is one that deletes a node. Mine is shown in Listing 13-4.

Code Listing 13-4

```
PROCEDURE delete_node

   FOR i = This.num_kids TO 1 STEP -1
      This[i].delete_node()
   ENDFOR

   LOCAL parent; parent = This.parent
   LOCAL i

   FOR i = This.num_in_parent TO parent.num_kids-1
      parent[i] = parent[i+1]
   ENDFOR

   * what we want to do now:
   * release parent[parent.num_kids]
   parent[parent.num_kids] = ''

   parent.num_kids = parent.num_kids - 1
   This.tree.size = This.tree.size - 1

* end of node::delete_node
```

This is the first of our recursive subroutines. It starts by calling itself to delete any children attached to the node we are deleting. That call would, in turn, call itself again to delete any children of those children, and so on down to the bottom of this branch of the tree.

The disadvantage of these recursive routines is that you have to read them twice to find out what they do. After calling itself as often as needed, this one gets to work on the node you originally specified.

It starts by moving all following children down a number. If you delete child 2, the former child 3 becomes the new child 2, the former 4 becomes the new 3, and so on.

You cannot release a property of an object in the current version of Visual dBASE, so this routine just assigns an empty string to the unneeded property. After that, it decrements the num_kids and size properties, appropriately.

On your own, put a call to this routine into your mainline to test it. You'll want to inspect() the tree before and after you delete. Once you're satisfied that it works, remove the delete testing code, returning to the full tree.

The final routines completing the node class are two that support the display code that we're coming to. Actually, it's just one method, next_node(), that uses its own subroutine to keep itself simple. Listing 13-5 shows these methods of the node class.

Code Listing 13-5

```
FUNCTION next_node

IF This.num_kids > 0 .AND. This.expanded
   RETURN This[1]
 ELSE
   RETURN This.next_right_up_node()
ENDIF


* end of next_node


FUNCTION next_right_up_node
* returns the next node in right/up part of depth-first
* traversal

* exception condition -- at root, return tree object
   IF This.depth = 1
      RETURN This.parent && prevents recursion past root
   ENDIF

* otherwise, return node
```

```
    IF This.num_in_parent < This.parent.num_kids

       * if not last sibling, return next sibling
       RETURN This.parent[This.num_in_parent+1]

    ELSE

       * if last sibling, return parent's next_right_up_node
       RETURN This.parent.next_right_up_node()

    ENDIF

 * end of node::next_right_up_node
```

The next_node() method participates in a depth-first traversal of the tree. You can start at any node and repeatedly call next_node(). It will return nodes in the depth-first order for the sub-tree that starts at the first calling node. Of course, if the first calling node is the tree's root, then next_node() will traverse the entire tree.

Programming the Tree_display_form Class

To display a tree, we'll use the outline style. The root will be the top line of the display. Fully contracted, the lines under the root will be the nodes that are direct children of the root. If you expand any one of those children, you get grandchildren of the root, and so on.

To do this, we'll attach an array of Text objects to the Form. The first Text will be line one, the next will be line two, and so on. We'll allow MAX_LINES, a constant you can define to suit your applications' requirements. A smaller MAX_LINES will, of course, handle smaller outlines, but it will run faster.

In the display code, we'll associate a node of the tree with each text object, until we come to the end of the tree. As we display the tree, we'll constantly be reassigning the node that is attached to each Text. When you expand a node, all the lower nodes are moved down to higher-numbered Text objects.

For example, assume that the root has two children and that they are not expanded. The text objects will be assigned in this order:

- 1 — Root

- 2 — First child

- 3 — Second child

Now let's mentally double-click the first child. Here's the expanded version:

- 1 — Root
- 2 — First child
- 3 — Grandkid a
- 4 — Grandkid b
- 5 — Grandkid c
- 6 — Second child

As you see, expanding or contracting any node means that we'll have to reassign all the lower nodes to different Text objects, so the best place for this assignment is in the display code.

Let's get started with the constructor.

The Tree_display_form Constructor

The constructor code has three distinct parts:

- Assigning properties
- Attaching Text objects
- Initializing the display

We'll build these in order.

Assigning Properties

The constructor for the tree_display_form begins, as usual, by assigning the passed parameters to the appropriate properties of the Form. Listing 13-6 shows this code.

Code Listing 13-6

```
CLASS tree_display_form(title, tp, lft, hght, wdth, tree);
   OF Form(title)

   * Built-in properties
   This.Top    = tp
   This.Left   = lft
   This.Height = hght
   This.Width  = wdth
   This.Text   = title

   This.ScrollBar = 2 && Auto

ENDCLASS && tree_display_form
```

To see what's happening, we'll want to change our test mainline at the top of the class. We won't need to inspect() the tree; we'll need to create and launch a tree_display_form with our test tree attached. Listing 13-7 shows the code that replaces the inspect() call:

Code Listing 13-7

```
         j2.make_child('Jeanne')

f = NEW tree_display_form("Family Tree", ;
    4, 15, 10, 40, test_tree)

f.Open()

CLASS tree(tname) OF Object
```

When you run this code, you'll get a small form that does nothing. Let's keep going.

The next job is to add some custom properties that we'll need, as shown in Listing 13-8.

Code Listing 13-8

```
   This.ScrollBar = 2 && Auto

   * Custom properties
```

Chapter 13   Building Tree Classes

```
   This.save_width = wdth
   This.tree = tree
   This.selected = 1
   This.OnSize = {;This.on_size() }

ENDCLASS && tree_display_form
```

The on_size() method will do two things. First, it will make sure that the Form shows only whole lines. If the user resizes the form to show, for example, 15.6 lines, it will snap to 16 full lines. Second, it will refuse to allow changes in the width. (You may not want this feature in every application. This will show you what happens when you include it.)

The save_width property is there to accommodate the width-retention behavior. The tree property is an object reference to the tree object that is being displayed. The selected property is the number of the Text that has been selected by the user, which we will let default to 1, the root.

You will get an error if you attempt to resize the tree Form at this point, since we haven't written an on_size() method yet.

Attaching Text Objects

Now we're ready to attach the Text objects that will display each node of the tree. Listing 13-9 shows the creation of the text objects.

Code Listing 13-9

```
   This.OnSize = {;This.on_size() }

   FOR i = 1 TO tree.size

      This[i] = NEW Text(This)
      This[i].Top          = i-1
      This[i].Left         = 0
      This[i].Height       = 1
      This[i].Width        = This.Width

      This[i].Text         = ''
      This[i].Alignment    = 3 && left center
      This[i].Border       = (i = 1)
      This[i].ID           = i
```

325

```
        This[i].OnLeftDblClick = class::left_double_click

        This[i].OnRightDblClick = ;
        {; IF TYPE('This.node')='O'; INSPECT(This.node); ENDIF}

        This[i].OnLeftMouseDown = class::left_click

        This[i].node = ''

ENDFOR

* end of constructor
```

This loop initializes one Text for each node in the tree, allowing you room enough to completely expand every node. (You must make sure that MAX_LINES is big enough to accommodate your tree.)

The Text property is initialized to a null string — it will be filled in by the display code. The border is turned on only for the selected Text, which is, for starters, Text number one. Each text is given an ID equal to its location in the set of Texts.

The left mouse actions are set up to handle the later addition of event handlers. For the moment, if you want to successfully compile this code, add dummy PROCEDURE statements, such as these:

```
* end of constructor

PROCEDURE left_click

PROCEDURE left_double_click

ENDCLASS && tree_display_form
```

The right mouse double click will eventually get changed. For instance, we could use the right double-click to launch a tabbed form set to the selected node. For the moment, it inspects the node, if the node is an object. (The user may have clicked below the last Text that holds a tree node. You couldn't inspect() something there.)

The last line in the loop sets the node property to a null string. This will be set to the node of the tree that corresponds to the Text by the display code.

Initializing the Display

Finally, we need to set up the initial display. This is done simply by calling the appropriate method. Listing 13-10 shows this call.

Code Listing 13-10

```
ENDFOR

This.display(This.tree.root, 1)

* end of constructor
```

Of course, you can't run this yet, since we haven't provided a display() method. That's our next order of business.

The Tree_display_form Display Methods

Conceptually, the display() method is simple. It starts at the current node/line pair and uses the tree object's next_node() method to keep displaying lines until it is done. Listing 13-11 shows the display() routine.

Code Listing 13-11

```
* end of constructor

PROCEDURE display(from_node, line_num)
LOCAL node, line

* 'This' is the tree_display_form (Form) object.

line = line_num
node = from_node

This.display_line(node, line)

DO WHILE line <= MAX_LINES
```

```
    * Does a depth-first traversal, possibly blocked
    * when node.expanded = .F.

    node = node.next_node()
    line = line + 1

    * exit if at root
      IF node.depth = 0
         EXIT
      ENDIF

    This.display_line(node, line)

ENDDO

* end of tree_display_form::display


PROCEDURE left_click

PROCEDURE left_double_click && expand/contract

ENDCLASS && tree_display_form
```

The parameters are copied into LOCAL variables at the beginning. Since parameters are passed by reference, this is a necessary step to be sure that you don't inadvertently change a parameter in the calling routine.

After that, the display_line() method is called to show the current line. This routine is written so that it can be called at the line/node combination on which the user double-clicks to expand or contract. We don't want to redisplay the whole tree if the user changes only the last node.

Then we loop over all the remaining lines, until we exit at the root. The MAX_LINES limit should never be reached, since that should be at least enough lines to show the whole tree. As each line/node combination is displayed, the line counter is incremented and the next_node() method is used to advance down the tree in our depth-first traversal.

The display_line() method consists of exactly two assignment statements. The first one, as shown in Listing 13-12, assigns the Text property of the Line object and the second one assigns the node property a reference to the current tree node object.

Code Listing 13-12

```
* end of tree_display_form::display


PROCEDURE display_line(node, line_num)
* displays from the specified node/line on down

* This is the parent form
* This[i] is the text object (1 thru MAX_LINES)

* line_num is global from tree_display_form::display()

This[line_num].text = ;
   SPACE( TAB_SIZE*(node.depth-1) ) + ;
   IIF(node.num_kids > 0, ;
      IIF(node.expanded, ' - ', '+ '), ;
      '   ' )+ ;
   node.name

This[line_num].node = node

* end of tree_display_form::display_line


PROCEDURE left_click
```

The first assignment statement is not trivial, but it's also not as complex as it looks at first glance. It has three parts.

First, it prints an appropriate number of spaces, indenting the text once for each level in the tree past one. Next, it prints either a "+," a "-," or a blank, for a node that can be expanded, contracted, or is childless, respectively. Finally, it adds the name of the node to the Text property of the Text object.

The node property is assigned an object reference to the current tree node so that we can cross-reference easily when the user clicks on a node. What looks to the user like clicking on a node is, in reality, clicking on a Text object. That Text object has to know which node it corresponds to.

Before you run this program, put two #defines up near the top, like these:

```
#define MAX_LINES 50
#define TAB_SIZE   5
```

You can adjust the actual values to suit yourself. The MAX_LINES constant specifies the largest tree that can be handled. It's a compromise between size and speed. The TAB_SIZE value determines the number of spaces to indent each text line under the outline's root.

When you run this program, you'll get a display like the one in Figure 13-2.

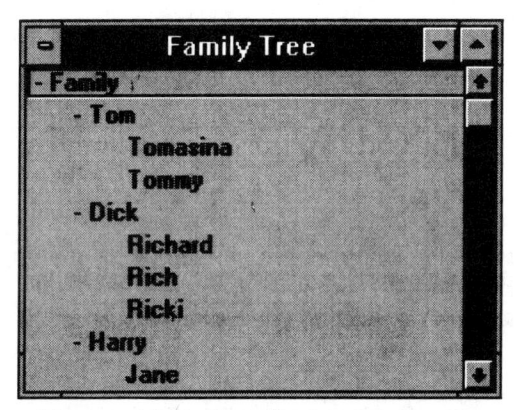

Figure 13-2: The first tree display

When you manipulate this form, you'll see that the elevator is hooked up and fully operational. On the other hand, if you double-click on a tree node, nothing happens.

Our next and last job with this class is hooking up event handlers so that you can manipulate the tree.

The Tree_display_form Event Handlers

To begin, let's hook up the node selection to the left mouse click. Text objects don't have an OnClick handler, but they do have an OnLeftMouseDown, which will serve nicely. Listing 13-13 shows the two methods to add, replacing the dummy left_click() procedure.

Code Listing 13-13

```
* end of tree_display_form::display_line


PROCEDURE left_click
```

Chapter 13 Building Tree Classes

```
* This is the rectangle that got the OnLeftMouseDown
Form.select(This.ID)

* end of tree_display_form::left_click


PROCEDURE select(line_num) && selects new node

Form[Form.selected].Border = .F.
Form.selected = line_num
Form[line_num].Border = .T.

* end of tree_display_form::select

PROCEDURE left_double_click && expand/contract
```

The left_click() method just calls the select() method. Select() changes the border of the formerly selected Text back to False. It then records the new selection and turns its Border property to True. You might want to try experimenting with other visual clues to selection, such as a contrasting color or by changing the font to include an underline.

Warning: a bug in the 0.638 version causes the text to not repaint when you change the border property. This is a workaround:

```
Form[Form.selected].Visible = .F.
Form[Form.selected].Border = .F. && this might not show
Form[Form.selected].Visible = .T.
...
Form[line_num].Visible = .F.
Form[line_num].Border = .T. && this might not show
Form[line_num].Visible = .T.
```

The next event to implement is OnSize(). For this I want to maintain the original width and to set the bottom border to show full lines only. Listing 13-14 shows the code.

331

Learn Visual dBASE Programming

Code Listing 13-14

```
* end of tree_display_form::select


PROCEDURE on_size

This.OnSize = {;} && turn self off

This.Height = ROUND(This.Height, 0) && show whole lines
This.Width  = This.save_width && don't adjust width

This.OnSize = tree_display_form::on_size && turn self on

* end of tree_display_form::on_size


PROCEDURE left_double_click && expand/contract
```

The only complication is that you cannot change the size of a form inside an OnSize() handler without being in danger of falling into an infinite loop. Making any assignment to the Height or Width property in a program is the same as dragging a border or corner — it triggers the OnSize() event. You don't want to do this in an OnSize() handler, or it will call itself, possibly forever.

That's why the first line of this routine assigns a null codeblock to the OnSize() event property. The last line reassigns a reference to itself. In between, the Height is adjusted to the nearest whole line number, and the Width is set to the save_width value.

There is one more event handler to implement, the left double-click that expands and contracts a node. This is relatively simple now that we've got a cast of supporting methods, but it still takes some work. Listing 13-15 shows the code.

Code Listing 13-15

```
* end of tree_display_form::on_size


PROCEDURE left_double_click && expand/contract
* This is the text object that read the double click

* ignore double clicks if no kids
   IF This.node.num_kids = 0
```

```
      RETURN
   ENDIF

This.node.expanded = .NOT. This.node.expanded

* close kids and clear following lines, when contracting
IF .NOT. This.node.expanded

   LOCAL oref; oref = This.node.next_right_up_node()
   oref.stop = .T.

   LOCAL nd; nd = This.node[1]

   LOCAL ond
   DO WHILE .NOT. nd.stop

      ond = nd
      nd  = nd.next_node()
      ond.expanded = .F.

   ENDDO

   IF nd.depth >= 1 && don't clear tree's stop
      nd.stop = .F.
   ENDIF

   LOCAL i
   FOR i = This.ID TO Form.tree.size
      Form[i].Text = ''
   ENDFOR

ENDIF

* Re-display the tree from here down
This.Parent.display(This.node, This.ID)

* end of tree_display_form::left_double_click

ENDCLASS && tree_display_form

* end of TREE.PRG
```

The first job is simple: if the node has no children, the method simply returns, doing nothing. You might want to add a dialog box here, if you have neophyte users. Experienced users will quickly catch on. After this check, the rest of the routine is sure that its job applies.

The first thing the routine does is flip the expanded property from one logical state to the other. Then it has a lot of work to do when you are contracting an expanded node. I'll get back to this.

In either case, the tree is redisplayed from the current Text/node on down, which only takes the one-line call to the display() method.

When you are expanding a node, the new display will wipe out all previous displays from the point of the change down, so your code doesn't have to worry about cleanup. The work inside the major IF block applies to contractions.

First, a LOCAL object reference is assigned to the next node to the right or up the tree. That node's stop property is set True to limit the following depth-first traversal.

Next, the LOCAL nd is set to the first child of the current node and the sub-tree is traversed, setting each child's expanded property to False. This means that the next time you expand this node, you'll see just its immediate children. You'll probably want to test this code with this work commented out to see if you want it behaving this way.

The last cleanup job is to set all the Text properties of the Text objects below the current node to blanks. The ones that will still be displayed are set to new values in the display process that follows.

When you run this code, you'll see that you now have a fully functional tree display class.

Warning: In the current release of Visual dBASE, you need to click on a node to select it before you can double-click to expand/contract it. This may be fixed in a later release.

This is a very sophisticated piece of object-oriented programming, and you can be justifiably proud of having come this far.

The Full Listing

The full listing follows, for those who don't have the disk. If you do have the disk, the full listing is included as L13-15.PRG.

Code Listing 13-16

```
* TREE.PRG -- tree and related classes
* copyright 1995, Martin L. Rinehart

#define MAX_LINES 50
#define TAB_SIZE   5

* test data and mainline code:
  test_tree = NEW tree('Family')
  r = test_tree.root

    t = r.make_child('Tom')
       t.make_child('Tomasina')
       t.make_child('Tommy')

    d = r.make_child('Dick')
       d.make_child('Richard')
       d.make_child('Rich')
       d.make_child('Ricki')

    h = r.make_child('Harry')
       h.make_child('Jane')
       j = h.make_child('June')
          j.make_child('Jillian')
          j.make_child('Jonathan')

       h.make_child('Jill')
       j2 = h.make_child('Jack')
       j2.make_child('John')
       j2.make_child('Jeanne')

f = NEW tree_display_form("Family Tree", ;
    4, 15, 10, 40, test_tree)

f.Open()


CLASS tree(tname) OF Object

    This.name     = tname
    This.tree     = This
    This.depth    = 0
```

335

```
   This.root          = NEW node(This, 1)
   This.root.name     = tname
   This.size          = 1
   This.stop          = .T.

ENDCLASS && tree


CLASS node(prnt_node, num) OF Object

   This.parent        = prnt_node
   This.tree          = prnt_node.tree
   This.num_in_parent = num
   This.num_kids      = 0

   This.depth = prnt_node.depth + 1

   This.expanded = .T.
   This.name     = ''
   This.stop     = .F.

   * kids are this[1]...this[num_kids]

   FUNCTION make_child(name)
      LOCAL kid

      This.num_kids = This.num_kids + 1
      kid = NEW node(This, This.num_kids)
      This[This.num_kids] = kid
      This[This.num_kids].name = name
      This.tree.size = This.tree.size + 1

   RETURN kid

   * end of node::make_child



   PROCEDURE delete_node

      FOR i = This.num_kids TO 1 STEP -1
         This[i].delete_node()
      ENDFOR
```

Chapter 13 — Building Tree Classes

```
   LOCAL parent; parent = This.parent
   LOCAL i

   FOR i = This.num_in_parent TO parent.num_kids-1
      parent[i] = parent[i+1]
   ENDFOR

   * what we want to do now:
   * release parent[parent.num_kids]
   parent[parent.num_kids] = ''

   parent.num_kids = parent.num_kids - 1
   This.tree.size = This.tree.size - 1

* end of node::delete_node



FUNCTION next_node

IF This.num_kids > 0 .AND. This.expanded
   RETURN This[1]
ELSE
   RETURN This.next_right_up_node()
ENDIF


* end of next_node



FUNCTION next_right_up_node
* returns the next node in right/up part of depth-first
* traversal

* exception condition -- at root, return tree object
   IF This.depth = 1
      RETURN This.parent && prevents recursion past root
   ENDIF

* otherwise, return node
IF This.num_in_parent < This.parent.num_kids

   * if not last sibling, return next sibling
```

```
        RETURN This.parent[This.num_in_parent+1]

   ELSE

      * if last sibling, return parent's next_right_up_node
      RETURN This.parent.next_right_up_node()

   ENDIF

   * end of node::next_right_up_node


ENDCLASS && node


CLASS tree_display_form(title, tp, lft, hght, wdth, tree);
   OF Form(title)

   * Built-in properties
   This.Top    = tp
   This.Left   = lft
   This.Height = hght
   This.Width  = wdth
   This.Text   = title

   This.ScrollBar = 2 && Auto

   * Custom properties
   This.save_width = wdth
   This.tree = tree
   This.selected = 1
   This.OnSize = {;This.on_size() }

   FOR i = 1 TO tree.size

      This[i] = NEW Text(This)
      This[i].Top           = i-1
      This[i].Left          = 0
      This[i].Height        = 1
      This[i].Width         = This.Width

      This[i].Text          = ''
```

```
   This[i].Alignment    = 3 && left center
   This[i].Border       = (i = 1)
   This[i].ID           = i

   This[i].OnLeftDblClick = class::left_double_click

   This[i].OnRightDblClick = ;
 {; IF TYPE('This.node')='O'; INSPECT(This.node); ENDIF}

   This[i].OnLeftMouseDown = class::left_click

   This[i].node = ''

ENDFOR

This.display(This.tree.root, 1)

* end of constructor


PROCEDURE display(from_node, line_num)
LOCAL node, line

* 'This' is the tree_display_form (Form) object.

line = line_num
node = from_node

This.display_line(node, line)

DO WHILE line <= MAX_LINES

   * Does a depth-first traversal, possibly blocked
   * when node.expanded = .F.

   node = node.next_node()
   line = line + 1

   * exit if at root
     IF node.depth = 0
        EXIT
     ENDIF
```

```
        This.display_line(node, line)

   ENDDO

   * end of tree_display_form::display


   PROCEDURE display_line(node, line_num)
   * displays from the specified node/line on down

   * This is the parent form
   * This[i] is the text object (1 thru MAX_LINES)

   * line_num is global from tree_display_form::display()

   This[line_num].text = ;
       SPACE( TAB_SIZE*(node.depth-1) ) + ;
       IIF(node.num_kids > 0, ;
           IIF(node.expanded, ' - ', '+ '), ;
           '   ' )+ ;
       node.name

   This[line_num].node = node

   * end of tree_display_form::display_line



   PROCEDURE left_click
   * This is the rectangle that got the OnLeftMouseDown
   Form.select(This.ID)

   * end of tree_display_form::left_click



   PROCEDURE select(line_num) && selects new node

   Form[Form.selected].Border = .F.
   Form.selected = line_num
   Form[line_num].Border = .T.

   * end of tree_display_form::select
```

```
PROCEDURE on_size

This.OnSize = {;} && turn self off

This.Height = ROUND(This.Height, 0) && show whole lines
This.Width  = This.save_width && don't adjust width

This.OnSize = tree_display_form::on_size && turn self on

* end of tree_display_form::on_size


PROCEDURE left_double_click && expand/contract
* This is the text object that read the double click

* ignore double clicks if no kids
   IF This.node.num_kids = 0
      RETURN
   ENDIF

This.node.expanded = .NOT. This.node.expanded

* close kids and clear following lines, when contracting
IF .NOT. This.node.expanded

   LOCAL oref; oref = This.node.next_right_up_node()
   oref.stop = .T.

   LOCAL nd; nd = This.node[1]

   LOCAL ond
   DO WHILE .NOT. nd.stop

      ond = nd
      nd  = nd.next_node()
      ond.expanded = .F.

   ENDDO

   IF nd.depth >= 1 && don't clear tree's stop
```

```
            nd.stop = .F.
    ENDIF

    LOCAL i
    FOR i = This.ID TO Form.tree.size
        Form[i].Text = ''
    ENDFOR

ENDIF

* Re-display the tree from here down
This.Parent.display(This.node, This.ID)

* end of tree_display_form::left_double_click


ENDCLASS && tree_display_form

* end of TREE.PRG
```

Summary

In this chapter you've taken a look at trees and seen that they are another way of looking at outlines, or that outlines are another way of looking at trees.

We've seen that you can traverse a tree either depth-first or breadth-first, and that the depth-first traversal is the same as reading an outline from top to bottom.

We've used recursive programming techniques to traverse the tree. You saw that these techniques are a good match for a recursive data structure, such as a tree, and that they can do a lot of work in very few lines of code.

After building our tree and node classes, using the object properties Inspector to check our work, we went on to build an outline display class that shows trees as an outline.

With this class, you can double-click on an outline topic and see it expanded or contracted. It's a sophisticated capability, built with sophisticated programming techniques.

The tree_display_form class you've built here uses the tree class which, in turn, is built from node objects. You've fit all these together into a useful form.

Congratulations! You're doing sophisticated, object-oriented programming.

Chapter 14

Critical Path Charting

In this final chapter, we're going to build our last class. It's a critical path calculating and charting routine that will do more sophisticated work with the screen and in calculations than we have seen up to this point. If you can complete this class, you'll have earned the right to call yourself an object-oriented dBASE programmer.

For serious project management there are several excellent commercial products but they all share a problem: they are designed for people who need to build an aircraft carrier or do a moon launch.

My needs for project management are very modest. I do projects that typically are measured in months involving a small number of people. I just need a simple tool to draw a project schedule and to reschedule when something takes too long.

It was easier for me to write the pchart class (Project CHARTing) than it would be for me to use one of the serious project management programs.

We'll start by building a form and some sample data. We'll add headings, then component labels, and then we'll draw the components themselves. Finally we'll add connecting lines showing the dependencies between project components.

After we've finished the drawing we'll address the calculations. First we'll make sure that project components follow each other in the order we specify, and then we'll go on to find the critical path.

Let's start by thinking about the design.

Designing the Class

I wanted a simple tool that I could use in multiple places. Object-oriented programmers always talk about code reuse, but aren't always good at achieving it. Some studies have found that object-oriented programming shops are no better at generating reusable code than procedural programming shops.

I think the easiest way to prevent your code from being reused is to make it sophisticated. By sticking to very simple things with very few options you just might succeed in writing code that can be used many times in many places.

A Simple Data Structure

With that in mind, I designed an almost trivially simple class. You organize your data in an array of arrays. Each member array has four elements:

- Component name
- Start time
- End time
- Precedent element

The start and end times are normalized so that time one is the first time of the first component or components. For a good-looking chart, you pick a unit of time that will make the chart 50 to 100 units wide (we'll be showing one character per unit of time).

I map my data into these units at one day per unit. You could just as easily use one week, one month, or one hour per unit. The pchart class won't even know.

The precedent element is the location in the array of arrays of the project component that must be completed before this element can start. For example, you had to learn to do object-oriented programming in Visual dBASE before you could begin this class. If Learn O-O dBWin was array 2, then 2 would be the precedent project in array 3, Write Critical Path Class.

Among the more useful extensions of sophisticated project software is the ability to have multiple precedent components. You often need to complete A, B, and C before you go on to D. In simple projects, however, you can almost always look at A, B, and C and pick the biggest one as the precedent for D. It's not theoretically sound, but it works on smaller jobs.

A Simple Class

With the project components in a single array, we've got a simple data structure. Next in the design is the class that works on that structure.

A pure object approach would have each object able to display itself with a method like object::draw(). But the chart should also have lines between the elements showing the dependencies. These lines would be separate objects if we were going to be purely object-oriented. So let's take another approach.

In this class, the code is almost all procedural, except that it uses the Visual dBASE objects to do the actual drawing. We'll just draw one element at a time and then fill in the connecting lines.

The only wrinkle is that we'll need to use a fixed-pitch font to neatly write headings over the chart. I've allowed three lines of heading and left the first one blank. The next two show the numbers 1 through whatever. Above them, any application can fill in whatever it likes just by assigning the header1.Text property.

Drawing the Chart

Ready to get to the code? As always, start with a copy of SKELETON.PRG, appropriately edited. Listing 14-1 shows my starting point.

Code Listing 14-1

```
* PCHART.PRG -- project chart class
* copyright 1995, Martin L. Rinehart
```

Learn Visual dBASE Programming

```
CLASS pchart(nm, tp, lf, ht, wd, proj_arr) ;
    OF Form(nm)

ENDCLASS

* end of PCHART.PRG
```

There's nothing new here. We're inheriting from the Form class since we want to put a chart on the screen. As always, we start the Form with a name and four parameters to position and size the form. Then we add the class-specific parameters.

In this case, there's only one class-specific parameter, the project data array.

Building a Test Project

Before we can go on to the next step, we'll need a project to work with. In Listing 14-2 you'll see how I built one. It's pretty trivial, but without it you can't make any progress.

Code Listing 14-2

```
* PCHART.PRG -- project chart class
* copyright 1995, Martin L. Rinehart


pdat = NEW Array(10)

* Each element of pdat (Project DATa) is a 4 element array:
*     pdat[?][1] = name of component
*     pdat[?][2] = Start point
*     pdat[?][3] = End point
*     pdat[?][4] = Precedent component

* Start and end points are normalized to chart grid values,
* e.g. 1 = first time, 2 = next, etc. These could be hours,
* days, months, ...

* Precedent component is the number in the array of the
* element which must be completed before this element is
* started. Zero == no precedent.
```

```
LOCAL i
FOR i = 1 TO pdat.Size
   pdat[i] = NEW Array(4)
   pdat[i][1] = 'Part '+LTRIM(STR(i))
   pdat[i][2] = (i-1)*3+1
   pdat[i][3] = pdat[i][2]+6
   pdat[i][4] = i-1
ENDFOR

pc = NEW pchart( 'Project Chart', ;
                3, 5, 15, 60, pdat )

pc.Open()


CLASS pchart(nm, tp, lf, ht, wd, proj_arr) ;
      OF Form(nm)

ENDCLASS

* end of PCHART.PRG
```

If you're entering these listings as you go along, and I hope you are, don't be tempted to skip the comments.

Tip: Always document your data structures when you don't use straight objects. Object constructors are largely self-documenting but most other structures need explanations.

If you have ever gone back to a program like this one after some time away from it, you'll need to read those comments. Without them the code won't make much sense.

One of the best features of object-oriented programming is that it goes a long way toward documenting itself. Compare these two fragments:

```
FOR i = 1 TO pdat.Size
  pdat[i] = NEW Array(4)
  pdat[i][1] = 'Part '+LTRIM(STR(i))
  pdat[i][2] = (i-1)*3+1
  pdat[i][3] = pdat[i][2]+6
```

```
    pdat[i][4] = i-1
ENDFOR

* object-oriented equivalent:

FOR i = 1 TO pdat.Size
  pdat[i] = NEW Array(4)
  pdat[i].name    = 'Part '+LTRIM(STR(i))
  pdat[i].start   = (i-1)*3+1
  pdat[i].stop    = pdat[i][2]+6
  pdat[i].follows = i-1
ENDFOR
```

The object version is more readable. But sometimes a procedural style gets the job done, and this is one of those times.

Creating the Form

The first item of business is to attach the parameters to the appropriate object properties. Listing 14-3 shows the beginning of the pchart class.

Code Listing 14-3

```
CLASS pchart(nm, tp, lf, ht, wd, proj_arr) ;           36
     OF Form(nm)                                       37
                                                       38
   LOCAL i                                             39
                                                       40
   #ifndef CHART_NAME_WIDTH                            41
      #define CHART_NAME_WIDTH 25                      42
   #endif                                              43
                                                       44
   #ifndef CHART_FONT_SIZE                             45
      #define CHART_FONT_SIZE    8                     46
   #endif                                              47
                                                       48
   This.Top    = tp                                    49
   This.Left   = lf                                    50
   This.Height = ht                                    51
   This.Width  = wd                                    52
                                                       53
   This.Scrollbar = 2 && Auto                          54
```

```
    This.ScaleFontName = "Courier"                          55
    This.ScaleFontSize = CHART_FONT_SIZE                    56
                                                            57
ENDCLASS                                                    58
                                                            59
* end of PCHART.PRG                                         60
```

The conditional preprocessor directive may be new to you. As you'll see here, this is a handy tool in the right spot. You can use either #ifdef, which means *if defined*, or #ifndef, which means *if not defined*.

In this case, I've defined both CHART_NAME_WIDTH and CHART_FONT_SIZE constants, but only if they are not already defined. That means that if there is any earlier definition of these constants, it will not be replaced by the new one. We'll use this shortly.

The value 2 for ScrollBar is *automatic*. This leaves the appearance of elevators up to the form. If a vertical or horizontal scrollbar is needed, the form will add one. If all your drawing fits in the form, the elevators disappear.

A final item that deserves comment is the choice of the Courier font as the ScaleFont for the form. Courier is a fixed-pitch, or monospaced, font. Each character is the same width. Without using a monospaced font, the header, which we're about to add, will be just about impossible to correctly align.

Tip: When you change the ScaleFont, you change the ratio of pixels to Turpins. You'll need to test each font name and size to find the correct values for pixel height and width.

With these lines in place, you can run PCHART. You'll get a big, empty Form.

Adding the Header Lines

We'll start with the header lines, or we won't be able to see where our project's components start and end. Before we can do this, we'll need to look ahead.

When we receive the data, the pchart class is going to recalculate starts and ends based on the precedence relationship. If component 1 has to be completed before component 2 can start, we'll check to see that the start of 2 comes after the end of 1. If we have to change the start time of a component, we'll change its end, too, so that it retains its specified length.

Learn Visual dBASE Programming

We'll need to do all those calculations so that we can find, among other things, the end of the project. We'll need to know the end of the project so that we can write header lines that reach the end.

This means that we need to do the calculations before we do the drawing. To make our life complicated, we'll find that the calculations are simple to check if we do the drawing first — you can see when things start and end and watch them move as you adjust the end time of precedent elements.

What comes first? The solution here is to do dummy calculations so that we'll have some data to draw with. So we'll step ahead, just a bit, and think about what the calculation routines will do.

The main calculator takes each element and stretches its array out to nine items, including recalculated start and end dates. Let's start with a dummy calculator, as shown in Listing 14-4.

Code Listing 14-4

```
This.ScaleFontSize = CHART_FONT_SIZE                    56
                                                        57
* end of constructor                                    58
                                                        59
                                                        60
PROCEDURE proj_calc(pa)                                 61
                                                        62
* adds five more elements to each member of pa:         63
*    pa[?][5] -- length (suggested stop-start+1)        64
*    pa[?][6] -- new start                              65
*    pa[?][7] -- new stop                               66
*    pa[?][8] -- logical, True if on critical path      67
*    pa[?][9] -- location in pa                         68
                                                        69
LOCAL i                                                 70
FOR i = 1 TO pa.Size                                    71
                                                        72
   pa[i].Resize(9) && add the new elements              73
                                                        74
   * dummy calculator!                                  75
     pa[i][6] = pa[i][2]                                76
     pa[i][7] = pa[i][3]                                77
     pa[i][8] = i > 5                                   78
   * end of dummy                                       79
                                                        80
```

Chapter 14   Critical Path Charting

```
    ENDFOR                                            81
                                                      82
    * end of pchar::proj_calc                         83
                                                      84
                                                      85
    FUNCTION proj_end(pa)                             86
                                                      87
    LOCAL i, last                                     88
    last = pa[1][7]                                   89
    FOR i = 2 TO pa.Size                              90
       last = MAX(last, pa[i][7])                     91
    ENDFOR                                            92
                                                      93
    RETURN last                                       94
                                                      95
    * end of pchart::proj_end                         96
                                                      97
                                                      98
ENDCLASS                                              99
                                                     100
* end of PCHART.PRG                                  101
```

All the code here is live, except those lines labeled "dummy calculator." These simply copy the original start time into the spot for the calculated start and similarly copy the end time.

The proj_end() function takes the calculated project component end times and finds the final point in the project. With these calculations filled in, we're ready to go back to drawing headings.

Listing 14-5 shows the three lines of header. To get them, we call the project calculator, then call the proj_end() function to find out the last time in the project. With that in hand we can find the width of the header.

Code Listing 14-5

```
This.ScaleFontSize = CHART_FONT_SIZE                  56
                                                      57
This.proj_calc(proj_arr)                              58
LOCAL last                                            59
last = This.proj_end(proj_arr)                        60
                                                      61
LOCAL cwid                                            62
```

351

```
cwid = CHART_NAME_WIDTH + This.proj_end(proj_arr)+ 3        63
                                                            64
This.header1  = NEW Text(This)                              65
This.header2  = NEW Text(This)                              66
This.header3  = NEW Text(This)                              67
                                                            68
This.header1.Top = 0                                        69
This.header2.Top = 1                                        70
This.header3.Top = 2                                        71
                                                            72
STORE CHART_NAME_WIDTH + 2 TO This.header1.Left, ;          73
         This.header2.Left, ;                               74
         This.header3.Left                                  75
                                                            76
STORE 1 TO This.header1.Height, ;                           77
         This.header2.Height, ;                             78
         This.header3.Height                                79
                                                            80
STORE cwid - CHART_NAME_WIDTH - 3 TO ;                      81
         This.header1.Width, ;                              82
         This.header2.Width, ;                              83
         This.header3.Width                                 84
                                                            85
STORE "Courier" TO ;                                        86
         This.header1.FontName, ;                           87
         This.header2.FontName, ;                           88
         This.header3.FontName                              89
                                                            90
STORE CHART_FONT_SIZE TO ;                                  91
         This.header1.FontSize, ;                           92
         This.header2.FontSize, ;                           93
         This.header3.FontSize                              94
                                                            95
This.header1.Text = '' && Assigned by calling routine
This.header2.Text = ''                                      97
This.header3.Text = ''                                      98
                                                            99
FOR i = 1 TO This.Header1.Width STEP 10                     100
                                                            101
   This.Header2.Text = This.Header2.Text + ;                102
       LEFT( STR(i+9,11), 10 )                              103
   This.Header3.Text = This.Header3.Text + '1234567890'
```

Chapter 14   *Critical Path Charting*

```
                                                         105
    ENDFOR                                               106
                                                         107
* end of constructor                                     108
```

The loop at lines 100 through 106 adds digits that show the number of your item's start and end, as you see in Figure 14-1.

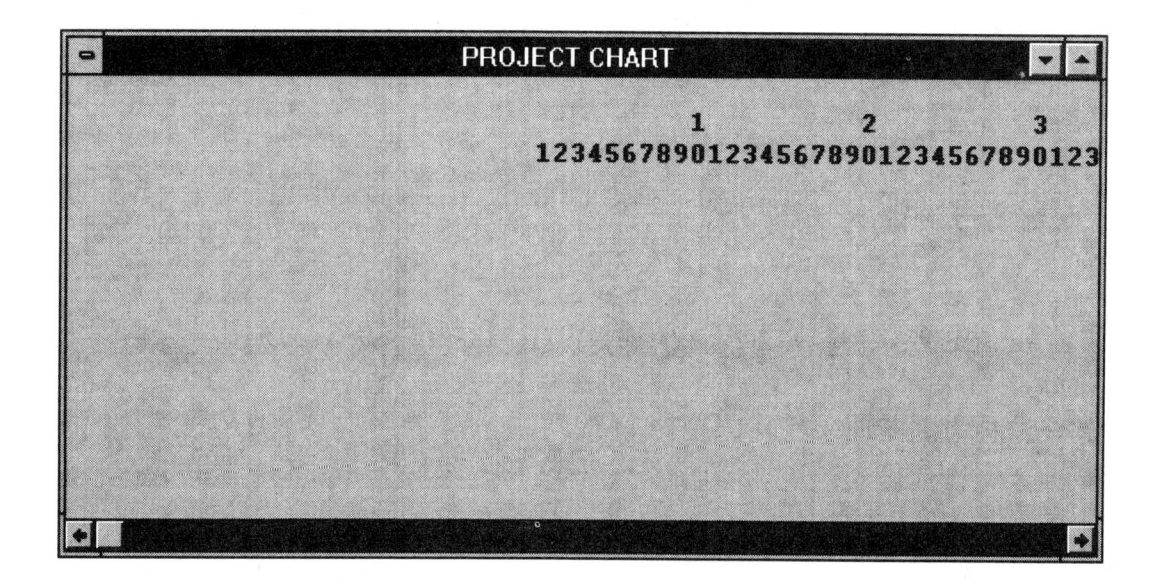

Figure 14-1: Header lines on the chart

If you comment out the assignment of Courier as the FontName, you'll see what happens with a proportional font (the default is MS Sans Serif).

Adding the Component Names

I've added text objects, starting with the form's index property 101, to show the project components' names. Listing 14-6 shows the new code.

Code Listing 14-6

```
    ENDFOR                                               106
                                                         107
```

353

Learn Visual dBASE Programming

```
FOR i = 1 TO proj_arr.Size                          108
                                                    109
   This[100+i] = NEW Text(This)                     110
   This[100+i].Top    = i + 2                       111
   This[100+i].Left   = 2                           112
   This[100+i].Height = 1                           113
   This[100+i].Width  = CHART_NAME_WIDTH            114
   This[100+i].Text   = proj_arr[i][1]              115
                                                    116
ENDFOR                                              117
                                                    118
* end of constructor                                119
```

When you run this you'll see that your 25 character name size is far more than you need for the names we're generating. I've added a new #define, which you see in Listing 14-7, to shrink this size.

Code Listing 14-7

```
ENDFOR                                              28
                                                    29
#define CHART_NAME_WIDTH 12                         30
                                                    31
pc = NEW pchart( 'Project Chart', ;                 32
            3, 5, 15, 60, pdat )                    33
```

I've added this line right after the mainline code that assigns all the project data values. As Figure 14-2 shows, this definition overrides the one we did conditionally (with #ifndef) in the class constructor.

Plotting the Project Components

With headings and names on your chart, it's time to actually draw in the project components. As you see in Listing 14-8, I use thick lines.

Code Listing 14-8

```
FOR i = 1 TO proj_arr.Size                          110
                                                    111
   This[100+i] = NEW Text(This)                     112
   This[100+i].Top    = i + 2                       113
   This[100+i].Left   = 2                           114
```

Chapter 14   Critical Path Charting

```
    This[100+i].Height = 1                              115
    This[100+i].Width  = CHART_NAME_WIDTH               116
    This[100+i].Text   = proj_arr[i][1]                 117
                                                        118
    This[200+i] = NEW Line(This)                        119
    This[200+i].Top    = i + 2.5                        120
    This[200+i].Left   = CHART_NAME_WIDTH + 1.5 + ;     121
                         proj_arr[i][6]                 122
    This[200+i].Bottom = i + 2.5                        123
    This[200+i].Right  = CHART_NAME_WIDTH + 1.5 + ;     124
                         proj_arr[i][7]                 125
    This[200+i].Width  = 7                              126
                                                        127
ENDFOR                                                  128
```

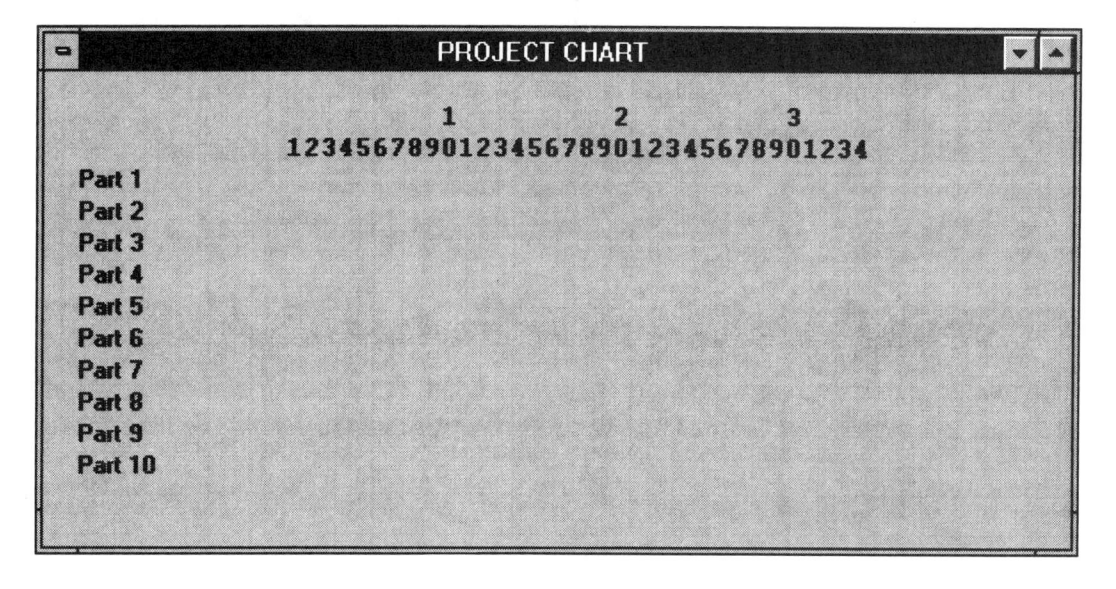

```
┌─────────────────── PROJECT CHART ───────────────────┐
                        1         2         3
               12345678901234567890123456789012 34
     Part 1
     Part 2
     Part 3
     Part 4
     Part 5
     Part 6
     Part 7
     Part 8
     Part 9
     Part 10
```

Figure 14-2: Names added and sized

These lines are drawn in the appropriate row with their left and right ends positioned to show the start and end of the project's component. The only wrinkle is the addition of .5s.

355

Learn Visual dBASE Programming

A line drawn at row 0 would be at the very top of the Form. Putting the line at 0.5 places it in the middle of the top row of characters. Similarly, writing it at column 10.5 starts it in the middle of the character rectangle.

Figure 14-3 shows the results this far.

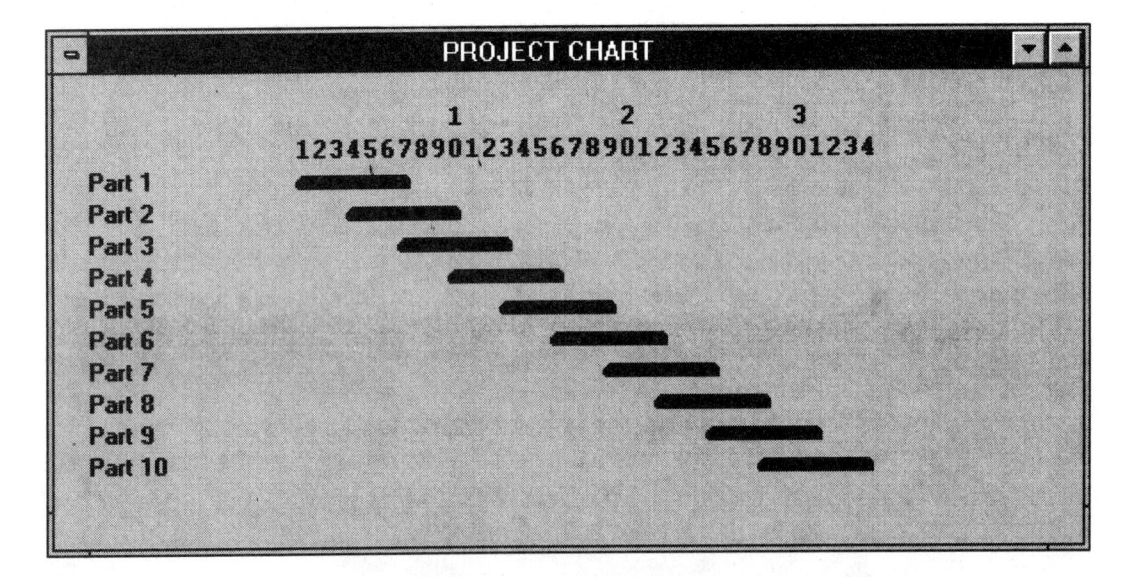

Figure 14-3: Project components drawn

Tip: dBASE 5.0 programmers often used thick lines, since the Shape object wasn't available before the release of Visual dBASE. The Shape object and its ShapeStyle properties are other possibilities here.

Before we continue, I've made some adjustments to the data to break up this neat pattern. As you can see in Listing 14-9, I've made project part 5 depend on part 2 and I've set part 7 to depend on part 1. I've also changed the start and end of parts 7 and 8.

Code Listing 14-9

```
ENDFOR                              28
                                    29
    pdat[5][4] = 2                  30
    pdat[7][2] = 8                  31
    pdat[7][3] = pdat[7][2]+12      32
```

Chapter 14   Critical Path Charting

```
    pdat[7][4] = 1                                      33
    pdat[8][2] = 20                                     34
    pdat[8][3] = pdat[8][2] + 3                         35
                                                        36
#define CHART_NAME_WIDTH 12                             37
                                                        38
pc = NEW pchart( 'Project Chart', ;                     39
               3, 5, 15, 60, pdat )                     40
```

When you run with this data, you'll get the result shown in Figure 14-4.

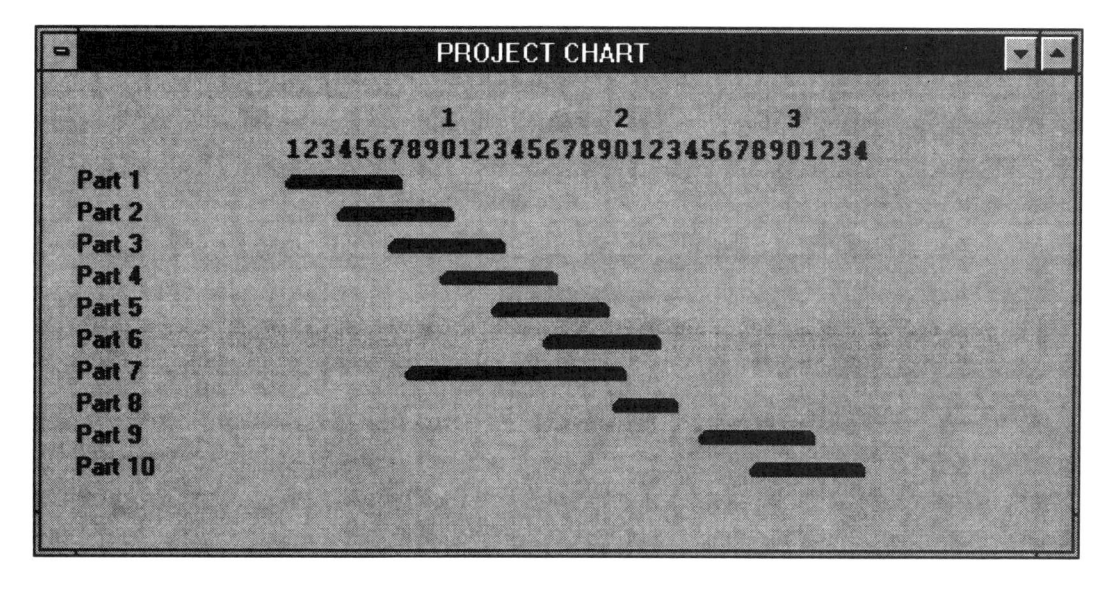

Figure 14-4: Data adjusted

Showing the Dependencies

What you can't see in Figure 14-4 is which project components depend on which others. We can show this by drawing thin lines from the end of one component to the start of the next. Listing 14-10 shows the addition of these dependency lines.

Learn Visual dBASE Programming

Code Listing 14-10

```
      This[200+i].Width = 7                              133
                                                         134
   LOCAL after                                           135
   after = proj_arr[i][4]                                136
   IF after > 0                                          137
      This[300+i] = NEW Line(This)                       138
      This[300+i].Top    = This[200 + after].Top         139
      This[300+i].Left   = This[200 + after].Right       140
      This[300+i].Bottom = This[200+i].Top               141
      This[300+i].Right  = This[200+i].Left              142
      * default width is 1                               143
   ENDIF                                                 144
                                                         145
ENDFOR                                                   146
                                                         147
* end of constructor                                     148
```

These lines are added for all the components except the ones that have a zero (no precedent) for the after value. They borrow their coordinates from the lines we have already drawn.

As you can see in Figure 14-5, these thin lines clearly show that we haven't done our calculations yet.

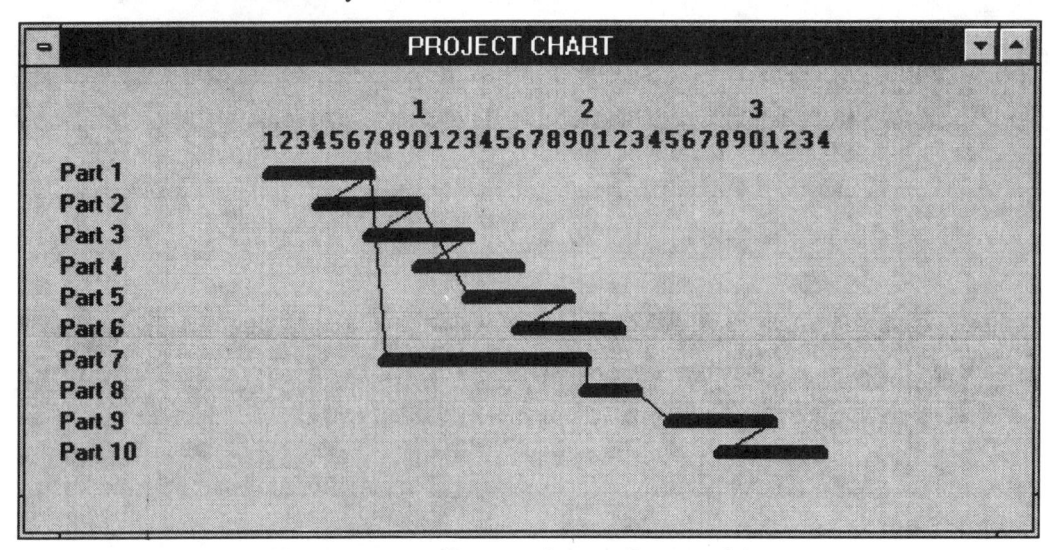

Figure 14-5: Dependency lines added

This brings us up to doing some calculations.

Doing the Calculations

We can't have a project component that is supposed to follow another actually beginning before the one it follows is completed. The calculations should take care of this for us.

There are two related calculations. First, we want to create a routine that can follow the project from beginning to end, assigning correct start and end times to each component. With that routine done we can then continue to find the critical path elements.

Following Dependencies

The calculations begin by finding the length of each component. That's stop minus start plus one, so that a project starting at time 7 and ending at time 8 takes 2 units of time. While we do this, we can initialize all the other elements that our calculations are filling in. The final element records the position of the component in the array of components.

The next job is to find the beginning component or components. These are the ones with a zero value in element 4. Their start and end times can be just copied from the original data. When we do this, we can check that there is at least one start component. We'll give up, displaying an appropriate message, if we don't find one.

We can place all the other (non-starter) elements in a separate set. Remember that internally when you make an array of arrays, you are storing references, not whole arrays, so this process is reasonably efficient.

For each element in the set of non-starters, we can check to see if it depends on an element for which we've already calculated the stop time. If it does, then we can calculate its start and end times.

The start time is the later of the original schedule or the time following the end of the precedent element. Its end time is the length of the component added to the start and then decremented by one. (If the job is 2 units long and starts at 7, you want it to end at 8.)

Every time we find an element whose times we can calculate, we remove it from the set that we are working on. Each pass through the set should find at least one component for which we can calculate start and end times. We'll just continue until the set of uncalculated components is emptied.

On each pass through the set of uncalculated components, we can check on the size of the set. If the size of the set doesn't shrink, we know that we've reduced the set as far as we can. If it's not empty, there's a circular relationship (A depends on B, B depends on C, and C depends on A). This is another type of error and all we can do is give up and write an appropriate message.

Ignoring errors, this is the algorithm in pseudo-code:

```
FOR ALL components
   calculate component length
   initialize other array elements
ENDFOR

FOR ALL components
   IF component has no precedent component
      copy its start and end from the original
   ELSE
      put component in Other set
   ENDIF
ENDFOR

DO WHILE Other set is not empty
   FOR ALL components in Other set
      IF component's precedent has times assigned
         calculate times for this component
         delete this component from the Other set
      ENDIF
   ENDFOR
ENDDO
```

When I wrote the code, I discovered that the loop over all components in the Other set was easier to do in reverse order. If you start with the first component and find you can calculate its values, you then delete it from the Other set. Of course, after you delete the first component, the next component to check is the first one in the reduced set. On the other hand, if you start at the end, you always do, for example, component 6 after you handle component 7. It doesn't change the order if you deleted 7 or left it in the Other set.

Listing 14-11 shows the code.

Code Listing 14-11

```
PROCEDURE proj_calc(pa)

* adds five more elements to each member of pa:
*    pa[?][5] -- length (suggested stop-start+1)
*    pa[?][6] -- new start
*    pa[?][7] -- new stop
*    pa[?][8] -- logical, True if on critical path
*    pa[?][9] -- location in pa

LOCAL i
FOR i = 1 TO pa.Size

   pa[i].Resize(9) && add the new elements

   pa[i][5] = pa[i][3] - pa[i][2] + 1
   pa[i][6] = 0
   pa[i][7] = 0
 * pa[i][8] = .F. && defaults to .F.
   pa[i][9] = i

ENDFOR

LOCAL starters, other_set
starters = 0
other_set = NEW Array(0)

FOR i = 1 TO pa.Size

   IF pa[i][4] = 0
      starters = starters + 1
      pa[i][6] = pa[i][2]
      pa[i][7] = pa[i][3]

   ELSE
      other_set.Add(pa[i])

   ENDIF

ENDFOR

IF starters = 0
```

```
      ? 'No starting components'                          192
      ? 'Critical path calculation impossible'            193
      RETURN                                              194
   ENDIF                                                  195
                                                          196
   LOCAL old_size                                         197
   old_size = other_set.Size                              198
                                                          199
   DO WHILE old_size > 0                                  200
                                                          201
      FOR i = other_set.Size TO 1 STEP -1                 202
                                                          203
         * is precedent item scheduled?                   204
                                                          205
         LOCAL after                                      206
         after = other_set[i][4]                          207
                                                          208
         IF pa[after][6] > 0                              209
                                                          210
            * schedule this item                          211
            other_set[i][6] = MAX( ;                      212
                  other_set[i][2], ;                      213
                  pa[ other_set[i][4] ][7]+1 )            214
            other_set[i][7] = ;                           215
                  other_set[i][6] + other_set[i][5] -  1
                                                          217
            * delete it from other_set                    218
            other_set.Delete(i)                           219
            IF other_set.Size > 1                         220
               other_set.Resize(other_set.Size - 1)       221
            ELSE                                          222
               other_set[1] = .F.                         223
               other_set.Size = 0                         224
            ENDIF                                         225
                                                          226
         ENDIF                                            227
                                                          228
      ENDFOR                                              229
                                                          230
      IF other_set.Size = old_size                        231
         ? 'Circular precedence:'                         232
                                                          233
```

Chapter 14 — Critical Path Charting

```
        FOR i = 1 TO other_set.Size                        234
            ?? ' ' + LTRIM( STR(other_set[i][9]) )         235
        ENDFOR                                             236
        ? 'Critical path calculation impossible'           237
        RETURN                                             238
     ENDIF                                                 239
                                                           240
     old_size = other_set.Size                             241
                                                           242
  ENDDO                                                    243
                                                           244
* end of pchar::proj_calc                                  245
```

Before you add this code, delete the dummy calculator in the proj_calc() method. When you run this, you'll get the result shown in Figure 14-6.

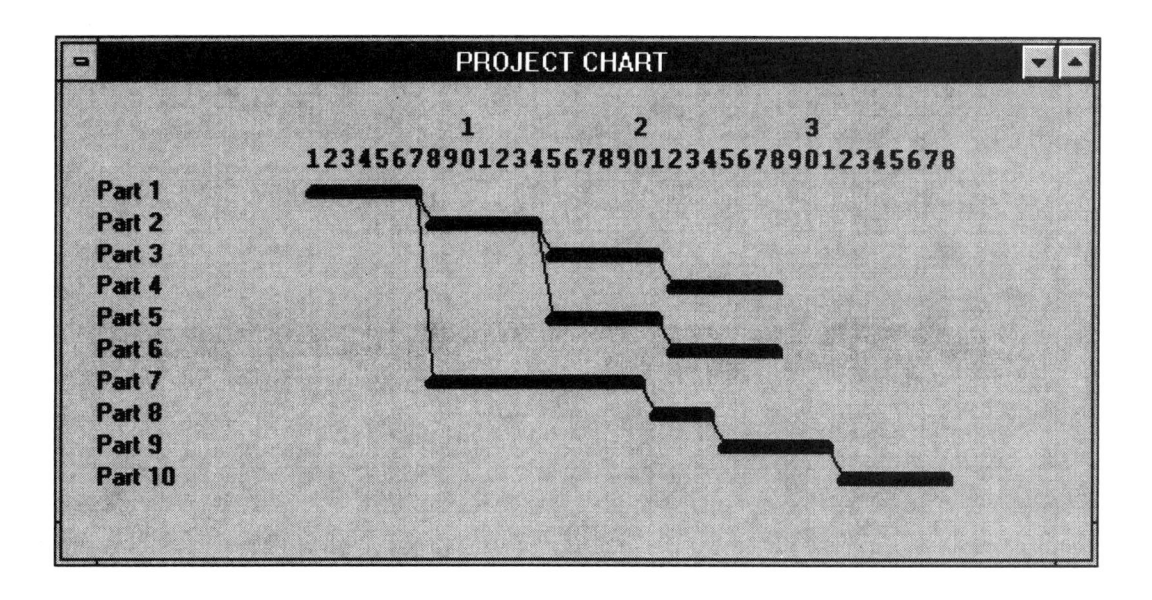

Figure 14-6: Dependencies calculated

As Figure 14-6 shows, the project components are now all adjusted so that the precedent components are completed before the following components are begun. All your dependency lines go from left to right, as they should.

Finding the Critical Path

The next calculation could be very complex or very simple. A component is on the _critical path if taking extra time for the component would delay the completion of the project.

The sophisticated way to calculate the critical path is to find each path to a component that has no following components. If you look at the project as a tree, you find each path to a leaf node. On each path you look for slack time — time between the end of a precedent component and the start of a following component, or time from the end of the leaf to the end of the whole project. Components preceding slack time are not in the critical path for the path you are analyzing.

For small projects, such as the ones we are going to handle, there's a simple way to find the critical path. Just add a unit of time to each component and see if it makes the project end one unit later. This is a crude, brute force algorithm, but it's all we need. Listing 14-12 shows this calculation.

Code Listing 14-12

```
   This.proj_calc(proj_arr)                                    67
   LOCAL last                                                  68
   last = This.proj_end(proj_arr)                              69
                                                               70
* critical path calculation:                                   71
   FOR i = 1 TO proj_arr.Size                                  72
                                                               73
      proj_arr[i][3] = proj_arr[i][3]+1                        74
      This.proj_calc(proj_arr)                                 75
      proj_arr[i][8] = last < This.proj_end(proj_arr)
      proj_arr[i][3] = proj_arr[i][3]-1                        77
                                                               78
   ENDFOR                                                      79
                                                               80
This.proj_calc(proj_arr)                                       81
                                                               82
LOCAL cwid                                                     83
cwid = CHART_NAME_WIDTH + This.proj_end(proj_arr)+ 3           84
...
      This[200+i].Width   = 7                                 145
                                                              146
   IF proj_arr[i][8]                                          147
      This[200+i].ColorNormal = 'R'                           148
```

Chapter 14   Critical Path Charting

```
       ENDIF                                          149
                                                      150
       LOCAL after                                    151
```

The extra proj_calc() at line 80 is thrown in to put the project back as you originally specified it.

In addition to doing the calculation, I've shown my critical path components in red, which is the job of the IF test at lines 147 through 149. When you run this code, you should see a highly visual critical path through your project.

We've made the calculation very simple, but unless you have a super-fast computer, you waited through a delay as the calculation was done. Even if you have a super-fast computer, you'll get a serious delay when you do this calculation for a more complex project than our simple one.

This should be covered by a display that tells you what is happening. I've added a new Form object that pops up when the calculation starts and shows a Text object that reports on the progress through each project component. The extra display work adds a lot of code and takes some extra time. The effect, however, is to make the calculation *seem* much faster.

Listing 14-13 shows the new display code.

Code Listing 14-13

```
       * critical path calculation:                    71
                                                        72
       LOCAL tempform, temptext                         73
       tempform = NEW Form()                            74
       tempform.Text = 'Critical Path Calculation'      75
                                                        76
       tempform.Top = 5                                 77
       tempform.Left = 20                               78
       tempform.Height = 5                              79
       tempform.Width = 60                              80
                                                        81
       temptext = NEW Text(tempform)                    82
       temptext.Top = 2                                 83
       temptext.Left = 1                                84
       temptext.Height = 1                              85
       temptext.Width = 58                              86
       temptext.Text = ''                               87
```

```
        temptext.Alignment = 4                                  88
                                                                89
        tempform.Open()                                         90
                                                                91
        FOR i = 1 TO proj_arr.Size                              92
                                                                93
            proj_arr[i][3] = proj_arr[i][3]+1                   94
            This.proj_calc(proj_arr)                            95
            proj_arr[i][8] = last < This.proj_end(proj_arr)
            proj_arr[i][3] = proj_arr[i][3]-1                   97
                                                                98
            temptext.text = proj_arr[i][1] + ;                  99
              IIF(proj_arr[i][8], ' IS',' IS NOT') + ;          100
              ' CRITICAL'                                       101
                                                                102
        ENDFOR                                                  103
                                                                104
        tempform.Close()                                        105
        RELEASE temptext, tempform                              106
                                                                107
    This.proj_calc(proj_arr)                                    108
```

Closing the Form

As a final touch, I like an OK or Close button on my Form. I've picked a non-standard position: the upper-left corner. The reason is that this area is empty space, not used by project components or heading lines.

At the top left, you don't have to worry about repositioning the button when the user adjusts the Form's size. Best, you don't have to worry about what happens during vertical or horizontal scrolling, which would be a definite challenge if you put the button at the bottom or on the right. Figure 14-7 shows the close button on my Form when I expanded the test data to a 20 part project.

Listing 14-14 shows the code to add the pushbutton.

Code Listing 14-14

```
    ENDFOR                                                      189
                                                                190
    DEFINE Pushbutton closer OF This;                           191
       PROPERTY;                                                192
```

```
        Top .5, ;                                       193
        Left 1.5, ;                                     194
        Height 1.25, ;                                  195
        Width 8, ;                                      196
        Text 'Close', ;                                 197
        OnClick { ;Form.Close() }                       198
                                                        199
* end of constructor                                    200
```

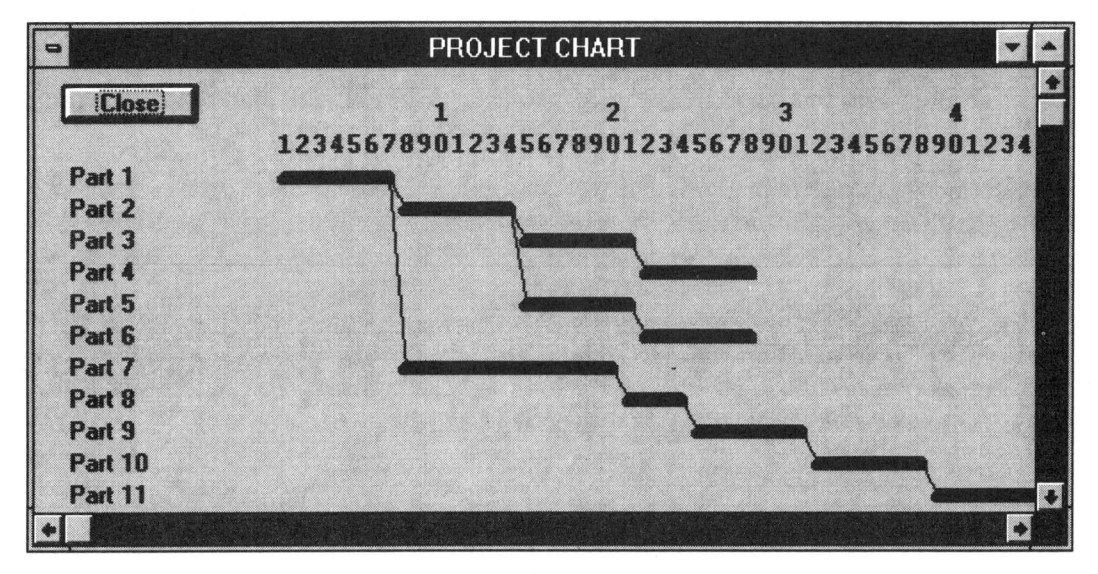

Figure 14-7: A Close button added

The Full Listing

For those without the accompanying disk, the full listing of the pchart code is shown in Listing 14-15. On disk it's L14-14.PRG.

Code Listing 14-15

```
* PCHART.PRG -- project chart class
* copyright 1995, Martin L. Rinehart


pdat = NEW Array(20)
```

```
* Each element of pdat (Project DATa) is a 4 element array:
*     pdat[?][1] = name of component
*     pdat[?][2] = Start point
*     pdat[?][3] = End point
*     pdat[?][4] = Precedent component

* Start and end points are normalized to chart grid values,
* e.g. 1 = first time, 2 = next, etc. These could be hours,
* days, months, ...

* Precedent component is the number in the array of the
* element which must be completed before this element is
* started. Zero == no precedent.

LOCAL i
FOR i = 1 TO pdat.Size
   pdat[i] = NEW Array(4)
   pdat[i][1] = 'Part '+LTRIM(STR(i))
   pdat[i][2] = (i-1)*3+1
   pdat[i][3] = pdat[i][2]+6
   pdat[i][4] = i-1
ENDFOR

   pdat[5][4] = 2
   pdat[7][2] = 8
   pdat[7][3] = pdat[7][2]+12
   pdat[7][4] = 1
   pdat[8][2] = 20
   pdat[8][3] = pdat[8][2] + 3

#define CHART_NAME_WIDTH 12

pc = NEW pchart( 'Project Chart', ;
                 3, 5, 15, 60, pdat )

pc.Open()


CLASS pchart(nm, tp, lf, ht, wd, proj_arr) ;
      OF Form(nm)
```

```
   LOCAL i

   #ifndef CHART_NAME_WIDTH
      #define CHART_NAME_WIDTH 25
   #endif

   #ifndef CHART_FONT_SIZE
      #define CHART_FONT_SIZE   8
   #endif

   This.Top    = tp
   This.Left   = lf
   This.Height = ht
   This.Width  = wd

   This.Scrollbar = 2 && Auto
   This.ScaleFontName = "Courier"
   This.ScaleFontSize = CHART_FONT_SIZE

   This.proj_calc(proj_arr)
   LOCAL last
   last = This.proj_end(proj_arr)

   * critical path calculation:

      LOCAL tempform, temptext
      tempform = NEW Form()
      tempform.Text = 'Critical Path Calculation'

      tempform.Top = 5
      tempform.Left = 20
      tempform.Height = 5
      tempform.Width = 60

      temptext = NEW Text(tempform)
      temptext.Top = 2
      temptext.Left = 1
      temptext.Height = 1
      temptext.Width = 58
      temptext.Text = ''
      temptext.Alignment = 4
```

Learn Visual dBASE Programming

```
      tempform.Open()

   FOR i = 1 TO proj_arr.Size

      proj_arr[i][3] = proj_arr[i][3]+1
      This.proj_calc(proj_arr)
      proj_arr[i][8] = last < This.proj_end(proj_arr)
      proj_arr[i][3] = proj_arr[i][3]-1

      temptext.text = proj_arr[i][1] + ;
         IIF(proj_arr[i][8], ' IS',' IS NOT') + ;
         ' CRITICAL'

   ENDFOR

   tempform.Close()
   RELEASE temptext, tempform

This.proj_calc(proj_arr)

LOCAL cwid
cwid = CHART_NAME_WIDTH + This.proj_end(proj_arr)+ 3

This.header1 = NEW Text(This)
This.header2 = NEW Text(This)
This.header3 = NEW Text(This)

This.header1.Top = 0
This.header2.Top = 1
This.header3.Top = 2

STORE CHART_NAME_WIDTH + 2 TO This.header1.Left, ;
         This.header2.Left, ;
         This.header3.Left

STORE 1 TO This.header1.Height, ;
         This.header2.Height, ;
         This.header3.Height

STORE cwid - CHART_NAME_WIDTH - 3 TO ;
         This.header1.Width, ;
         This.header2.Width, ;
```

```
            This.header3.Width

STORE "Courier" TO ;
        This.header1.FontName, ;
        This.header2.FontName, ;
        This.header3.FontName

STORE CHART_FONT_SIZE TO ;
        This.header1.FontSize, ;
        This.header2.FontSize, ;
        This.header3.FontSize

This.header1.Text = ''  && Assigned by calling routine
This.header2.Text = ''
This.header3.Text = ''

FOR i = 1 TO This.Header1.Width STEP 10

   This.Header2.Text = This.Header2.Text + ;
       LEFT( STR(i+9,11), 10 )
   This.Header3.Text = This.Header3.Text + '1234567890'

ENDFOR

FOR i = 1 TO proj_arr.Size

   This[100+i] = NEW Text(This)
   This[100+i].Top    = i + 2
   This[100+i].Left   = 2
   This[100+i].Height = 1
   This[100+i].Width  = CHART_NAME_WIDTH
   This[100+i].Text   = proj_arr[i][1]

   This[200+i] = NEW Line(This)
   This[200+i].Top    = i + 2.5
   This[200+i].Left   = CHART_NAME_WIDTH + 1.5 + ;
                        proj_arr[i][6]
   This[200+i].Bottom = i + 2.5
   This[200+i].Right  = CHART_NAME_WIDTH + 1.5 + ;
                        proj_arr[i][7]
   This[200+i].Width  = 7
```

```
      IF proj_arr[i][8]
         This[200+i].ColorNormal = 'R'
      ENDIF

      LOCAL after
      after = proj_arr[i][4]
      IF after > 0
         This[300+i] = NEW Line(This)
         This[300+i].Top    = This[200 + after].Top
         This[300+i].Left   = This[200 + after].Right
         This[300+i].Bottom = This[200+i].Top
         This[300+i].Right  = This[200+i].Left
         * default width is 1
      ENDIF

ENDFOR

DEFINE Pushbutton closer OF This;
   PROPERTY;
      Top .5, ;
      Left 1.5, ;
      Height 1.25, ;
      Width 8, ;
      Text 'Close', ;
      OnClick { ;Form.Close() }

* end of constructor


PROCEDURE proj_calc(pa)

* adds five more elements to each member of pa:
*   pa[?][5] -- length (suggested stop-start+1)
*   pa[?][6] -- new start
*   pa[?][7] -- new stop
*   pa[?][8] -- logical, True if on critical path
*   pa[?][9] -- location in pa

LOCAL i
FOR i = 1 TO pa.Size

   pa[i].Resize(9) && add the new elements
```

Chapter 14 — Critical Path Charting

```
      pa[i][5] = pa[i][3] - pa[i][2] + 1
      pa[i][6] = 0
      pa[i][7] = 0
    * pa[i][8] = .F. && defaults to .F.
      pa[i][9] = i

ENDFOR

LOCAL starters, other_set
starters = 0
other_set = NEW Array(0)

FOR i = 1 TO pa.Size

   IF pa[i][4] = 0
      starters = starters + 1
      pa[i][6] = pa[i][2]
      pa[i][7] = pa[i][3]

   ELSE
      other_set.Add(pa[i])

   ENDIF

ENDFOR

IF starters = 0
   ? 'No starting components'
   ? 'Critical path calculation impossible'
   RETURN
ENDIF

LOCAL old_size
old_size = other_set.Size

DO WHILE old_size > 0

   FOR i = other_set.Size TO 1 STEP -1

      * is precedent item scheduled?
```

```
         LOCAL after
         after = other_set[i][4]

         IF pa[after][6] > 0
            * schedule this item
              other_set[i][6] = MAX( ;
                    other_set[i][2], ;
                    pa[ other_set[i][4] ][7]+1 )
              other_set[i][7] = ;
                    other_set[i][6] + other_set[i][5] - 1

            * delete it from other_set
              other_set.Delete(i)
              IF other_set.Size > 1
                 other_set.Resize(other_set.Size - 1)
              ELSE
                 other_set[1] = .F.
                 other_set.Size = 0
              ENDIF

         ENDIF

      ENDFOR

      IF other_set.Size = old_size
         ? 'Circular precedence:'

         FOR i = 1 TO other_set.Size
            ?? ' ' + LTRIM( STR(other_set[i][9]) )
         ENDFOR
         ? 'Critical path calculation impossible'
         RETURN
      ENDIF

      old_size = other_set.Size

ENDDO

* end of pchar::proj_calc
```

```
FUNCTION proj_end(pa)

LOCAL i, last
last = pa[1][7]
FOR i = 2 TO pa.Size
   last = MAX(last, pa[i][7])
ENDFOR

RETURN last

* end of pchart::proj_end


ENDCLASS

* end of PCHART.PRG
```

Summary

In this chapter we've built a project chart class that handles simple projects where some components can't be started until others are completed. It does the calculations and displays the data.

We've used a basically procedural style of code, drawing first one component and then another. The calculations are also procedural, although we've made extensive use of the Array object for our data structures.

We built the drawing portion of the class first, using dummy calculation routines. The drawing gives us a nice display of the data that is very useful for testing the calculation routines.

While we've been building this class, you've again been working with an array of arrays and making good use of Array object methods such as add(), delete() and resize().

Now it's time for congratulations!

Your course in event-driven, object-oriented programming with Visual dBASE is now complete. You've learned to create objects that the user controls, and you've seen that your underlying program doesn't really lose control in this new paradigm.

Along the way you've used many of Visual dBASE's built-in objects and properties. We started with the purely visual objects (remember how strange this all was when you put the first lines on your calendar?) and progressed to the lowest-level objects, the Object and the Array.

You've been using new techniques and tools, such as hooking codeblocks to event handlers. You've used object programming language components such as function pointers and the scope resolution operator. And you've used visual programming tools, such as the object properties Inspector and the Form Designer.

You've also begun a personal library of reusable objects, such as your calendar, speed bar, and your outline manipulator. You're not just thinking about objects anymore — you've been building them.

I hope you've enjoyed the journey. Now you're ready to continue on your own. Here's a project to test yourself: write a multi-window, multi-file text editor.

Here's a hint to get you started: using getfile() and the Editor object, a single-file, single-window text editor should take about a dozen lines of code. (The DataSource property of an editor can be a text file.)

A good C++ programmer can do the whole job in 5,000 lines of code. A good Visual dBASE programmer can do it in under 500.

Enjoy your Visual dBASE programming!

Index

Accelerators (shortcut keys), 241, 242
ACTION_D routines, 106
Applications
  beginning, 219–60
  completing, 256–59
  creating an Empty Form, 221–25
  creating a Menu System, 231–46
  creating a Scratch Form, 220–31
  Form Designer output, 226–31
  help about Menu Objects, 244–46
  launching the Form Designer from Command window, 221–23
  launching Form Designer from Navigator, 223–24
  launching the Form Expert directly, 224–25
  Modal Windows, 247–59
  modifying the menu, 256–59
  saving forms, 225–26
  skeleton, 256
  using Form Designer, 219
  using Menu Designer, 219
ASCII characters, 92

BASIC programming, 57
Bitmaps, 266
Borland
  C++, 77
  language packages, 11
  naming Turpin unit, 156
  shortcut keys named by, 241
  SpeedBar, 113, 261
  Two-Way Tool, 226

Calculator, dummy, 351
Calendar, 139–61
  adding date objects, 151–57
  adding a grid of objects, 141–45
  class, complete, 157–61
  class creation, 140–41
  drawing the horizontal lines, 144–45
  drawing the vertical lines, 142–44
  labeling the days of the week, 148–51
  letting user resize, 146–48
Calendar, completing, 193–218
  adding new buttons, 203–6
  adjusting the buttons, 202–6
  full listing, 207–18
  GDI (Graphics Device Interface) resources, 197
  GPFs (General Protection Fault) and other crashes, 197
  handling keystrokes, 197–99
  how not to handle keystrokes, 194–97
  how not to use Calendar, 196–97
  how not to use This, 195–96
  keystroke events, 194–202
  miscellaneous keystrokes, 199–202
  moving existing buttons, 202–3
Calendar, designing, 163–91
  adding Home and End pushbuttons, 179–82
  days
    adding color, 167
    improving spacing, 167–69
    moving selected, 165–67
  full listing, 182–90
  highlighting selected dates, 164–65
  months
    adding pushbuttons, 174–75
    adjusting, 169–79
    changing, 173–79
    changing correctly, 178–79
    displaying, 169–73

Calendar, designing *continued*
  MONTH_WIDTH constant, 172
  selecting dates with mouse, 164–69
  years, adjusting, 179–82
CALENDAR.PRG
  completing calendar class, 157
  and deletions, 148
  developing routines such as, 197
  modifications, 153
  starting, 140
Charting, critical path, 343–76
  adding the component names, 353–54
  adding the header lines, 349–53
  building a test project, 346–48
  closing the form, 366–67
  creating the form, 348–49
  designing the class, 344–45
  doing the calculations, 359–66
  drawing the chart, 345–59
  finding the critical path, 364–66
  following dependencies, 359–63
  full listing, 367–75
  plotting the project components, 354–57
  showing the dependencies, 357–59
  a simple class, 345
  simple data structure, 344–45
CLASS/ENDCLASS, 47, 84–85
Classes
  building Visual dBASE, 2
  constructor, 124
  creating new, 123–25
  and objects, 5–6
  scopes, 132
Clipper programming, 1, 57
Codeblocks
  expression, 132–33
  null, 134–35
  statement, 133–34
  and subroutines, 132
Codes
  dBASE and Fox programmers, 22
  debugging, 23
  keeping sound, 49–50
  old-fashioned, 21
  pchart, 367

  procedural, 21–46
Command windows
  arranging Visual dBASE, 114–16
  dot prompt equivalent, 3
  launching Form Designer, 221–23
Compiler and linker, 11
Constructor
  assigning properties, 125
  functions, 6
Constructor, tree_display_form, 323–27
  assigning, 323–25
  attaching text objects, 325–26
  initializing the display, 327
Control construct, CLASS/ENDCLASS, 47
Coordinates, pixel-sized, 266–70
Critical path charting, 343–76
Crystal reports, 12

Date objects
  adding, 151–57
  adding date calculation functions, 151–53
  calling with a date parameter, 153
  creating day objects, 153–54
  drawing the day objects, 155–56
  improving performance, 156–57
  setting the day objects, 154–55
dBASE
  and Fox programmers, 22
  object-oriented Visual, 2
  See also Visual dBASE
DBASEWIN forum (CompuServe), 54
DBASEWIN.INI
  SpeedBar stored in, 114
  startup file, 111
DBF and Form Expert, 13
Debugging code, 23
Dependencies, following, 357–63
Designer, Form, 13
Diagrams, action, 49–50
  adding properties, 57–58
  defining, 50
  design for debugging, 54
  designing a utility, 51–54
  implementing the lexer, 54–63
  keeping code sound, 49–50

Index

lexer, 51–52
output machinery, 54
parser, 52–53
scrambling sound code, 50
stack machinery, 53
test loop, 55
tokenizer, 51
using object class object, 55–56
Dialog boxes
   titling, 36
   Windows, 34
DO/UNTIL loop, 47
DOS editors, 10
Dot operator, 6, 7
Dummy calculator, 351

Editor, 9–11
   built-in, 10
   DOS, 10
   GUI programming, 9
   Program, 13, 27
   and small test programs, 10
ELSEIF, 106
End user preferences, Navigator, 112
Error_on() procedure, 79–83
Event Handlers
   assigning properties in, 126–28
   responding to a move event, 126
   STATIC finds recursion in, 129
   STATIC scope in, 129–30
Event handlers, tree_display_form, 330–34
Event Handlers
   using STATIC variables in, 128–30
   writing, 126–30
Event-driven programming, 121–38
Experts, Form, 12–13
Expression Builder tools, 13
Expression codeblocks, 132–33
Extensions
   .LST, 35
   .TMP, 35

Files
   building test, 24
   writing output, 28–30

Fonts, defaults, 4
FOR Loops, 88–89
Form Designer, 11–12, 13
   extension .WFM, 226
   launching from Command window, 221–23
   launching from the Navigator, 223–24
   using, 219
Form Designer output, 226–31
   Header and General .WFM output, 227–31
   plain form, 226–27
Form Experts, 221
   and .DBF, 13
   launching the, 224–25
Forms
   basics, 122–25
   saving, 225–26
Fox programming, 1, 22, 57
Functions
   constructor, 6
   defined, 30
FUNCTIONs, statement, 41

GDI (Graphics Device Interface) resources, 197
GETFILE(), 34, 35
GPFs (Windows General Protection Fault) and other crashes, 197
GUI
   environment, 220
   programming editor, 9
   working program, 294

Hacking, 267
Handlers, ON KEY, 194
Help, about Menu Objects, 244–46
Help/About Window, 254–56
HPIX_SIZE units, 274

I/O routines, low level, 23
Input file, reading, 27–28
Interfaces, user, 33–37

Keys
   mnemonic, 241
   shortcut, 241
Keystrokes, how not to handle, 194–97

379

Lexer (lexical analysis routine), 48, 51–52
  adding a, 55
  implementing, 54–63
Line numbering, 30–33
  structuring, 30–32
Linker and compiler, 11
LISTER, 26, 30, 33, 34, 36–39
LISTER.PRG
  creating, 25–26
  launching, 27
LISTER program, improving, 43–45
Listings
  numbered, 22–39
  procedural codings, 38–39
LOCAL parameters, declaring, 41–42
Local or private variables, 43
LOCAL variables, 39–42
Look() method, improving, 79
Loops, DO/UNTIL, 47
LST extensions, 35

Menu Designer
  features, 240–43
  finding, 232–34
  learning, 235–38
  output, 238–40
  using, 219, 234–43
  See also Menu System
Menu Objects, help about, 244–46
Menu System
  creation, 231–46
  extensions .MNU files, 231
  See also Menu Designer
Message, closing with a, 36–37
Method properties, 71
Methods
  class, 71–72
  defined, 6–7
MFC (Microsoft Foundation Classes), 77
Microsoft, C++, 77
Mnemonic keys, 241
Modal Windows
  creating, 247–59
  Not_Yet Windows, 247–53
    adding an OK Pushbutton, 250–53

adding the Text Object, 247–50
Help/About Window, 254–56
Mousaholic, 9
Mouse, selecting dates with, 164–69

Names, testing, 34–36
Navigator, 3, 8, 112, 223–24
Null codeblocks, 134–35
Numbering, line, 30–33
Numbers, neat, 32–33

Object properties and methods, 6–7
Object reference variables, 5
Object-oriented
  dBASE, 2
  event-driven programming, 109–20, 121–38
Objects
  analysis, 47–66
  attaching, 135–37
  and classes, 5–6
Objects generation, 67–107
  adding tokens, 78
  building the prefix, 92–95
    choosing prefix characters, 92
    a new mainline, 92–94
    new pop and push routines, 94–95
  CLASS/ENDCLASS, 84–85
  completing DO CASE blocks, 100–105
    adding the new stack, 101–2
    adding the pushy words to pusher(), 104–5
    handling the keywords in Stack_em(), 102–3
    modifying mainline, 101
  Error_on() procedure, 79–83
  file input in the mainline, 68–69
  fixing FOR Loops, 88–89
  improving the Look() method, 79
  output machinery, 89–105
  PROCEDUREs and FUNCTIONs, 85–87
  stack machinery, 69–89
    testing and fixing, 96–100
    first test, 96
    fixing the silence, 99–100
    implementing fixes, 97–98
ON KEY handlers, 194
Operator, scope resolution, 132

Index

Output file, writing, 28–30
Output machinery, simple output, 90–92
OWL (Object Windows Library), 77

Parameters, LOCAL, 41–42
PARAMETERS, statement, 31, 41
Parser (grammatical analysis routine), 48
   completing, 65–66
   generator, 63
   implementing, 63–66
   output, 64–65
pcharts
   classes, 344
   codes, 367
   running, 349
Pixel-sized coordinates, 266–70
PRIVATE or LOCAL variables, 43
PRIVATE variables, 39–40
Procedural codings, 21–46, 38–39
Procedure defined, 30
PROCEDUREs
   and FUNCTIONs, 85–87
   statements, 41
Productivity, level of, 2
Program Editor, 13, 27, 116–19
Programmer preferences, Windows, 112
Programmers
   dBASE, 22
   Fox, 22
Programming
   assigning proprieties in the constructor, 125
   attaching objects, 135–37
   BASIC, 57
   C++, 18
   class
      constructor, 124
      creating a new, 123–25
   Clipper, 57
   Clipper basics, 1
   event-driven, 121–38
   form basics, 122–25
   Fox, 57
   Fox basics, 1
   FoxPro 2.x, 18
   learning by doing, 2
   mastering the tools, 8–13
   object-oriented, 1, 121–38
   object-oriented, event-driven, 109–20
      Command Window, 114–16
      DBASEWIN.INI, 111
      the Navigator, 112
      Program Editor, 116–19
      setup, 110–18
      SpeedBar, 113–14
      windows, 110–11
   tree classes, 314–22
   tree_display_form class, 322–34
   UNIX-based tool (YACC), 63
   Windows, intelligent, 123
   writing Event Handlers, 126–30
   Xbase, 2
Programs
   building skeletons, 24–25
   LISTER, 38–39, 43–45
   writing, 7–8
Project CHARTing, 344
Properties, 6, 71

Query tools, 13

Reading input files, 27–28
Recursion, 311–14
   breadth-first traversals, 312
   depth-first traversals, 311–12
   eliminating, 132
   non-recursive routines, 313–14
   routines, 312–13
Reference variables, 130–32
Reports, crystal, 12
RESOURCE.DLL, scrolling through bitmaps in, 266
Routines
   ACTION_D, 106
   Show_stack(), 77–78
   Stack_em(), 75–77

SCAN/ENDSCAN, 106
Scopes
   resolution operators, 132
   Visual dBASE, 39–45

381

Learn Visual dBASE Programming

Scratch Form, creating, 220–31
SKELETON.MNU, running a, 243
SKELETON.PRG
   creating a calendar class, 140
   creating LISTER.PRG, 25
   critical path charting, 345
SKELETON.WFM
   comparing to listing, 259
   launching, 256
Skeletons, 26, 54
   application, 256
   building program, 24–25
   finding menu designer, 232–34
Software Development Kit (SDK), 5
Sparse array notation defined, 142
SpeedBar (Borland), 113–114, 261. *See also* Speed_bar
SPEEDBAR.PRG
   additions, 280
   entering changes and clean_up() calls, 302
Speed_bar
   building visual components, 276–84
   calling a clean_up() method, 301–4
   completing, 275–89, 293–308
   designing, 275
   drawing the buttons, 279–84
   error-proofing, 300–304
   full listing, 289–92, 304–8
   launching, 276–79
   operating, 285–89
      acting on the clicks, 289
      clicking the buttons, 285–88
   spacing, 294–97
      surround width, 294–97
   status messages
      for buttons, 297–300
      setting, 298–300
      unsetting, 299–300
Speed_bar Class
   building, 261–92
   Button Object, 262–75
      adding the image, 265–75
      bouncing rectangles, 263–65
      drawing the image, 270–72

      pixel-sized coordinates, 266–70
      putting a wiggle in the image, 272–75
Stack class, 70–74
   constructor code, 71
   implementation, 72–73
   inheritance, 70–71
   methods, 71–72
   Show_stack() routine, 77–78
   Stack_em() routine, 75–77
   testing, 73–74
   using, 74–78
Stack machinery, 53, 69–89
Statements
   codeblocks, 133–34
   FUNCTION, 41
   PARAMETERS, 31, 41
   PROCEDURE, 41
   PROCEDUREs and FUNCTIONs, 85–88
STATIC variables, 43, 102, 128–30, 149
Subroutines, 30
   class scope, 132
   and codeblocks, 132
   reference variables, 130–32
   scope resolution operator, 132
   using named, 130–35

Test files, building, 24
TESTIN.PRG
   not processing, 33
   opening, 24, 29
TESTOUT.TMP, 24, 29
Text, 6
TMP extensions, 35
Tokenizer, 51
Tokenizing, 58–63
   defined, 51
   obtaining the first keyword, 58–61
   routines, 57
Tools, 21–46
   Expression Builder, 13
   Query, 13
   UNIX-based (YACC), 63
   using, 13–18

Index

Tree classes
  building, 309–42
  depth property, 316, 317
  designing the tree, 310–14
  detailed design, 310–11
  full listing, 334–42
  LOCAL variables, 328
  mainline, 318
  make_child() routine, 318
  MAX_LINES, 322, 328, 330
  name property, 317
  nodes, 315
  node's constructor, 316
  num_in_parent property, 317
  num_kids property, 317
  overall object design, 310
  programming, 314–22
  programming the tree_display_form class, 322–34
  recursion, 311–14
  root property, 316
  size property, 316
  SKELETON.PRG, 314
  stop property, 317
  TAB_SIZE, 330
  tree constructor, 316
  TREE.PRG, 314, 320
  tree_display_form constructor, 323–27
  tree_display_form display methods, 327–30
  tree_display_form event handlers, 330–34
Turpin, Bill, 156
Turpin defined, 156
Two-Way Tool, 226

UNIX-based tool (YACC), 63
User interface, 33–37

Variables
  LOCAL, 39–42
  object reference, 5
  PRIVATE, 39–40
  PRIVATE or LOCAL, 43
  reference, 130–32
  STATIC, 43, 102, 128–30, 149
Visual dBASE
  classes, 2
  object-oriented, 2
  scopes, 39–45
  See also dBASE
VPIX_SIZE units, 274

Windows
  Command, 3
  dialog box, 34
  Help/About, 254–56
  intelligent, 123
  Modal, 247–59
  Navigator, 3, 8
Windows programs
  classes and objects, 5–6
  compiler and linker, 11
  constructor functions, 6
  crystal reports, 12
  the editor, 9–11
  first, 1–19
  form designer, 11–12
  menus and dialogs, 12–13
  object properties and methods, 6–7
  simple, 3–7
  using tools, 13–18
Writer, third-party report, 12
Writing
  Event Handlers, 126–30
  output file, 28–30

Xbase programming, 2

YACC (Yet Another Compiler Compiler), 63

Addison-Wesley warrants the enclosed disk to be free of defects in materials and faulty workmanship under normal use for a period of ninety days after purchase. If a defect is discovered in the disk during this warranty period, a replacement disk can be obtained at no charge by sending the defective disk, postage prepaid, with proof of purchase to:

Addison-Wesley Publishing Company
Editorial Department
Trade Computer Books Division
One Jacob Way
Reading, MA 01867

After the ninety-day period, a replacement will be sent upon receipt of the defective disk and a check or money order for $10.00, payable to Addison-Wesley Publishing Company.

Addison-Wesley makes no warranty or representation, either express or implied, with respect to this software, its quality, performance, merchantability, or fitness for a particular purpose. In no event will Addison-Wesley, its distributors, or dealers be liable for direct, indirect, special, incidental, or consequential damages arising out of the use or inability to use the software. The exclusion of implied warranties is not permitted in some states. Therefore, the above exclusion may not apply to you. This warranty provides you with specific legal rights. There may be other rights that you may have that vary from state to state.